Occupational Therapy Practice Guidelines for

Productive Aging for Community-Dwelling Older Adults

Natalie Leland, PhD, OTR/L, BCG
Assistant Professor
University of Southern California
Los Angeles

Sharon J. Elliott, DHS, GCG, OTR/L, BCG, FAOTA
Adult Therapy Services Coordinator
Therapeutic Life Center
Greenville, NC

Kimberly J. Johnson, MS, MSW
Research Associate
University of Massachusetts–Boston
Department of Gerontology
Boston

AOTA PRESS

The American
Occupational Therapy
Association, Inc.

AOTA Centennial Vision

We envision that occupational therapy is a powerful, widely recognized, science-driven, and evidence-based profession with a globally connected and diverse workforce meeting society's occupational needs.

AOTA Vision Statement

The American Occupational Therapy Association advances occupational therapy as the pre-eminent profession in promoting the health, productivity, and quality of life of individuals and society through the therapeutic application of occupation.

AOTA Mission Statement

The American Occupational Therapy Association advances the quality, availability, use, and support of occupational therapy through standard-setting, advocacy, education, and research on behalf of its members and the public.

AOTA Staff

Frederick P. Somers, *Executive Director*
Christopher M. Bluhm, *Chief Operating Officer*

Chris Davis, *Director, AOTA Press*
Ashley Hofmann, *Development/Production Editor*
Victoria Davis, *Digital/Production Editor*

Beth Ledford, *Director, Marketing*
Amanda Fogle, *Marketing Specialist*
Emily Zhang, *Technology Marketing Specialist*
Jennifer Folden, *Marketing Specialist*

The American Occupational Therapy Association, Inc.
4720 Montgomery Lane
Bethesda, MD 20814
301-652-AOTA (2682)
TDD: 800-377-8555
Fax: 301-652-7711
www.aota.org

To order: 1-877-404-AOTA (2682)

Disclaimers

This publication is designed to provide accurate and authoritative information in regard to the subject matter covered. It is sold or distributed with the understanding that the publisher is not engaged in rendering legal, accounting, or other professional service. If legal advice or other expert assistance is required, the services of a competent professional person should be sought.
—*From the Declaration of Principles jointly adopted by the American Bar Association and a Committee of Publishers and Associations*

It is the objective of the American Occupational Therapy Association to be a forum for free expression and interchange of ideas. The opinions expressed by the contributors to this work are their own and not necessarily those of the American Occupational Therapy Association.

ISBN-13: 978-1-56900-332-9
Library of Congress Control Number: 2012936497

Cover design by Jennifer Folden
Composition by Maryland Composition, Laurel, MD
Printing by Automated Graphics Systems, White Plains, MD

Contents

Appendixes 59

References 141

Figures and Tables Used in this Publication

Acknowledgments

The series editor for this Practice Guideline is

Deborah Lieberman, MHSA, OTR/L, FAOTA
Program Director, Evidence-Based Practice Project
Staff Liaison to the Commission on Practice
American Occupational Therapy Association
Bethesda, MD

The issue editor for this Practice Guideline is

Marian Arbesman, PhD, OTR/L
President, ArbesIdeas, Inc.
Consultant, AOTA Evidence-Based Practice Project
Clinical Assistant Professor, Department of
    Rehabilitation Science
State University of New York at Buffalo

The authors acknowledge the following individuals
for their contributions to the evidence-based literature
review:

Dana Burns, MS, OTR/L
Carla Chase, EdD, OTR/L
Wanda I. Colón, PhD, OTR/L
Teresa Hallenen, MS, OTR/L
Emily Hawthorne, MS, OTR/L
Shira Kirshenbaum, MS, OTR/L

Jennifer Lane, MS, OTR/L
Kathryn Mann, MS, OTRL
Letha J. Mosley, PhD, OTR/L, FAOTA
Elsa M. Orellano, PhD, OTR/L, ATP
Stephanie Ramey, MS, OTR/L
Wendy Stav, PhD, OTR/L, SCDCM, FAOTA
Sarah Wasek, MS, OTRL

The authors acknowledge and thank the following
individuals for their participation in the content review
and development of this publication:

Coralie Glantz, OT/L, BCG, FAOTA
Elizabeth Gomes, MS, OTR/L
Christine Kroll, MS, OTR
Susan Murphy, ScD, OTR
Elsa M. Orellano, PhD, OTR/L, ATP
Samia H. Rafeedie, OTD, OTR/L, CBIS
Regula Robnett, PhD, OTR/L
Lauren M. Rosenberg, OTR/L
Wendy Stav, PhD, OTR/L, SCDCM, FAOTA
Missi Zahoransky, MSHS, OTR/L
V. Judith Thomas, MGA
Christina A. Metzler
Madalene Palmer

Introduction

Purpose and Use of This Publication

Practice guidelines have been widely developed in response to the health care reform movement in the United States. Such guidelines can be a useful tool for improving the quality of health care, enhancing consumer satisfaction, achieving measurable outcomes, promoting appropriate use of services, and reducing costs. The American Occupational Therapy Association (AOTA), which represents nearly 140,000 occupational therapists, occupational therapy assistants (see Appendix A), and students of occupational therapy, is committed to providing information to support decision making that promotes a high-quality health care system that is affordable and accessible to all.

Using an evidence-based perspective and key concepts from the second edition of the *Occupational Therapy Practice Framework: Domain and Process* (AOTA, 2008b), this guideline provides an overview of the occupational therapy process for productive aging among community-dwelling older adults. It defines the occupational therapy domain and process and interventions that occur within the boundaries of acceptable practice. This guideline does not discuss all possible interventions, and although it does recommend some specific occupational therapy interventions, the occupational therapist makes the ultimate judgment regarding the appropriateness of a given intervention in light of a specific client's circumstances, needs, and available evidence to support the intervention.

AOTA intends, through this publication, to help occupational therapists and occupational therapy assistants, as well as the people who manage, reimburse, or set policy regarding occupational therapy services, to understand the contribution of occupational therapy in treating community-living older adults to facilitate productive aging. Although this practice guideline was written with the objective of presenting the current evidence on productive aging for community-dwelling older adults, the evidence presented may be applicable to other populations of older adults. Readers should be cognizant of the generalizability of these practice guidelines when working with older adult populations in other settings (please refer to the Methodology section in Appendix E for details of inclusion and exclusion criteria). This guideline also can serve as a reference for health care professionals, health care facility managers, education and health care regulators, third-party payers, and managed care organizations to assist in understanding the role of occupational therapy services in the community. Selected diagnostic and billing code information for evaluations and interventions is provided in Appendix B and Appendix C.

This document may be used in any of the following ways:

- To assist occupational therapists and occupational therapy assistants in communicating about their services to external audiences
- To assist other health care practitioners, case managers, clients, families and caregivers, and health care facility managers in determining whether referral for occupational therapy services is appropriate
- To assist third-party payers in understanding the therapeutic need for occupational therapy services
- To assist legislators; third-party payers; federal, state, and local agencies; and administrators in understanding the professional education, training, and skills of occupational therapists and occupational therapy assistants

- To assist health and social services planning teams in determining the scope, benefits, and need for occupational therapy services
- To assist program developers; administrators; legislators; federal, state, and local agencies; and third-party payers in understanding the scope of occupational therapy services
- To assist researchers, occupational therapists, occupational therapy assistants, program evaluators, and policy analysts in this practice area in determining outcome measures for analyzing the effectiveness of occupational therapy intervention
- To assist policy, education, and health care benefit analysts in understanding the appropriateness of occupational therapy services to support productive aging among community-living older adults
- To assist policymakers, legislators, and organizations in understanding the contribution occupational therapy can make in prevention, health promotion, remediation of impairments, program development, and health care reform to support productive aging among community-living older adults
- To assist occupational therapy educators in designing appropriate curricula that incorporate the diverse roles of occupational therapy within productive aging.

The introduction to this guideline continues with a brief discussion of the domain and process of occupational therapy. This discussion is followed by a detailed description of productive aging as well as the occupational therapy process for productive aging among community-living older adults, including a summary of evidence from the literature regarding best practices. Embedded within these descriptions are summaries of the results of systematic reviews of evidence from the scientific literature regarding best practices in occupational therapy intervention for this population. Finally, the appendixes contain the meth-

odology and evidence tables for the review, guidelines related to using *International Classification of Diseases (ICD)* and *Current Procedural Terminology (CPT)* codes for billing, and examples of alternative funding sources for productive aging services.

Domain and Process of Occupational Therapy

Occupational therapists' expertise lies in their knowledge of occupation and their understanding of how occupational engagement can be used to support health and participation in home, education (e.g., lifelong learning), workplace, and community life (AOTA, 2008b).

In 2008, the AOTA Representative Assembly adopted the *Occupational Therapy Practice Framework: Domain and Process* (2nd edition). Informed by the first edition of the *Occupational Therapy Practice Framework: Domain and Process* (AOTA, 2002), the previous *Uniform Terminology for Occupational Therapy* (AOTA, 1979, 1989, 1994), and the World Health Organization's *International Classification of Functioning, Disability, and Health* (*ICF;* WHO, 2001), the *Framework* outlines the profession's domain and the process of service delivery within this domain.

Domain

A profession's *domain* articulates its sphere of knowledge, societal contribution, and intellectual or scientific foundation. The occupational therapy profession's domain focuses on helping others participate in daily life activities. The broad term that the profession uses to describe daily life activities is *occupation.* As outlined in the *Framework,* occupational therapists and occupational therapy assistants[1] work collaboratively with people, organizations, and populations (clients) to engage in everyday activities

---

[1] *Occupational therapists* are responsible for all aspects of occupational therapy service delivery and are accountable for the safety and effectiveness of the occupational therapy service delivery process. *Occupational therapy assistants* deliver occupational therapy services under the supervision of and in partnership with an occupational therapist (AOTA, 2009a).

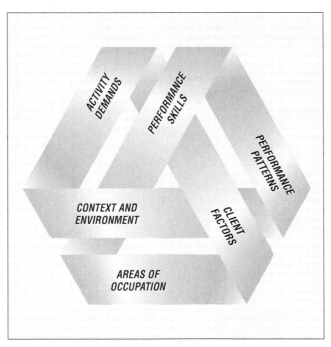

Figure 1. Occupational therapy's domain.

Reprinted from "Occupational Therapy Practice Framework: Domain and Process" (2nd ed., p. 627), by American Occupational Therapy Association, 2008, *American Journal of Occupational Therapy, 62,* 625–683. Used with permission.

or occupations that they want and need to do in a manner that supports health and participation (see Figure 1). Using occupational engagement as both the desired outcome of intervention and the intervention itself, occupational therapy practitioners[2] are skilled at viewing the subjective and objective aspects of performance and understanding occupation simultaneously from this dual, yet holistic, perspective. The overarching mission to support health and participation in life through engagement in occupations circumscribes the profession's domain and emphasizes the important ways in which environmental and life circumstances influence the manner in which people carry out their occupations. Key aspects of the domain of occupational therapy are defined in Figure 2.

Process

For the purpose of the practice guideline, the client can be defined to include an individual, organization (e.g., community senior center), or population (e.g., community-living older adults in a defined community or region; Moyers & Dale, 2007). Many professions use the process of evaluating, intervening, and targeting outcomes that is outlined in the *Framework.* Occupational therapy's application of this process is made unique, however, by its focus on occupation (see Figure 3).

The process of occupational therapy service delivery typically begins with the occupational profile. The *occupational profile* is an assessment of the client's occu-

---

[2]When the term *occupational therapy practitioner* is used in this document, it refers to both occupational therapists and occupational therapy assistants (AOTA, 2006b).

AREAS OF OCCUPATION	CLIENT FACTORS	PERFORMANCE SKILLS	PERFORMANCE PATTERNS	CONTEXT AND ENVIRONMENT	ACTIVITY DEMANDS
Activities of Daily Living (ADL)* Instrumental Activities of Daily Living (IADL) Rest and Sleep Education Work Play Leisure Social Participation	Values, Beliefs, and Spirituality Body Functions Body Structures	Sensory Perceptual Skills Motor and Praxis Skills Emotional Regulation Skills Cognitive Skills Communication and Social Skills	Habits Routines Roles Rituals	Cultural Personal Physical Social Temporal Virtual	Objects Used and Their Properties Space Demands Social Demands Sequencing and Timing Required Actions Required Body Functions Required Body Structures
*Also referred to as *basic activities of daily living (BADL)* or *personal activities of daily living (PADL)*.					

Figure 2. Aspects of occupational therapy's domain.

Reprinted from "Occupational Therapy Practice Framework: Domain and Process" (2nd ed., p. 628), by American Occupational Therapy Association, 2008, *American Journal of Occupational Therapy, 62,* 625–683. Used with permission.

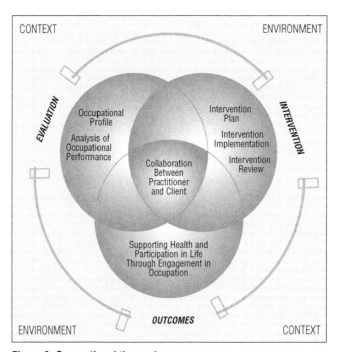

Figure 3. Occupational therapy's process.

Reprinted from "Occupational Therapy Practice Framework: Domain and Process" (2nd ed., p. 627), by American Occupational Therapy Association, 2008, *American Journal of Occupational Therapy, 62,* 625–683. Used with permission.

pational needs, problems, concerns, desires, and priorities and the analysis of occupational performance, which includes the skills, patterns, contexts and environments, activity demands, and client factors that contribute to or impede the client's satisfaction with his or her ability to engage in valued daily life activities. Therapists then plan and implement intervention using a variety of approaches and methods in which occupation is both the means and ends (Gray, 1998; Trombly, 1995). Occupational therapists continually assess the effectiveness of the intervention and the client's progress toward targeted outcomes. This ongoing intervention review informs decisions to continue or discontinue intervention and any need to make referrals to other agencies or professionals.

The occupational therapy intervention approaches for community-living older adults to support productive aging may include promotion, restoration, maintenance, compensation, or prevention (AOTA, 2008b). *Promotion interventions* seek to support health and augment contextual and activity experiences that enhance performance in the client's life (AOTA, 2008b). Interventions seek to support a client's goals to enhance or improve body functions, performance skills, or performance patterns to sustain health and performance in occupations. One example of promotion is group intervention focusing on behavioral strategies targeting participation in desired occupations for community-dwelling older adults with chronic pain.

Restorative intervention seeks to change client variables that affect performance in areas of occupation (AOTA, 2008b; Dunn, McClain, Brown, & Youngstrom, 1998). Intervention focuses on attaining restorative goals when the person shows potential and desire for change in body functions, performance skills, or patterns of performance. Restorative interventions include the use of selected therapeutic procedures designed to promote recovery or change in body functions, such as muscle strength or cognitive ability. Restorative intervention also includes therapeutic practice to improve performance skills and performance patterns.

Maintenance interventions include those interventions focusing on preserving a client's occupational performance, which may decline without intervention (AOTA, 2008b). One example of a maintenance intervention is an occupational therapy practitioner educating a community-living older adult about independently completing a home exercise program to maintain current strength gained during an occupational therapy plan of care. The functional exercise program can be integrated into the client's daily routines and occupations (e.g., emptying the dishwasher, washing windows).

Compensatory interventions include adaptations to activity demands and the performance environment that enable a person to resume performance of valued occupations even when deficits in body functions, performance skills, or performance patterns are not amenable to change (Dunn et al., 1998). Compensatory intervention approaches also involve teaching the client skills and strategies that enable him or her to use preserved abilities to "work around" impairments. By modifying the activity demands, patterns of performance, or environment, the community-living older adult may be able to continue to engage in valued occupations. For example, people with arthritis who report having difficulty participating in gardening tasks, specifically holding on to the tools and kneeling to work at ground level, may benefit from a compensatory gardening intervention incorporating adapted gardening equipment with built-up handles (to address difficulty holding tools) and raised flowerbeds (to compensate for difficulty kneeling) to facilitate participation in this desired activity. Similarly, an individual with arthritis may have difficulty caring for a pet, including opening food containers, reaching water and food bowls on the ground, and grooming the pet. The occupational therapy practitioner may educate the client on strategies to address pet grooming activities, including the use of alternative equipment such as a wide handle can opener to assist with opening food containers and alternative strategies for food placement to limit bending and kneeling. These compensatory strategies (e.g., modified equipment) address the limitations in body function caused by the arthritis that may otherwise prevent the individual's participation.

Preventive approaches include designing interventions with the objective of preventing occurrence or progression of barriers to performance (AOTA, 2008b). There are three levels of prevention: (1) primary, (2) secondary, and (3) tertiary. *Primary prevention* interventions are focused on addressing risk factors, maintaining health, or addressing potential characteristics that may place a person at potential risk of an illness or event before its onset (Mausner & Bahn, 1974). One example of a primary prevention program would be a home safety assessment to reduce the risk of falls and home safety accidents.

Secondary prevention is defined as the early detection and treatment of a disease or disability with the rationale that early intervention will limit or prevent the further progression of the disease or disability (Mausner & Bahn, 1974; Patrick, Richardson, Starks, Rose, & Kinne, 1997). An example of secondary prevention can include instructing older adults with a history of arthritis on strategies and adaptive equipment to perform activities of daily living (ADLs) and instrumental activities of daily living (IADLs) without putting undue strain on joints to minimize further decline in function (AOTA, 2008b).

Tertiary prevention includes minimizing the impact of an existing disease or disability in an effort to maximize existing quality of life (Clark et al., 2011; Mausner & Bahn, 1974). This may include educating a person who has low vision and diabetes about specialized equipment and techniques (e.g., talking blood glucose monitors, insulin syringe magnifier) to manage his or her diabetes successfully and minimize acute episodes.

The intervention review process is based on carefully observing the client's response to intervention and tracking and analyzing the client's progress, which can contribute to the science of productive aging by providing replicable case examples. Therapists select outcome measures that are valid, reliable, and appropriately sensitive to the client's occupational performance, satisfaction, adaptation, role competence, culture, health and wellness, prevention, self-advocacy, quality of life, and occupational justice (i.e., access to and opportunities for participation in the full range of meaningful and enriching occupations afforded to others within the community to satisfy personal, health, and societal needs [adapted from Townsend & Wilcock, 2004]).

Productive Aging

Background

The population in the United States is aging; by 2030, it is estimated that 20% of the U.S. population will be 65 years of age or older (U.S. Bureau of the Census, 2009). Among people 65 years or older, the fastest-growing segment of the population is those 85 years or older. Further, women live longer than men. The aging population is expected to be more diverse than previous cohorts of older adults, with Hispanics making up the fastest-growing segment of the aging population (He, Sengupta, Velkoff, & Debarros, 2005; Shrestha, 2006). The diversity of this aging U.S. population not only captures racial and ethnic differences among older adults but also highlights the existence of health disparities (Agency for Healthcare Research and Quality, 2008; Betancourt & King, 2003; Betancourt, Maina, & Soni, 2005; Nickens, 1986; Yen, Michael, & Perdue, 2010). Specifically, variations in available social and financial resources can influence the client's access to and use of preventive health care and chronic disease management (Institute for the Future, 2003).

The baby boomer generation and the current generation of older adults are living longer than previous generations, with life expectancy having almost doubled over the last 100 years (National Center for Health Statistics, 2011). In 1900, life expectancy was 47.3 years of age; life expectancy had increased to 77.9 as of 2007 (He, Sengupta, Velkoff, & Debarros, 2005; National Center for Health Statistics, 2011; Shrestha, 2006). Chronic conditions are expected to be the leading cause of disability globally by 2020 (World Health Organization, 2010). In addition, those people 85 years of age or older have the highest rates of health care use and have been associated with higher rates of morbidity and disability (Breyer, Costa-Font, & Felder 2010; Christensen, Doblhammer, Rau, & Vaupel, 2009).

As the number of older adults continues to increase, the proportion of older adults living with one or more chronic conditions continues to grow. To support productive aging and continued partici-pation, despite occupational shifts in habits, roles, and routines, preventive care models are needed. These programs should include self-management programs or strategies to support participation that will support older adults in the management of their chronic conditions and the prevention of illness and injury. The facilitation of productive aging among community-living older adults includes the continued participation in desired occupations and maximizing quality of life while minimizing acute episodes that result in hospitalizations.

Definition and Historical Context

Productive aging, a term introduced by Robert Butler in 1983, broadly refers to a variety of activities that mark the multiple ways people contribute to their own health and life, to their families and communities, and to society as they age (Butler, 2002; Butler & Gleason, 1985). Using nationally representative data from the American Changing Lives Survey, Hinterlong and colleagues (2008) estimated that 85% of Americans age 60 years or older participated in one or more productive activities (e.g., paid work, volunteering, caregiving, providing informal assistance to others) at some point over a 9-year period. The same study found that time engaged in productive aging declined with advancing age (Hinterlong, 2008). Butler framed this topic as a positive alternative to the existing dominant perception of older adults as frail, withdrawn, and dependent on society (Butler & Gleason, 1985, p. xii).

Underpinning the conceptualization of productive aging is the idea that remaining engaged in paid or voluntary roles, and their associated activities, has benefits for the aging individual as well as society (Hinterlong & Williamson, 2006/2007). Butler, Gleason, and their colleagues recognized the diversity of the aging experience and the interconnectedness of health, activity, and social attitudes toward the aged. Their goal was to explore ways older people could continue to work, participate in their communities, volunteer, remain physically active, and engage in self-care. In turn, productive activity would allow older adults to shape the public perceptions of aging beyond the stereotype of dependency (Butler & Gleason, 1985).

Over the past three decades, much has changed in relation to productive aging through recognition of the activities engaged in by older adults (e.g., raising grandchildren, paid work, volunteering); yet, there is still much more to be done to engage people productively across the expanding life course (Rowe, 2007). As scholars have investigated productive aging, there has been some question about the activities that should be considered productive. Although paid work, volunteering, and family caregiving have been accepted activities within the productive aging paradigm and have received the most attention in the literature, the definitions of productive aging have varied. This differentiation in definitions has altered the activities included in this area of research. Moreover, many studies focus on a single activity, such as labor force participation; this in turn has led to many specific areas of inquiry with limited studies examining productive aging in a more holistic or broad perspective (Hinterlong, 2008).

One early definition emphasized social and economic forces by defining productive aging as participation in any activity that resulted in supplying a good or service without which an alternative product or service would have to be purchased (Herzog, Kahn, Morgan, Jackson, & Antonucci, 1989). In addition to the activities of paid employment, volunteer work, and caregiving, this definition of productive aging included informal volunteering or helping, home maintenance, and housework.

Another definition of productive aging developed by Caro, Bass, and Chen (1993) characterized productive aging as any paid or unpaid activity an older adult engaged in that "contributes to producing goods or services, or develops the capacity to produce them" (p. 6). According to this definition, housework and leisure-time activities are excluded, whereas education and job training became part of the discussion of productive aging. The inclusion of education acknowledged that older adults may need or desire to continue to learn new skills and take on new work challenges as they approach and pass retirement. Rowe and Kahn (1998) suggested that productive aging include any paid or unpaid activity performed by an aging individual that provides "valued" goods or services in society (p. 47). In this context, productive activities—paid work, volunteering, civic engagement, housework, and caregiving—are placed within an individual context of remaining socially engaged with life.

Although the activities included in the definitions of productive aging vary, a common element across definitions is the recognition of the age-related changes in habits, roles, and routines that are influenced by familial responsibilities, health, financial security, labor force participation, and personal preferences that lead older adults to engage in valued activities as they age. Supporters of a productive aging approach are interested in ways to facilitate participation among older adults. In fact, the term *productive aging* is popularly used to note a positive view of aging and the importance of socially engaging older adults (Bass & Caro, 2001).

Productive Aging and Occupational Therapy: A Holistic Perspective

The sociological concept of productive aging described in the previous section is closely tied to the *Occupational Therapy Practice Framework* (AOTA, 2008b) and the tenets of the profession that postulate that engagement in occupation promotes health and well-being across the care continuum (Meyer, 1922; Peloquin, 1991a, 1991b). Consistent with the sociological definitions of productive aging, AOTA stated, "Productive aging involves care of self and others, management of home, engagement in leisure and physical activities, civic engagement, and social interaction which can involve travel, entertaining, and visiting with friends" (AOTA, 2010a). AOTA's definition of productive aging offers a more holistic and expansive perspective than past literature on productive aging by encompassing a wider range of IADLs. This practice guideline focuses on providing clinicians information using this broader perspective.

Three factors influence an individual's ability to engage in productive aging: (1) mental and physical functioning, (2) the degree of social relations and friendships with others, and (3) an individual's educational obtainment and sense of mastery (Rowe & Kahn, 1998). Focusing on these factors is not meant to diminish the role that public policy, global economic factors, and negative attitudes (or ageism) can have on the ability of an individual to productively age (Bass & Caro, 2001) but rather to focus attention on individual factors affecting occupation as people age. For example, screening tools for depression, vision loss, and cognitive decline can be effective tools for determining the level of an individual's participation in instrumental, leisure, and social activities (Perlmutter, Bhorade, Gordon, Hollingsworth, & Baum, 2010). Such participation can influence an individual's ability to productively age. Occupational therapy practitioners have the training to identify and develop interventions focusing on the factors that affect participation in desired occupations and therefore influence productive aging (AOTA, 2008b).

Stav, Hallenen, Lane, and Arbesman (2012) conducted a systematic review of the relationship between occupational performance and health in older adults. This review was designed to examine the engagement of community-dwelling older adults in various occupations and activities (e.g., IADLs, work, social activity, leisure activity, sleep) and the affect of health and well-being.

Factors Influencing Productive Aging

Older adults in the United States who strive to age productively are faced with multiple obstacles, including the challenges of the aging process, societal norms and expectations, changes in financial and caregiving resources, and environmental challenges, that can affect their ability to remain in their homes, engage in the community, and participate in desired occupations. Occupational therapy practitioners need to be cognizant of the multiple factors affecting older adults' ability to participate in desired occupations

and embrace a holistic perspective when developing and implementing interventions to address productive aging among community-dwelling older adults.

The Aging Process

Aging is universal, but how an individual ages varies from person to person, because each individual is influenced by his or her environment, heredity, lifestyle, and illness (Busse, 1969; Masoro & Austad, 2006). *Primary aging* and *secondary aging* are terms that distinguish between the universal aging trajectory experienced by all (primary aging) and the impact of disease process, impairments, and disability on aging (secondary aging; Busse, 1969). Primary aging includes the changes that occur even in the absence of disease (Busse, 1969). Examples of primary aging include decreasing bone strength, decreasing reaction time, slowing of the metabolism, thinning of the skin, and decreasing muscle mass. Secondary aging includes age-related changes caused by environmental characteristics (e.g., sedentary lifestyle, poor diet, smoking) and disease (e.g., macular degeneration, osteoporosis; Masoro & Austad, 2006).

Approximately 50% of older U.S. adults have at least two chronic health conditions (secondary aging changes), and 20% of older adults in the United States have a chronic disability (He et al., 2005; Shrestha, 2006). Many factors can cause chronic disability among older adults. For example, cognitive decline (e.g., Alzheimer's disease) contributes to disability and limitations in occupational performance (Letts et al., 2011). Race, ethnicity, socioeconomic status, gender, and marital status have been associated with disability in the United States. Specifically, women experience more disability then men (Chappell & Dujela, 2008). People with lower education (Verbrugge, 1991), people who are not married, and Black Americans have been found to have the highest rates of disability (Kominski et al., 2002; Verbrugge, 1991).

The prevalence of disability also has been associated with increased age and decreased occupational performance. Seventy-eight percent of people age 85 years or older have difficulty performing their daily self-care routine (American Geriatric Society, n.d.). As people age, they also can experience increased difficulty in participating in IADLs, including home management, financial management; meal preparation and clean-up; shopping, caregiving; pet care; child rearing; religious observance; safety and emergency maintenance; and community mobility. In addition, other areas of occupation that may be affected by the aging process include sleep, work (paid and volunteer), education (i.e., lifelong learning), leisure, and social participation (Orellano, Colón, & Artesman, 2012).

Participation in desired occupations also may be limited because of changes in performance patterns or because of an incompatibility between the older adult and his or her context and environment. Lifelong routines of older adults may become more challenging to perform because of aging changes (either primary or secondary aging processes). Occupational therapy practitioners are uniquely qualified to address the influences of these aging changes on the participation of older adults, given their knowledge of factors that affect occupational performance. The occupational therapy practitioner can use occupation-based interventions with the older adult when modifying existing roles, routines, habits, and rituals to facilitate participation in the desired occupations. Similarly, the occupational therapy practitioner can develop interventions and work collaboratively with the older adult to identify appropriate changes to his or her contexts and environments to maximize safety, facilitate independence and confidence, and limit fall risk to support participation in desired occupations.

Occupational therapy practitioners have a long history of working with older adults within the medical model to address ADL and IADL limitations after an acute medical event. Guided by the same principles of the *Framework,* occupational therapy practitioners have specialized knowledge and skills to address occupational participation with community-living older adults outside the traditional medical setting. For example, an occupational therapist can develop and administer a disease self-management program for people in an assisted living facility or for

an Area Agency on Aging that serves all the senior centers within its region.

Societal Norms and Expectations

Society's norms and expectations are additional important factors that affect older adults. Neugarten (1974) introduced three temporal categories of older adults—the young old, the old old, and the oldest old—to operationalize the societal norms and expectations of older adults. Clinicians should be aware of these temporal categories of older adults when designing and implementing interventions to support productive aging. These temporal categories can provide clinicians with a framework for societal norms and expectation for the older adult population.

The *young old* includes people ages 65 to 74 years who may be transitioning from work to retirement (Neugarten, 1974). The young old have been described as being active in leisure roles and socialization (Federal Interagency Forum on Aging-Related Statistics, 2010), as well as grandparenting, and have fewer physical and cognitive impairments than people 75 years of age or older (Federal Interagency Forum on Aging-Related Statistics, 2010). The young old have a higher likelihood of living with their spouse (Fields & Casper, 2001).

The *old old* (people 75–84 years of age) are more likely to live alone, have a higher likelihood of experiencing loss of significant others, and may experience modification of occupational role performance (e.g., requiring assistance with certain occupations; Fields & Casper, 2001; He et al., 2005). People in the *oldest old* category (85 years of age or older) have been associated with multiple chronic conditions, decreased participation in leisure activities, limited ADLs and IADLs, increased risk of institutionalization, and increased health care use (Campion, 1994; Federal Interagency Forum on Aging-Related Statistics, 2010).

Clinicians also should be aware that frequent societal shifts that occur (e.g., economic climate changes, policy changes) may alter the norms and expectations of older adults, as described by Neugarten (1974). The national economic shift has led to delayed retirement (U.S. Bureau of Labor Statistics, 2011), adult children returning home to live with parents (Pettersson & Malmberg, 2009), and grandparents raising grandchildren (U.S. Bureau of the Census, 2008). These could be examples of alternate expectations and norms that may occur among older adults and that are not captured in Neugarten's operationalization of older adults. For example, a 78-year-old client may seek occupational therapy services to facilitate productive aging. The societal norms for an individual categorized in the old old group would not be seeking interventions to return to the paid workforce, based on Neugarten's work (1974). During better economic times, this person may express a goal of being able to participate in desired volunteer activities. In light of the current economic climate in the United States (a societal shift), this same person may now express a goal of needing to return to work, and the intervention would incorporate performance skills related to returning to paid work instead of skills required to participate in desired volunteer activities. Within the context of this societal shift, this goal of returning to paid work may be perceived as a new norm or accepted expectation, whereas this desire to return to work in different economic times may not be perceived as an accepted norm or expectation.

Work

Work is another important factor clinicians should be aware of when intervening with community-dwelling older adults. Older adults who retire at the United State's traditional retirement age of 65 can spend 30 or more years in retirement (Benartzi, 2010; Johnson, Soto, & Zedlewski, 2008; Wallace, 2008). Although more people are choosing to work past age 65 (Johnson et al., 2008; U.S. Bureau of Labor Statistics, 2011), increasing life expectancy requires them to have planned financially over the life course, building up enough financial resources to potentially support their lifestyle for three decades in retirement. In addition, research has shown that savings have decreased over time and Social Security is making up a larger proportion of older adults' retirement income (AARP & American Council of Life Insurers, 2007; Benartzi, 2010; Butrica, 2008; Butrica, Murphy, & Zedlewski, 2008; Clark et al., 2001; Johnson et al., 2008). The accumulated impact

of smaller accrued savings, recent economic changes, and limited financial planning for retirement has created the need for many older adults to work past the traditional retirement age or return to the workforce after they retire. As of 2009, 6.5 million people 65 years of age or older were in the labor force, and this number is expected to increase to 11.1 million by 2018 (U.S. Bureau of Labor Statistics, 2011).

Understanding the financial status of older adults is essential for the occupational therapy clinician when addressing productive aging. For older adults with a goal of returning to work or continuing to work, occupational therapy practitioners may focus interventions on limitations that may affect the older adult's ability to participate in the workforce or modifications to the job site or tasks to improve performance (Gupta & Sabata, 2010; O'Hayer, 2009). Alternatively, for older adults who have retired and do not plan to return to the workforce, clinicians need to be aware of the older adult's financial resources, especially when recommending equipment or modifications.

Volunteering

Older adults may also engage in unpaid work as well as paid work, and the occupational therapy practitioner can play a role in supporting engagement in volunteer activities. *Volunteering* is a flexible, unpaid activity performed by a person, by choice, to assist another person or group of people (Wilson, 2000). Formal volunteering, or community-based volunteering, is organized by an institution (e.g., hospital, religious organization, senior center) and designed for the direct or indirect benefit of others (Wilson & Musick, 1997). Volunteering can involve a wide scope of activities that may offer opportunities for older adults to contribute to others in their communities and to remain socially engaged (Fischer & Schaffer, 1993). Volunteering can be a meaningful occupation for older adults and a mechanism to help structure their time or a routine leading to an enhanced purpose to their life or a sense of belonging or incorporation into a social network (Musick & Wilson, 2003; Wilson, 2000).

According to the U.S. Bureau of Labor Statistics, in 2010, approximately 24% of adults 65 years of age or older provided some form of volunteer work for a community organization, and these people most frequently engaged in volunteering through a religious institution. Although rates of volunteerism are highest among adults ages 35 to 44, on average, volunteers 65 or older devote the most time annually (96 hours) to volunteer work (U.S. Bureau of Labor Statistics, 2011). Recent research has supported the idea that volunteering for a community organization has a positive effect on the mental and physical health of older adults, and many policymakers would like to see an increase in the rates of volunteering as the baby boom generation retires (Grimm, Spring, & Dietz, 2007).

Informal volunteering, also referred to as *helping* or *informal social assistance,* usually involves providing aid to a friend or neighbor. Helping might involve driving a friend to an appointment or mowing a neighbor's lawn; these forms of volunteering are usually less structured than formal volunteer activities (Wilson, 2000; Wilson & Musick, 1997). Because of the unstructured nature of this form of volunteerism, less is known about this valued activity and its impact. However, studies suggest that this informal assistance is a common activity for people 55 or older (Hinterlong, 2008; Rowe & Kahn, 1998).

Although volunteering has been linked to positive outcomes for people engaged in this occupation, they must possess the capacity to perform the volunteer activity to participate (Thoits & Hewitt, 2001). Occupational therapy practitioners can help facilitate volunteer participation by increasing the congruency between the older adult and the volunteer work (AOTA, 2008b). For example, occupational therapy practitioners can help older adults identify volunteer opportunities that match their abilities, perform volunteer site assessments, make recommendations for volunteer site and task modification, and improve older adults' performance skills or client factors to facilitate volunteer work performance.

Caregiving

Other factors that affect older adults are becoming a caregiver or a care recipient. Many older adults serve as caregivers for spouses or significant others (Johnson & Schaner, 2005), children, and grandchildren (U.S. Bureau of the Census, 2008). The number of older adults who are primary caregivers for grandchildren has been increasing. As of 2008, 6.4 million grandparents in the United States had grandchildren younger than age 18 living with them, of which 2.6 million are responsible for providing the primary caregiving to these grandchildren. Approximately 1.6 million grandparents also were working while caring for their grandchildren (U.S. Bureau of the Census, 2008). Occupational therapy practitioners can work with older adults to support and facilitate participation in caregiving activities.

Families make up a large portion of informal caregiving resources (Stephens & Franks, 2009). Changes in family structures affect the caregiving resources available to older adults. The changing family structures have been influenced by the decline in the U.S. fertility rates (i.e., people not having as many children or any children) and changes in marital trends, including an increase in the divorce rate and an increase in the number of people who never married. Among adults 65 years of age or older, in 2003, 7% of men and 8.6% of women were divorced or never married (He et al., 2005). In addition, the global economy has resulted in adult children and parents living geographically further apart, resulting in an increase in distant caregiving (Neal, Wagner, Bonn, & Niles-Yokum, 2008). Adult children also are coping with balancing caregiving for aging parents while continuing to maintain other roles, such as worker and parent, which limit their ability to cope with the stress these multiple roles can create, often draining their energy and time (Dilworth & Kingsbury, 2005; Riley & Bowen, 2005).

Changing dynamics with respect to the family structure (e.g., fewer or no children) and proximity of family caregivers has significant implications for the availability of caregiving resources among older adults. Without family members to assist with caregiving, older adults will be required to use other resources as they age. Occupational therapy practitioners can work with older adults and their significant others to support and facilitate participation in caregiving activities by educating the caregiver on strategies to reduce caregiver burden and working with the care recipient to maximize their occupational performance.

Community Mobility and Driving

Age-associated changes in vision (Owsley, Stalvey, Wells, & Sloane, 1999), reflexes, muscle strength, or disease (Wang, Kosinksi, Schartzberg, & Shanklin, 2003) may limit a person's ability to drive safely in the community (Centers for Disease Control and Prevention, 2011). Alternatively, the person may experience secondary aging changes, which limit functional mobility in and around the home and hinder community mobility because of decreased endurance, strength, balance, and reaction time as a result of disease progression. When a person's functional mobility is impaired and he or she is no longer able to drive, walk in the community, or access public transportation, the opportunities for occupational engagement outside the home for that older adult can be limited (Dickerson et al., 2007). Although this practice guideline touches on community mobility and driving as it relates to productive aging, the reader is encouraged to consult the *Occupational Therapy Practice Guidelines for Driving and Community Mobility for Older Adults* (Stav, Hunt, & Arbesman, 2006), which provides a thorough overview of the evidence on driving assessment and intervention for older adults.

Aging in Place

In the United States, most older adults reside in the community and prefer to remain in the community as they age (Gitlin, 2003). The proportion of older adults living alone increases with age, particularly among women. For example, 29% of women 65 to 74 years of age live alone compared with 57% of women 85 years of age or older (He et al., 2005). Living alone, in an environment with multiple hazards that do not support the individual's optimal functioning (Gill, Williams, Robison, & Tinetti, 1999; Gitlin, 2003), experiencing a fall, or experiencing increased difficulty in participating in ADLs are all characteristics that place an individual at increased risk for institutionalization (Stel, Smit, Plujim, & Lips, 2004; Stevens, Corso, Finkelstein, & Miller, 2006; Tinetti & Williams, 1997). In addition, research suggests that older people living alone are at higher risk of social isolation; decreased level of social support and loneliness; and poorer mental, emotional, and physical health than their counterparts living with others (Cheng, Fung, & Chan, 2008; Cornwell & Waite, 2009; Kharicha et al., 2007; Routasalo, Savikko, Tilvis, Strandberg, & Pitkälä, 2006; St. John, Blandford, & Strain, 2006; Theeke, 2009; Yeh & Lo, 2004; You et al., 2009; You & Lee 2006).These statistics have significant implications for occupational therapy practitioners working with older adults. Occupational therapy practitioners can facilitate productive aging in place through interventions targeting the older adults' own environment and matching the needs of the individual with the demands of the environment in which they live (AOTA, 2011c).

Policies

Many policies are in place that affect the access and care of older adults. Occupational therapy practitioners need to be aware of federal and state policies that affect the lives of older adults, especially policies regarding Social Security benefits (e.g., old age survivor benefits, Supplemental Social Security Disability Insurance) and access to health care (e.g., Medicare Prescription Drugs, Improvement, and Modernization Act of 2003, the 2010 Patient Protection and Affordable Care Act; ACA). Although there has long been a belief in the three-legged stool of retirement financial security (i.e., personal savings, Social Security, and employer pension plan; Herd, 2009), recent research shows that Social Security benefits are often the primary income for older adults (McNamarra, Dobbs, Healey, & Kane, 2007). The passage of 1983 legislation that was targeted at addressing the solvency of Social Security resulted in the gradual transition of the Social Security eligibility age for full payment from ages 65 to 67 (Social Security Administration, 1984). Anyone born before 1937 is still eligible to access his or her full Social Security benefit at age 65. People born after 1937 and before 1960 are subject to the gradual age increase, which is currently being implemented by the Social Security Administration with the goal of achieving access to full benefits at age 67 (Social Security Administration, 2011). For example, those born between 1943 and 1954 are eligible for full benefits at age 66. The gradual age increase for Social Security eligibility is optimized at age 67. Anyone born in 1960 or later must be 67 years of age to access full Social Security benefits (Social Security Administration, 2011).

Two recent pieces of legislation that affect health care for older adults and occupational therapy services for older adults are the Medicare Prescription Drug, Improvement, and Modernization Act of 2003 (Center for Medicare Advocacy, 2004; Center for Medicare and Medicaid Services, Office of Legislation, 2004) and the 2010 ACA (Kaiser Family Foundation, 2011). The Medicare act included the introduction of a drug benefit for Medicare beneficiaries as well as the incorporation of coverage for certain preventive services (e.g., an initial welcome to Medicare physical, cardiovascular screening, diabetes screening) for Medicare beneficiaries (Center for Medicare Advocacy, 2004). Practitioners also need to have an understanding of the ACA, because the programs and policies associated with this bill are developed and implemented over time. In particular, occupational therapy practitioners should be aware of rehabilitation and habilitation inclusion under the health insurance exchange plans, how payments are made, and how accountable care organizations may affect reimbursement and practice patterns.

Other Factors Affecting Older Adults

Numerous other factors affect older adults, including loss, depression, and substance abuse. All of these factors can limit the ability of adults to age productively. Older adults may experience many losses as they age, such as a loss in roles (e.g., worker to retiree, caregiver to care receiver), a reduction of support networks as a result of deaths of loved ones and friends, and a loss in independence. Older adults are also at a higher risk for depression when they experience a decline in their functioning (National Institute of Mental Health, 2007).

The proportion of people 65 years old or older with depressive symptoms is higher than any other younger age groups (Federal Interagency Forum on Aging-Related Statistics, 2010). Older adults also are more

likely to die by suicide compared with other age groups (National Institute of Mental Health, 2007). Clinicians also should be aware of the growing trend of substance abuse among older adults, which is sometimes used with a result of depression (Johns Hopkins Medicine, 2009). A recent study found increased abuse of prescription drugs, illegal drugs (e.g., heroin, cocaine), and alcohol among older adults (Substance Abuse and Mental Health Services Administration, Office of Applied Studies, 2009). Occupational therapy practitioners can play a role in facilitating occupational engagement to limit loss in roles, improve functioning, and support health and well-being (Stav et al., 2012).

Summary

This practice guideline highlights a few of the factors that affect older adults as a foundation for understanding the role occupational therapy practitioners can play in facilitating productive aging. The factors highlighted here are not exhaustive but touch on the diversity of issues affecting older adults and the need for occupational therapy practitioners to have a holistic perspective to facilitate productive aging. This practice guideline presents the current evidence on productive aging for community-dwelling older adults. The authors also acknowledge that the evidence presented is within the context of productive aging for community-dwelling older adults; people seeking detailed evidence on specific populations (i.e., Alzheimer's disease, low vision) or detailed evidence related to community mobility can refer to AOTA's practice guidelines focusing on these three topic areas. The *Occupational Therapy Practice Guidelines for Adults With Alzheimer's Disease and Related Disorders* (Schaber, 2010) provides a comprehensive perspective on the current evidence on Alzheimer's disease, approaches, and interventions. The *Occupational Therapy Practice Guidelines for Older Adults With Low Vision* (Kaldenberg & Smallfield, in press) provides detailed information on low vision approaches, and interventions. The *Occupational Therapy Practice Guidelines for Driving and Community Mobility for Older Adults* (Stav et al., 2006) provides a thorough overview of the evidence on driving assessment and intervention for older adults.

Occupational Therapy Process to Facilitate Productive Aging

Settings

Services for community-dwelling older adults to facilitate productive aging may occur at an individual, organization, and population level in a variety of facilities and community-based settings. The types of facilities where occupational therapy practitioners may provide services to community-dwelling older adults include home, inpatient rehabilitation, outpatient settings, continuing care retirement communities, transitional care units, or short-term rehabilitation in a skilled nursing facility. A few examples of community settings where occupational therapy practitioners may work with community-dwelling older adults includes homes, senior centers, Area Agencies on Aging, and Councils on Aging (AOTA, 2006a; Brachtesende, 2005a, 2005b; Ratnoff, Becker-Omvig, Elliott, O'Sullivan, & Talley, 2002).

In addition, occupational therapy practitioners also have a role in facilitating productive aging at the individual, organizational, or population level while consulting or working in settings such as low vision centers (Gourley, 2007), assisted living facilities, work sites (Brachtesende, 2005a, 2005b; Evans et al., 2008), group homes (AOTA, 2010c), transportation boards or driver assessment clinics (Stav, Arbesman, & Lieberman, 2008), adult day centers (Easton & Herge, 2011; Kaminsky, 2010), fitness centers (AOTA, 2010c), and senior housing complexes or retirement communities (including naturally occurring retirement communities; Elbert & Neufeld, 2010; Farrell & Murphy, 2010; Grisbrooke & Scott, 2009). Working in nontraditional settings or with nontraditional populations may require alternative funding sources (refer to Appendix D).

Occupational therapy practitioners need to be aware of legislation in their state that may determine the need for a physician's order or certification to evaluate and provide interventions to older adults, particularly when working outside the traditional medical model (e.g., direct access) where there is no qualifying hospital stay or medical event initiating the services (Robinson-Brown & Robinson, 2010). State practice acts and licensure/certification regulations offer guidance and specific regulations regarding referral requirements, because these regulations vary from state to state. Many states allow for direct access to occupational therapy services, but some states do require a physician's order. Many of these laws have exemptions for practice in nontraditional or "nonmedical" settings (AOTA, 2010c).

Screening

Screening is defined as "obtaining and reviewing data relevant to a potential client to determine the need for further evaluation and intervention" (AOTA, 2010d, p. 2). Screening approaches can include interviews, structured observations, informal testing, and record reviews (Collier, 1991; Hinojosa, Kramer, & Crist, 2010). The objective of the screening process is to identify whether a person is experiencing difficulty with participation in desired occupations and may benefit from an occupational therapy evaluation and possible intervention. The occupational therapist is responsible for the screening process; the occupational therapy assistant can contribute to the screening process within the parameters of state and federal legislation (AOTA, 2010d). A variety of standardized screening tools (e.g., Model of Human Occupation Screening Tool; Kielhofner et al., 2009) can be used to identify whether a client has limitations or problems that occupational therapy can address or perhaps refer to another provider. Table 1 provides examples of the screening process conducted at the individual, organizational, and population level.

Older adults and their significant others or the occupational therapist then would discuss the results

Table 1. Examples of Screening the Client

Background: Twenty percent of adults in the United States have arthritis (Hootman & Helmick, 2006; Murphy, Nyquist, Strasburg, & Alexander, 2006). Arthritis is a common cause of disability and health care use (Brault, Hootman, Helmick, & Theis, 2009; Hootman & Helmick, 2006; Murphy et al., 2006; Yelin et al., 2007). Interventions found to be effective in managing arthritis include providing education in self-management of arthritis, increasing physical activity, and managing weight/minimizing obesity (Arthritis Foundation, 2011a; Arthritis Foundation, Association of State & Territorial Health Officials, & Centers for Disease Control and Prevention, 1999; Murphy, Lyden, Smith, Dong, & Koliba, 2010).

Client With Arthritis

Individual	Organization	Population
Mr. Jones has been attending senior center activities for the past year, since he retired. His former occupation was a machinist for a military contracting company. Mr. Jones's primary hobby is working in his shop in his garage repairing electrical equipment. His arthritis and his current hand pain have made participation in this desired occupation more difficult.	As the **occupational therapy consultant** for a local assisted living facility (ALF) chain, **James** has been asked to conduct an organizational level screening of the ALF chain to identify whether he can assist the organization to better meet the needs of its residents with arthritis. ■ James set up a meeting with the manager overseeing all of this organization's ALFs. ■ In the meeting, the manager reviewed his concerns about the residents with arthritis at his chain's ALFs and the current services offered to all residents.	*Healthy People 2020* (U.S. Department of Health and Human Services, 2010) identified reducing the number of people with arthritis experiencing limitations in ADLs and IADLs as one of its priorities. The state health department has embraced this initiative and tasked each county in the state with developing an arthritis action plan.
Deirdre, an occupational therapist, met Mr. Jones at a health fair he attended at the local senior center where Deirdre was providing occupational therapy screenings for attendees. Deirdre completed the screening through a brief interview with Mr. Jones. She focused on the identifying the following items: ■ Daily activities and routines (occupations) that are impaired by his arthritis pain ■ His current abilities and impairments (e.g., Does he feel that his strength has decreased? Is it harder for him to repair electrical equipment than it was before his arthritis flare-up?) ■ His current pain level and its affect on his daily routine and occupations.	■ James inquired whether any of the facilities had conducted a needs assessment regarding services for people with arthritis. ■ James also inquired whether each facility tracks the number of residents with arthritis and their abilities to perform daily activities over time. He also inquired as to whether strategies are in place to prevent or improve any functional decline. ■ James discussed with the manager the necessity of conducting a needs assessment to determine which needs are and are not being met. ■ He also discussed the need to develop a tracking and screening system for people with arthritis to identify changes in their abilities to perform daily activities. ■ James discussed the need to identify any existing contextual and environmental barriers for residents with arthritis.	The state health department would like **Sabrina, the occupational therapist,** to conduct a population-level screening with the county health department representatives to determine whether a full evaluation and intervention is required to meet the initiative. Sabrina set up a meeting with the county health department representatives. During the meeting, she inquired about the county's arthritis prevalence and the type of services that currently exist. The meeting representatives stated that services vary in different parts of the county and that they are unaware of some services being provided because they do not come under the umbrella of their organization.
Deidre and Mr. Jones discussed the results of his screening and determined that an occupational therapy evaluation was warranted. Mr. Jones stated he would ask the physician next week, during his regular appointment with the rheumatologist, about a prescription for an occupational therapy evaluation.	■ James discussed the need to identify existing services and systems for ALF residents with arthritis to support current level of performance and prevent decline in occupational participation. ■ James offered to meet with the administrators and directors of nursing at each facility to discuss their concerns and review evidence-based intervention and programs beneficial to people with arthritis. The manager at the ALF and James agreed that James should conduct an organizational level evaluation based on the results of the screening.	During the meeting, Sabrina discussed conducting a countywide needs assessment to identify existing services for people with arthritis in the county she was tasked with screening. The needs assessment would help her identify existing exercise and health education community programs and resources for this population and help her determine other services people with arthritis need and would like offered. Sabrina also found out that the county does not have a tracking system in place to identify the prevalence of people with arthritis and related disability. The county health department representatives and Sabrina decided that she should conduct a population-level evaluation on the basis of the screening results.

Note. ADLs = activities of daily living; IADLs = instrumental activities of daily living.

of the completed screening with their physicians to determine whether a referral for occupational therapy services is needed. During the screening process, occupational therapy clinicians should educate the older adults and their caregivers about the screening process, results of the screening, and recommendations and education about occupational therapy or relevant other services on the basis of the screening results (AOTA, 2010d). This education cannot only empower older adults to advocate for needed services but also encourage them to seek future screenings as they experience age-associated changes or difficulties performing meaningful occupations.

Referral

A referral for occupational therapy services for community-living older adults to facilitate productive aging will vary on the basis of the setting, state regulations, insurance requirements, and the client. The referral sources for occupational therapy services will differ based on the client (i.e., individual, organization, population) and the client's needs.

Individuals

In community-based settings, referrals can originate from many different sources, such as physicians, case managers, nurses, organizations and agencies (e.g., adult day care centers, councils on aging, senior centers) or institutions (e.g., skilled nursing facilities, assisted living facilities) and from other health care professionals. In many community-based settings, the client may self-refer. However, a physician referral still may be needed for insurance reimbursement and to comply with state regulations. Occupational therapists also need to be aware of the purpose of the referral (i.e., private pay preventive intervention vs. a referral initiated because of a decline in occupational performance). A referral may be initiated with the expectation that an occupational therapy evaluation will be conducted and followed by direct services as appropriate. Alternatively, the referral may be consultative in nature, requiring an evaluation with recommendations for other providers or services.

When receiving referrals, the occupational therapist needs to be aware of state policies related to occupational therapy direct access (e.g., the state practice act, licensure regulations), and whether the interventions will be billed through Medicare, private insurance, or privately. Working in a state where an occupational therapist has direct access, the clinician may not need a physician's referral if the occupational therapy interventions will be paid for privately and if the occupational therapist is not a Medicare provider. If the treatment sessions (e.g., skilled rehabilitation provided by home health care) are covered by insurance (e.g., private insurance, Medicare), even if they are provided in a state where the occupational therapy practitioner has direct access, the insurance company often requires a physician's referral and a plan of care approved by the physician for reimbursement of services. Occupational therapy practitioners should check their state practice acts and licensure laws for regulations concerning referrals and direct access.

Organizations and Populations

Occupational therapists working with a client who is defined as an organization or a population may provide services in a variety of settings (e.g., senior centers, adult day centers, health clubs). Requests for consultation or ongoing occupational therapy services for organizations, which involve community-living older adults, may come directly from the organization itself. For example, an occupational therapist may provide input into environmental design for a newly proposed senior apartment complex, integrating the occupational therapy practitioner's knowledge of the person–environment fit with the Americans with Disabilities Act (ADA, 1990) guidelines to facilitate optimal participation in desired occupations among community-living older adults. Because these types of services often are not covered by insurance and may not be provided on an individual basis, a physician's referral may not be needed. However, therapists will need to refer to their state practice act and licensure regulations to ensure they are abiding by appropriate regulations.

Occupational therapy referrals also may relate to populations or groups of people who have similar conditions (e.g., older adults with arthritis). For example, an occupational therapist may run a chronic disease self-management group for older adults with osteoporosis who were referred by a physician or another health care provider or self-referred. Occupational therapists should review their licensure laws and state practice acts to determine whether they can provide services in nontraditional areas without a physician's order.

Evaluation

Occupational therapists perform evaluations in collaboration with the client family or caregiver/significant others and target information specific to the client's desired outcomes. The two major elements of the occupational therapy evaluation are (1) the occupational profile and (2) the analysis of occupational performance (AOTA, 2008b). Occupational therapists working with older adults to facilitate productive aging may use standardized and nonstandardized assessments specifically designed for use with community-living older adults.

The clinician needs to stay current in the use of standardized assessment tools used in his or her area of practice, ensuring that the assessment tools selected were designed or validated for use with the population worked with (e.g., community-living older adults). The use of a standardized assessment tool such as the Functional Independence Measure™ (FIM), designed for an inpatient rehabilitation population, would not provide valid and reliable results for treating a community-living older adult in a home setting. Occupational therapists should validate clinical observations with data from standardized assessments. The use of standardized assessments allows for retrospective analysis of client outcomes contributing to the evidence supporting practice. Standardized assessments also can be used to demonstrate engagement in occupations and provide evidence to support reimbursement for treatment. Table 2 provides an overview of commonly used selected assessments for community-living older adults.

The purpose of the occupational profile is to determine who the client or clients are (i.e., an individual, an organization, a population), identify

their needs or concerns, and ascertain how these concerns affect engagement in occupational performance. Information for the occupational profile is gathered through formal and informal interviews with the client and significant others and may occur in one finite time period or over a period of time. Conversations with the client help the occupational therapist gain perspective of how the client spends his or her time; what activities the client wants or needs to do; and how the environment in which the client lives, works, and socializes supports or hinders occupational engagement. Examples of information gathered in an occupational profile at the individual, organizational, and population level are depicted in the case studies in Table 3. Developing the occupational profile involves the following steps (AOTA, 2008b):

1. *Identify the client or clients.*
2. *Determine why the client is seeking services.* Through interviews or checklists, the occupational therapist assists the client in identifying the current concerns relative to the areas of occupation and performance. This is a critical part of the evaluation. Assessments such as the Canadian Occupational Performance Measure (COPM; Law, et al., 1998) may be helpful in setting client-centered goals for occupational performance (Jenkinson, Ownsworth, & Shum, 2007; Phipps & Richardson, 2007; Trombly, Radomski, & Davis, 1998).
3. *Identify the areas of occupation that are successful and the areas that are causing problems or risks.* Based on the client's current concerns, the occupational therapist identifies possible motor, cognitive, and behavioral impairments and environmental barriers and supports related to occupational performance. When working with community-living older adults to support productive aging, clinicians should consider health promotion, wellness, and prevention goals to support continued participation in desired occupations, in addition to identifying impairments in occupational performance.

Table 2. Examples of Standardized Screening Tools and Assessments

Screening Tools and Assessments	Reference
Occupational Performance/Participation Assessments	
Activity Card Sort (ACS)	Baum, C. M., & Edwards, D. (2008). *Activity card sort (ACS)*. Bethesda, MD: AOTA Press.
Canadian Occupational Performance Measure (COPM)	Law, M., Baptiste, S., McColl, M. A., Carswell, A., Polatajko, H., & Pollock, N. (2005). *Canadian Occupational Performance Measure* (3rd ed.). Toronto, Ontario: CAOT Publications CAE.
National Institutes of Health Activity Record (ACTRE)	Gerber, L., & Furst, G. (1992). Validation of the NIH activity record: A quantitative measure of life activities. *Arthritis Care Research, 5,* 81–86.
Occupational Questionnaire	Smith, N. R., Kielhofner, G., & Watts, J. H. (1986). The relationships between volition, activity pattern, and life satisfaction in the elderly. *American Journal of Occupational Therapy, 40*(4), 278–283.
Assessment of ADLs and IADLs	
Assessment of Living Skills and Resources (ALSAR)	Williams, J. H., Drinka, T. J. K., Greenberg, J. R., Farrell-Holtan, J., Euhardy, R., & Schram, M. (1991). Development and testing of the Assessment of Living Skills and Resources (ALSAR) in community-dwelling veterans. *The Gerontologist, 31,* 84–91.
Assessment of Motor and Process Skills (AMPS)	Doble, S. E., Fisk, J. D., Lewis, N., & Rockwood, K. (1999). Test–retest reliability of the Assessment of Motor and Process Skills (AMPS) in elderly adults. *Occupational Therapy Journal of Research, 19,* 203–215.
Melbourne Low Vision ADL Index	Haynes, S. A., Johnson, A. W., & Heyes, A. D. (2001). Preliminary investigation of the responsiveness of the Melbourne Low Vision ADL Index to low-vision rehabilitation. *Optometry and Vision Science, 78*(6), 373–380.
Performance Assessment of Self-Care Skills	Rogers, J. C., & Holm, M. B. (1989). *Performance Assessment of Self-Care skills (PASS–Home)*. Unpublished tests. Pittsburgh: University of Pittsburgh.
Work Assessments	
Blankenship System (TBS) Functional Capacity Evaluation	Narro, P., & Clarke, E. (2007). The sensitivity and specificity of the Blankenship FCE System's indicators of sincere effort. *Journal of Orthopaedic and Sports Physical Therapy, 37*(4), 161–168.
DSI Work Solutions Functional Capacity Assessment	Isernhagen, S. J. (n.d.). *A brief history of the Isernhagen–DSI Work Solutions Functional Capacity Assessment*. Retrieved March 9, 2011, from http://dsiworksolutions.com/history.htm
Workwell Systems Functional Capacity Evaluation	Soer, R., Van der Schans, C. P., Geertzen, J. H., Groothoff, J. W., Brouwer, S., Dijkstra, P. U., & Reneman, M. F. (2009). Normative values for a functional capacity evaluation. *Archives of Physical Medicine and Rehabilitation, 90*(10), 1785–1794.
Leisure Assessments	
Idyll Arbor Leisure Battery (IALB) Leisure Assessment Inventory	*Idyll Arbor Leisure Battery*. (2010). Retrieved March 9, 2011, from http://www.idyllarbor.com/agora.cgi?p_id=A145&xm=on
Older Americans Resources and Services (OARS) Multidimensional Functional Assessment Questionnaire (OMFAQ)	Fillenbaum, G. G. (2005). *Multidimensional functional assessment of older adults: The Duke Older American Resources and Services Procedures*. Hillsdale, NJ: Lawrence Erlbaum.
Social Participation and Quality of Life Assessments	
Satisfaction with Performance Scaled Questionnaire	Yerxa, E. J., Burnett-Beaulieu, S., Stockin, S., & Azen, S. P. (1988). Development of the satisfaction with performance scaled questionnaire. *American Journal of Occupational Therapy, 42,* 215–221.
Performance Skills: Motor Assessments	
Activities-Specific Balance Confidence Scale (ABC)	Powell, L. E., & Myers, A. M. (1998). The Activities-Specific Balance Confidence (ABC) Scale. *Journal of Gerontology, Medical Sciences, 50*(1), M28–M34.

(continued)

Table 2. Examples of Standardized Screening Tools and Assessments *(cont.)*

Screening Tools and Assessments	Reference
Disabilities of the Arm, Shoulder and Hand (DASH)	Institute for Work and Health. (2006). *The DASH outcome measure: Disabilities of the arm, shoulder, and hand*. Retrieved March 9, 2011, from http://www.dash.iwh.on.ca/conditions.htm
Dynamic Gait Index	Shumway-Cook, A., & Woollacott, M. (1995). *Motor control theory and applications*. Baltimore: Lippincot Williams & Wilkins.
Falls Efficacy Scale (FES)/ Falls Efficacy Scale International (FESI)	Tinetti, M., Richman, D., & Powell, L. (1990). Falls efficacy as a measure of fear of falling. *Journal of Gerontology, 45*, 239.
Fall Risk for Older People-Community setting [FROP–Com]	Russell, M. A., Hill, K. D., Blackberry, I., Day, L. M., & Dharmage, S. C. (2008). The reliability and predictive accuracy of the Falls Risk for Older People in the Community assessment (FROP–Com) tool. *Age and Ageing, 37*, 634–639.
Fullerton Advanced Balance Scale (FAB):	California State University, Fullerton, Center for Successful Aging. (2008). *Fullerton Advanced Balance (FAB) Scale*. Retrieved March 23, 2011, from http://hhd.fullerton.edu/csa/CenterProducts/center products_assessment.htm
Functional Reach	Duncan, P. W., Weiner, D. K., Chandler, J., & Studenski, S. (1990). Functional reach: A new clinical measure of balance. *Journal of Gerontology, 45*(6), M192–M197.
Modified Clinical Test of Sensory Interaction in Balance	California State University, Fullerton, Center for Successful Aging. (n.d.). *Modified Clinical Test of Sensory Interaction in Balance*. Retrieved March 13, 2012, from http://www.patientsafety.gov/SafetyTopics/ fallstoolkit/resources/educational/Balance_Assessment_Handbook.pdf
Senior Fitness Test	Rikli, R. E., & Jones, C. J. (2001). *Senior Fitness Test manual*. Champaign, IL: Human Kinetics.
Six Minute Walk Test	Enright, P. L., McBurnie, M. A., Bittner, V., Tracy, R. P., McNamara, R., Arnold, A., & Newman, A. B. (2003). The 6-Minute Walk Test: A quick measure of functional status in elderly adults. *Chest, 123*(2), 387–398.
Timed Up and Go (TUG)	Podsiadlo, D., & Richardson, S. (1991). The Timed Up and Go: A test of basic functional mobility for frail elderly persons. *Journal of the American Geriatrics Society, 39*(2), 142–148.

Performance Skills: Psychological Assessments

Caregiver Strain Index	Robinson, B. C. (1983). Validation of a Caregiver Strain Index. *Journal of Gerontology, 38*, 344–348.
Short Comprehensive Assessment and Referral Evaluation (SHORT–CARE)	Gurland, B., Golden, R. R., Teresi, J. A., & Challop, J. (1984). The SHORT–CARE: An efficient instrument for the assessment of depression, dementia, and disability. *Journal of Gerontology, 39*, 166–169.
Geriatric Depression Scale	Sivrioglu, E. Y., Sivrioglu, K., Ertan, T., Ertan, F. S., Cankurtaran, E., Aki, O., … Kirli, S. (2009). Reliability and validity of the Geriatric Depression Scale in detection of poststroke minor depression. *Journal of Clinical and Experimental Neuropsychology, 31*(8), 999–1006.

Performance Skills: Cognitive Assessments

Executive Function Performance Test	Baum C. M., Connor L. T., Morrison T., Hahn, M., Dromerick A. W., & Edwards, D. F. (2008). Reliability, validity, and clinical utility of the Executive Function Performance Test: A measure of executive function in a sample of people with stroke. *American Journal of Occupational Therapy, 62*(4), 446–455.
Montreal Cognitive Assessment	Nasreddine, Z. (2011). *Montreal Cognitive Assessment (MoCA)*. Retrieved February 29, 2011, from http://www.mocatest.org/
Short Blessed Test	Katzman, R., Brown, T., Fukd, P., Peck, A., Schechter, R., & Shimmel, H. (1983). Validation of a short orientation–memory–concentration test of cognitive impairment. *American Journal Psychiatry, 140*(6), 734–739.

Performance Patterns: Assessments of Roles, Habits, and Routines

Role Change Assessment	Rogers, J. C., & Holm, M. B. (1989). *Performance Assessment of Self-Care skills (PASS–Home)*. Unpublished tests. Pittsburgh: University of Pittsburgh.

Table 2. Examples of Standardized Screening Tools and Assessments *(cont.)*

Screening Tools and Assessments	Reference
Context and Environment	
Home Assessment Profile (HAP)	Chandler, J., Duncan, P., Weiner, D., & Studentski, S. (2001). The Home Assessment Profile—A reliable and valid assessment tool. *Topics in Geriatric Rehabilitation, 16,* 77–88.
Home Environment Assessment Protocol (HEAP)	Gitlin, L. N., Schinfeld, S., Winter, L., Corcoran, M., Boyce, A. A., & Hauck, W. (2002). Evaluating home environments of persons with dementia: Interrater reliability and validity of the Home Environmental Assessment Protocol (HEAP). *Disability and Rehabilitation, 24,* 59–71.
Home Falls and Accidents Screening Tool (Home Fast)	Mackenzie, L., Byles, J., & Higginbotham, N. (2002). Reliability of the Home Falls and Accidents Screening Tool (HOME FAST) for measuring falls risk for older people. *Disability and Rehabilitation, 24,* 266–274.
Safety Assessment of Function and the Environment for Rehabilitation (SAFER)	Oliver, R., Blath Wayt, J., Brackley, C., & Tamaki, T. (1993). Development of the Safety Assessment of Function and the Environment for Rehabilitation (SAFER) tool. *Canadian Journal of Occupational Therapy, 60,* 78–82.
Westmead Home Safety Assessment (WeHSA)	Cooper, B., Letts, L., Rigby, P., Stewart, D., & Strong, S. (2005). Measuring environmental factors. In M. Law, C. Baum, & W. Dunn (Eds.), *Measuring occupational performance: Supporting best practice in occupational therapy* (2nd ed., pp. 326–327). Thorofare, NJ: Slack.

4. *Discuss significant aspects of the client's occupational history.* Significant aspects can include life experiences (e.g., medical interventions, employment history, vocational preferences), occupational roles, interests, and previous occupational patterns that provide meaning to the client's life. These experiences may shape how the person deals with everyday routines and occupations.

5. *Determine the client's priorities and desired outcomes.* Although addressed at the initiation of occupational therapy services and at various times throughout the care process, the occupational therapist and client will discuss and prioritize outcomes so that the therapist's evaluation and intervention will align with the client's desired outcomes. The occupational therapist may need to refer the client to additional professionals to achieve some of the desired outcomes.

Analysis of Occupational Performance

Information from the occupational profile is used by the occupational therapist to focus on the specific areas of occupation and the context and environment in which the client (i.e., individual, organization, population) will live and function.

Individuals as Clients

- For individual clients, observe the client performing the occupations in the natural or least-restrictive environment (AOTA, 2009b), and note the effectiveness of the client's performance skills (e.g., motor and praxis, sensory–perceptual, cognitive, communication and social) and performance patterns (e.g., habits, routines, rituals, roles).

- Select specific assessments and evaluation methods that will identify and measure the factors related to the particular aspects of the domain (refer to Figure 1) that may be influencing the client's performance. These assessments may focus on the client's body structures and functions, activity performance, or community participation. See Table 2 for examples of selected assessments.

- Interpret the assessment data to identify what supports or hinders performance.

- Develop or refine a hypothesis regarding the client's performance (i.e., identify underlying impairments or performance skill limitations that

Table 3. Case Studies

Case A* — Use of Occupation/Activities to Improve IADL Performance

Background: Individual	Occupational Therapy Evaluation	Occupational Therapy Intervention
Mrs. Adam is a vivacious, friendly, and talkative 81-year-old woman who recently developed rotator cuff tendonitis in her dominant right shoulder. This condition is hindering her occupational performance. She also complained of increased stress from being a caretaker for her husband. *Referral:* Mrs. Adam went to her physician to inquire about her right shoulder pain. He gave her a cortisone injection and a prescription for occupational and physical therapy services. Mrs. Adam called an outpatient therapy center and made an appointment for an evaluation.	Mrs. Adam's occupational profile revealed the following: ■ She worked as a bookkeeper for more than 50 years at a local grocery store and retired approximately 10 years ago. She is married to her husband of 52 years and lives in a single-family home in a rural area. She has 1 son and 4 grandchildren who live in the same neighborhood. ■ Mrs. Adam loves to cook and is constantly experimenting with various recipes and foods. ■ She kept an impeccable house until 6 months ago, when her husband had a stroke. She says she needs to help him get up from any surface, and she thinks this is how she hurt her shoulder. ■ Before her recent injury and her husband's stroke, Mrs. Adam's activities consisted of managing the home finances, shopping, maintaining the house, working in the flower beds, preparing meals, swimming at a local gym, meeting her female friends for lunch, and traveling with her husband. ■ Since her husband had the stroke, she says she does not feel comfortable leaving him alone during the day because he may have trouble standing up from the couch. ■ Mrs. Adam is able to perform her IADLs independently and occasionally uses a cane for long-distance ambulation. The Canadian Occupational Performance Measure (COPM; Law et al., 2005) revealed the main areas Mrs. Adam wants to work on in occupational therapy are as follows: ■ Learning about caregiving resources and how to help her husband without injuring herself ■ Managing the finances electronically (pain in her right dominant shoulder is hindering her ability to write) ■ Preparing meals, cleaning up after meals, grocery shopping (pain hinders this), maintaining a clean household (pain hinders completing laundry, floor cleaning), watering plants, and maintaining flowers (hindered by shoulder pain). Her performance according to the COPM (Law et al., 2005) was 6.4, whereas her average satisfaction with current performance was 4.0. On the Disabilities of the Arm, Shoulder and Hand (DASH); (Institute for Work and Health, 2006), results indicated Mrs. Adam had ■ Severe difficulty (4/5) performing recreational activities that require arm movement or force ■ Moderate (3/5) to severe (4/5) right shoulder pain ■ Mild (2/5) to moderate (3/5) right arm weakness ■ Moderate difficulty (3/5) changing sheets, carrying objects over 10 lbs., washing hair, and driving ■ Mild difficulty (2/5) opening heavy doors, writing, carrying bags, and donning a pullover sweater.	■ **Susan, Mrs. Adam's occupational therapist,** provided services in the home under Medicare Part B because they both felt this location would be the best on the basis of Mrs. Adam's goals and her living situation. ■ Susan worked collaboratively with Mrs. Adam and her husband to help educate them on home modifications to support and improve Mrs. Adam's IADL independence and help her to identify and resolve issues that arise during IADL performance (Gitlin et al., 2006, 2008). ■ Susan provided functional task exercise interventions (de Vreede et al., 2004, 2005) to improve Mrs. Adam's ability to perform IADLs and to reduce her shoulder pain (e.g., putting away groceries, folding laundry, watering plants). Mrs. Adam and her husband learned available adaptive equipment and various compensatory techniques to improve IADL performance. ■ Susan worked with Mrs. Adam and her husband on types of ergonomic suitcases that would be easier and lighter to maneuver and reduce stress on her shoulder. ■ Mrs. Adam was educated on techniques to prevent further flare up of her rotator cuff muscles, including educating her on proper lifting techniques and having her husband use higher seating surfaces to decrease strain on her shoulder muscles when helping her husband. ■ Susan suggested Mr. and Mrs. Adam talk with Mr. Adam's physician about therapy to improve his ability to transfer.

Table 3. Case Studies *(cont.)*

Cases B1* and B2* — Effectiveness of Home Modification and Fall Prevention Interventions on Performance

Case B1: Client as an Individual

Background	Occupational Therapy Evaluation	Occupational Therapy Intervention
Mr. Brown is a tall, thin, 63-year-old widowed man with a history of a mild stroke a few years ago. His eye doctor also recently diagnosed him with cataracts in both eyes. *Referral:* His medical doctor referred him to outpatient occupational and physical therapy during a routine visit when he asked Mr. Brown questions about falls and conducted a brief balance and ambulation screening.	Mr. Brown's occupational profile revealed the following: ■ He has 2 grown children and 4 grandchildren who live nearby and are supportive. His son lives in the home behind him and is concerned about his father's safety moving within the home. ■ He ambulates without a device in the home and has mild weakness in his right arm. He uses a cane for long-distance ambulation outside the home. ■ He has had more difficulty keeping his balance over the last year when standing to put his pants on, climbing over the bathtub, performing yardwork, and getting the mail from his rural mailbox. He also said his decreased balance is affecting his ability to work as an electrician (e.g., climb ladders), walk safely around his home, and ascend and descend stairs. ■ He has difficulty performing home-maintenance tasks such as carrying the trashcans to the curb and raking the yard. ■ He stated he is able to complete his other IADLs and ADLs independently, although slowly. Fullerton Advanced Balance Scale (FAB): (California State University, Fullerton, Center for Successful Aging, 2008) ■ The long FAB form score of 20/40 points (50%) indicated Mr. Brown was at risk for falls. Modified Clinical Test of Sensory Interaction in Balance (California State University, Fullerton, Center for Successful Aging, n.d.) assesses different sensory systems involved in balance. ■ Mr. Brown was unable to maintain his balance standing on a compromised surface with or without his vision, indicating impairments in his visual or vestibular systems to help maintain his balance. ABC scale identifies balance confidence to perform 16 functional tasks (Powell & Myers, 1998) ■ Mr. Brown scored a 55% confidence, indicating he was at risk for falling (Lajoie & Gallagher, 2004) and that intervention may help improve his balance confidence (Myers, Fletcher, Myers, & Sherk, 1998). Westmeade Home Safety Assessment (WeHSA; Clemson, 1997) ■ Mr. Brown stated he walked in his stocking feet during the day at home. He fell 6 times in the past year but had no falls before that time. ■ Decreased lighting was noted throughout the home, especially in the hallway where his bathroom was located.	■ Mr. Brown participated in outpatient occupational therapy. **Ben, his occupational therapist,** also conducted a home safety assessment in conjunction with Mr. Brown and his son. ■ Ben instructed Mr. Brown on multifactorial fall prevention strategies that have been found effective in reducing fall risk (Beswick et al., 2008; Chang et al., 2004; Davison, Bond, Dawson, Steen, & Kenny, 2005; Gillespie et al., 2009; Logan et al., 2010; Skelton, Dinan, Campbell, & Rutherford, 2005). ■ Ben educated Mr. Brown and his son on Mr. Brown's fall risk factors and ways Mr. Brown can reduce his risk of falling. ■ Ben discussed recommendations for home and yard modifications and durable medical equipment to reduce the risk of falls and improve safety, especially due to Mr. Brown's cataracts and decreased balance (Gillespie et al., 2009; Steultjens et al., 2004). ■ Ben worked with Mr. Brown on functional balance exercises to reduce his fall risk. ■ Ben discussed possible IADL modifications to improve safety and independence, reduce the risk of falls, and lessen the fear of falling. ■ Ben also facilitated behavioral changes in Mr. Brown to reduce the fear of falling by trying to incorporate fall risk reduction strategies into Mr. Brown's current routines and habits and working with him on safely performing tasks that created a fear of falling to increase his confidence (Peterson & Clemson, 2008; Peterson & Murphy, 2002; Zijlstra et al., 2009).

*Case study provides abbreviated examples of assessments/intervention.

(continued)

Table 3. Case Studies *(cont.)*

Case Study B2: Client as an Organization		
Background	Occupational Therapy Evaluation	Occupational Therapy Intervention
Denise worked part-time at the **local Area Agency on Aging (AAA)** treating older adults on site who required occupational therapy services, consulting as needed for program development, and providing education to AAA staff and participants about various topics. Recently, several people attending the senior centers within the AAA's region had falls necessitating hospitalization. The head of the AAA met with Denise to talk about the occupational therapy programming, which could be provided at the center to address the fall risk of their participants. The head of the AAA requested that Denise provide their staff and consumers with information on fall prevention and asked if she could perform a fall safety assessment in all the senior centers in their region to help prevent other participants from falling. The organization head also inquired whether Denise could offer their consumers fall risk screenings quarterly at all their senior centers as part of her regular job at the center. Denise agreed this was feasible because she could educate participants about fall prevention during the fall risk screenings.	The organizational (AAA) occupational profile revealed the following: ▪ The AAA was responsible for services in 5 adjacent counties, including services at 15 senior centers. ▪ Each senior center followed the same regulations and policies as the AAA. ▪ Although each senior center offered similar exercise and social programs, each also had its own unique offerings not available at the other senior centers. ▪ A program manager was on site daily at each of the senior centers. ▪ The senior centers operated on various schedules but generally opened at 9:00 a.m. and ran programs until 4:00 p.m. ▪ Each senior center offered a meal and snack to its participants. ▪ On average, between 15 and 35 participants attended each senior center daily. Denise conducted an occupational therapy evaluation and worked collaboratively with the facility to set goals. ▪ Denise conducted a needs assessment and reviewed the incident reports of the individuals who had fallen in the center. ▪ She met with the head of the AAA and her staff to identify any specific staff concerns. ▪ She also met with a group of seniors who attended the various senior centers to obtain input for her assessment. ▪ She conducted a fall safety assessment at each of the senior centers.	▪ Denise provided occupational therapy services at an organizational level, "designed to affect the organization to more efficiently and effectively meet the needs of the clients or consumers or stakeholders" (AOTA, 2008b, pp. 653–655). ▪ Denise educated the staff and seniors at each of the senior centers regarding risk factors for falls and strategies to prevent falls. ▪ She recommended several environmental modifications at each of the senior centers to decrease falls and improve the safety of those that worked or attended the centers. ▪ She conducted fall risk screenings quarterly at each senior center. ▪ She recommended a few senior center attendees talk to their physicians about a referral for rehabilitation services to reduce their risk of falling. ▪ She conducted a program evaluation periodically to evaluate the effectiveness of the screenings and the environmental recommendations.

Table 3. Case Studies *(cont.)*

Cases C1* and C2* — Use of Occupation and Activity-Based Health Management/Maintenance Interventions to Improve Performance

Case Study C1: Client as an Individual

Background	Occupational Therapy Evaluation	Occupational Therapy Intervention
Mrs. Conte is a 68-year-old retired woman who lives with her 68-year-old husband in a single-family home in a small city. She had a hip fracture 1 year ago and has gradually shown a decline in function over this past year. Recently, she developed pneumonia and bronchitis necessitating hospitalization for a week. She was also recently diagnosed with high blood pressure. *Referral:* Her physician referred her to home health occupational therapy to help her regain her strength, improve her function, and reduce her risk of developing fractures from the progression of her recently diagnosed osteopenia.	Mrs. Conte's occupational profile indicates the following: ■ Mrs. Conte is a retired truck driver, like her husband. She and her husband have 2 grown children (a daughter and son). The son lives out of state and visits 2–3 times a year. The daughter and her 2 children live around the corner and visit regularly. ■ Mrs. Conte is able to dress herself independently; however, she needs assistance from her husband to step over the tub and does not have enough energy to stand and shower. ■ She was ambulating independently without any device until the physical therapist at the hospital recommended she use a walker with wheels and a seat until she becomes stronger. Mrs. Conte stated she does not know how to maneuver the walker to prepare meals, wash and dry the laundry, or carry items from place to place. ■ She previously loved to travel by car but has not done so since she and her husband retired. ■ She also enjoyed working in the garden with her husband of 40 years, but she cannot comfortably reach her ground-level flowerbeds to weed them. ■ Although she loves taking care of "Peppy," her pet dog, her husband has been the usual one walking the dog each day, while Mrs. Conte watches television. Mrs. Conte reluctantly admitted she had become sedentary most of the day and progressively weaker since she retired a few years ago. She admits this has become much worse since her hip fracture last year. On recommendation of the physician, Mr. Conte bought his wife a home blood pressure machine before her recent bout of pneumonia. However, they both state they do not know how to use it. Mr. Conte is fearful because his wife has not been consistently taking her blood pressure medication because "it's new and I haven't gotten used to taking it." ■ Mrs. Conte is also worried about developing a hunched posture like her mother. ■ She stays up past midnight watching television and has difficulty getting to sleep and remaining asleep once she falls asleep. Scores on the Geriatric Depression Scale (Sivrioglu et al., 2009) indicated possible depressive symptoms. ■ Mrs. Conte said she sometimes feels "down" about her inability to do some of her favorite activities. The occupational therapist gathered occupational history information using the Activity Card Sort (Baum & Edwards, 2008). ■ Mrs. Conte's favorite activities included gardening, taking care of her dog, watching her grandchildren (ages 2 and 4), driving, and reading. ■ She mentioned currently she is unable to garden and walk her dog, and she has difficulty keeping up with the grandchildren.	Occupational therapy services for Mrs. Conte were provided by a home health agency. The **occupational therapist** collaboratively worked with Mrs. Conte and her husband on the following: ■ Using her existing daily routines and behaviors to integrate new health management routines (e.g., taking her blood pressure and her blood pressure medication) ■ Integrating physical activity into Mrs. Conte's habits, routines, and meaningful occupations to improve activity levels, health, and feelings of self-efficacy (Leveille et al., 1998; Rejeski et al., 2003, 2008) ■ Increasing her knowledge about osteopenia and instructing her how to integrate functional weight-bearing exercises into her physical activity routine (Fisher & Li, 2004) ■ Educating her on energy conservation techniques, adaptive strategies, safety equipment, and functional ambulation to improve her independence and safety during IADLs ■ Developing a bedtime routine and learning relaxation exercises to help her sleep (Green, 2008) ■ Recommending a referral to her physician to assess her for depression ■ Recommending a referral to a local community group to help her learn how to manage her chronic conditions.

*Case studies provide abbreviated examples of assessments/intervention.

(continued)

Table 3. Case Studies *(cont.)*

Cases C1* and C2* — Use of Occupation and Activity-Based Health Management/Maintenance Interventions to Improve Performance

Case Study C1: Client as an Individual *(cont.)*

The occupational therapist also used selected subtests from the Senior Fitness Test (Rikli & Jones, 2001) to assess Mrs. Conte's physical activity levels. Compared with people her age/gender, Mrs. Conte scored below average in all areas with percentile ranks as follows (Rikli & Jones, 2001):
- Chair stand test (lower-extremity strength): <5%
- Arm curl test (upper-extremity strength): 5%
- Chair sit and reach test (lower-extremity flexibility): 5%
- Back scratch test (upper-extremity flexibility): 15%

Case Study C2: Client as a Population

Background	Occupational Therapy Evaluation	Occupational Therapy Intervention
The **owner of a retirement community** placed an ad in the local newspaper for a consultant to develop and implement health promotion programs at his retirement community. The first program the owner wanted to start was a Chronic Disease Self-Management program, developed by the Stanford School of Medicine (2011), to assist in improving the health of the retirement community residents, which would help them live in his community for longer periods of time. **Mary is a licensed occupational therapist** who is board certified in gerontology through AOTA and has been trained in the Chronic Disease Self-Management program. She responded to the ad.	Mary educated herself about the retirement community and reviewed the results of the needs assessment the owner had conducted. The occupational profile indicated the following: • The retirement community had 50 homes, each with 1–2 residents. • Most residents were independent or required minimal assistance of a loved one to help them perform their ADLs/IADLs. • The residents' most prevalent chronic conditions were arthritis, diabetes, heart disease, and chronic obstructive pulmonary disease. Mary conducted an occupational therapy evaluation and worked collaboratively with the owner to set program goals: • A needs assessment revealed that at least 50% of the residents would benefit from the Chronic Disease Self-Management program. • Residents self-identified whether they would like to participate in the program. • Potential program participants discussed the program with their physicians and obtained a physician referral to participate in the program. • Each program participant's physician completed a medical history profile and described limitations in physical activity. • Participants completed a profile indicating their current level of physical activity and rated their pain on a 0–10 numeric pain rating scale (McCaffery & Beebe, 1993). • Participants also completed information about their current dietary habits. • Mary used the Activity Card Sort (Baum & Edwards, 2008) with each potential participant to determine the types of occupations group members currently and previously participated in and to help set goals for program participation.	• Mary used evidenced-based information to implement the Chronic Disease Self-Management program. • She educated the residents and the retirement community staff about the benefits and criteria of being referred to the program and created flyers to market the program. • Per the protocol of the Chronic Disease Self-Management program, Mary held classes 2.5 hours weekly for 6 weeks. • The classes were offered every quarter in combination with a trained lay leader. • Mary followed the typical group session topics within the Chronic Disease Self-Management program, including medication management, coping strategies, exercises, effective communication, nutrition, and how to appraise new treatments (Stanford School of Medicine, 2011). • After completing the program, attendees completed a satisfaction questionnaire. • Mary completed a program evaluation periodically to assess the program. • If Mary thought an individualized occupational therapy evaluation or treatment would benefit a program participant, she suggested he or she speak to a physician.

Table 3. Case Studies *(cont.)*

Cases D1* and D2*—Participation in Occupations/Activities Supports Health		
Case Study D1: Client as a Population		
Background	Occupational Therapy Evaluation	Occupational Therapy Intervention
This case study discusses a population-based arthritis exercise intervention. To illustrate this case study, Mrs. Danworth was chosen as a representative participant of the arthritis exercises classes given by an occupational therapist at a local health club. Mrs. Danworth is a 75-year-old, widowed woman who lives alone and has mild rheumatoid arthritis. She has a steady male companion, Mr. James, with whom she ballroom dances weekly. Mrs. Danworth is a retired teacher and elementary school principal. She is an active member of the community, is on the local city council, and fights strongly for education issues. She also enjoys attending church weekly and volunteers in the women's group at her church. Mr. James often attends church with her, and they go out to breakfast after church. Mrs. Danworth enjoys sewing and quilting and is currently making quilts for her grandchildren. *Referral:* Mrs. Danworth saw an advertisement to participate in arthritis exercise classes geared toward adults age 60 years and older. She called and inquired about the classes and asked to sign up. There was a set fee to attend the classes.	▪ **Joshua, an occupational therapist** who works part-time at a **health club,** spoke to the owner of the club about offering more programming specifically for older adults. The occupational profile of the health club revealed the following: ▪ The health club averaged 300 members each day. ▪ Approximately 50% of its members were adults 50 years of age or older. ▪ The health club was 5 years old and had a sufficient number of exercise machines and classes suitable for people younger than the age of 50. ▪ Currently, no exercise or health promotion classes were specifically focused on adults ages 50 or older. ▪ The owner of the club oversees the daytime, nighttime, and weekend managers. ▪ The health club is open from 5:00 a.m. until 12:00 a.m. daily. A large classroom with seating is available for providing educational programs for up to 30 people at a time. Joshua conducted an occupational therapy evaluation and worked collaboratively with the health center staff to set goals for program development: ▪ Joshua conducted a needs assessment in his community and determined there was a need for preventative programming, especially for people with arthritis. ▪ Joshua reviewed the literature and spoke to his supervisor at the health club about becoming an instructor for the Arthritis Foundation Exercise Program (Arthritis Foundation, 2011b). ▪ He informed his supervisor this program was designed to reduce the stiffness associated with arthritis, improve joint movement, and maintain strength (Arthritis Foundation, 2011a). ▪ He contacted the Arthritis Foundation and found out that this type of class was not currently offered in his area. ▪ He completed the instructor training and started preparing for his Arthritis Foundation Exercise class. ▪ Joshua created flyers and marketed the Arthritis Foundation exercise classes, especially noting the benefits of class participation.	▪ After receiving the instructor training, Joshua set up his first Arthritis Foundation exercise class session at the health club that Mrs. Danworth attended. ▪ Joshua conducted the arthritis exercise classes 2 times a week for 6–8 weeks, several times a year. ▪ He discussed the benefits of physical activity related to reducing morbidity (Glass, Mendes de Leon, Marottoli, & Berkman, 1999; Gregg et al., 2003); and how to maintain functional abilities (Keysor, 2003; Seeman & Chen, 2002). ▪ Each group member, at the conclusion of the program, completed a satisfaction questionnaire. ▪ Joshua conducted a program evaluation periodically to assess the effectiveness of the program and changes that might need to be made. ▪ Joshua also made referrals to other health care professionals as needed, for follow-up services.

*Case studies provide abbreviated examples of assessments/intervention.

(continued)

Table 3. Case Studies (cont.)

Case Study D2: Client as an Individual		
Background	Occupational Therapy Evaluation	Occupational Therapy Intervention
Mr. Dempsey is a 74-year-old-man who lives alone in a mobile home. His wife died from cancer several years ago. Mr. Dempsey has been healthy most of his life, but he states he is moving much slower than when he was younger and that his back pain hinders his ability to perform tasks. He also feels lonely and does not have any friends who live nearby. Mr. Dempsey said he wants to meet and socialize more with people his own age. Mr. Dempsy had a recent exacerbation of severe low back pain from an old sports injury, which necessitated a short hospitalization and then short-term rehabilitation at a skilled nursing facility (SNF) for 1 week. The occupational therapist at the SNF began training Mr. Dempsey in self-care techniques he could use that would not exacerbate his back pain. Mr. Dempsey's daughter, who lives out of state, spoke to the therapist yesterday and stated she was worried about his safety at home. The occupational therapist said she planned to recommend a home safety assessment and short-term home health occupational therapy upon discharge. The physician discussed Mr. Dempsey's physical condition and emotional state with Mr. Dempsey and his daughter. *Referral:* Mr. Dempsey's physician wrote an occupational therapy home health evaluation and treatment order (in addition to other services) and ordered a home safety assessment.	**Martha, an occupational therapist** working at a home health agency, received the order for Mr. Dempsey and made an appointment with him once he returned home and it was appropriate for her to enter the case. Mr. Dempsey's daughter also was present for the evaluation. Martha conducted an interview and completed an occupational profile with Mr. Dempsey. Mr. Dempsey's occupational profile revealed the following: ■ He has been lonely since his wife died and wishes he had more company. He gave up driving recently and uses a van service in town to get from place to place, although getting out of his home and up and down the rickety stairs is difficult. Martha also completed a functional occupational therapy evaluation with Mr. Dempsey. Results of the occupational therapy evaluation revealed the following: ■ Mr. Dempsey had reduced overall strength, reduced endurance, and moderate low back pain hindering his ability to transfer into and out of the tub safely, get into and out of bed, get up and down from a chair or toilet, and bathe and dress himself. ■ He stated he slept and watched television most of the day due to his back pain. He informed Martha he used to like to read, but he was having trouble seeing the printed material. For the home safety assessment, Martha used the Cougar Home Safety Assessment (Fisher, Civitella, & Perez, 2006). Results indicated the following: ■ He did not have any emergency calling system or a cellular phone for emergencies. ■ Lighting was low throughout the home, hindering his ability to read, one of his prior favorite occupations. ■ The home was cluttered and unkempt with dirty dishes in the sink, floors that were unclean, and piles of laundry on the chairs. ■ The electrical cable for his television went across the bedroom doorway. ■ The stairs to the mobile home were in disrepair, hindering his ability to get out of the home to engage in occupations. ■ The water temperature was 140° F, and Mr. Dempsey admitted he burned himself a few times when showering. ■ The bathroom lacked grab bars and a nonskid surface on the shower floor, hindering his ability to shower safely. ■ The bed was too high for Mr. Dempsey to get up onto safely. ■ He had no fire extinguisher, and both smoke alarms had nonworking batteries. ■ His home lacked a carbon monoxide detector.	■ Martha made recommendations on the basis of the evaluation and reviewed the recommendations with Mr. Dempsey and his daughter. ■ Martha worked with Mr. Dempsey on improving his overall strength and instructing him in proper body mechanics and compensatory techniques to perform self-care tasks. She also instructed him in proper body mechanics when getting on and off his bed and made recommendations for adaptations to increase his safety and independence. ■ Martha taught Mr. Dempsey energy conservation techniques to maximize his limited endurance. ■ She provided instruction on a functional home exercise program and made suggestions to improve his safety while performing ADLs and IADLs. ■ Martha encouraged Mr. Dempsey to perform regular cognitive activities to help challenge his thinking skills and to use as a leisure activity and provided him with strategies to complete this (Wilson et al., 2002). ■ Martha also suggested Mr. Dempsey be assessed for services with the local Area Agency on Aging and provided Mr. Dempsey and his daughter with this information. She spoke to him about attending the senior center once he finishes therapy and his endurance was improved. Martha explained that attending the senior center a few times a week would help increase his engagement in activities and his socialization, which may have a positive affect on his life (Barnes, Mendes de Leon, Wilson, Bienias, & Evans, 2004; Crooks, Lubben, Petitti, Little, & Chiu, 2008; Dahan-Oliel, Gélinas, & Mazer, 2008; Mendes de Leon et al., 1999; Mullee, Coleman, Briggs, Stevenson, & Turnbull, 2008; Silverstein & Parker, 2002; Wang, Karp, Winblad, & Fratiglioni, 2002). ■ Attendance at the senior center also may help him engage in regular physical activity, which may improve his functioning (Seeman & Chen, 2002). ■ Martha provided Mr. Dempsey and his daughter with community resources to help change the smoke detector batteries, maintain the cleanliness of his home, repair his stairs, and obtain and install grab bars in the bathroom. ■ Mr. Dempsey's daughter bought all the needed equipment and ensured any requested home recommendations were made. ■ Martha rechecked the home after changes were made and trained Mr. Dempsey on the safety equipment. ■ The home modifications and safety equipment helped facilitate Mr. Dempsey's ability to engage more safely in daily activities.

*Case studies provide abbreviated examples of assessments/intervention.

Note. ADLs = activities of daily living; IADLs = instrumental activities of daily living.

may be influencing occupational performance in multiple areas, such as memory impairments affecting hygiene, home management tasks, work tasks, and social interaction).

- Develop goals in collaboration with the client and relevant others that address the client's desired outcomes.
- Identify potential intervention approaches, guided by best practice and the evidence, and discuss them with the client.
- Document the evaluation process and communicate the results to the client or relevant others, and appropriate team members, organizations, or community agencies.

Organizations and Agencies as Clients

- For clients that are organizations, clinicians evaluate, observe, and try to gain an understanding of the organization or agency's "mission, values, organizational culture and structure, policies and procedures, and built and natural environments" (AOTA, 2008b, p. 655).
- Interpret the assessments to understand the organization's facilitators and barriers of effective functioning of people within the organization (AOTA, 2008b).
- Develop or refine a hypothesis regarding the organization or agency's performance (i.e., identify underlying organizational barriers that may be influencing their customer's performance within multiple areas, such as architectural barriers hindering potential customers from entering the organization).
- Develop goals in collaboration with the organization or agency and relevant other partners that address the organization's desired outcomes.
- Identify potential intervention approaches, guided by best practice and the evidence, and discuss them with the client.
- Document the evaluation process and communicate the results to the client and appropriate team members, organizations, or community agencies.

Populations as Clients

- For clients that are populations, the evaluation process is aimed toward members of the population as a whole rather than to each specific individual (AOTA, 2008b). Analyzing occupational performance for populations often focuses on conditions or occupational performance issues specific to that particular population (AOTA, 2008b).
- The occupational therapist should evaluate and observe the population as a whole and interpret the assessments to develop an understanding of the types of concerns that particular population has, as well as the population's strengths and impairments.
- Develop or refine a hypothesis regarding the population's performance (i.e., identify underlying barriers that may be influencing the population's performance within multiple areas, such as a lack of support groups for people who have multiple sclerosis).
- Develop goals in collaboration with the population and relevant other partners that address the desired outcomes.
- Identify potential intervention approaches, guided by best practice and the evidence, and discuss them with members of the population.
- Document the evaluation process and communicate the results to the client, relevant organizations, and community agencies.

Another part of the evaluation process involves the occupational therapist using a top-down approach (Gray, 1998; Trombly, 1993) to complete an analysis of the client's occupational performance, including gathering information on areas of occupation, performance skills, client factors, performance patterns, contexts and environments, and activity demands to collaboratively develop an intervention plan and work in conjunction with the client to facilitate productive aging.

Areas of Occupation

When working with a community-living older adult to facilitate productive aging, all areas of occupation should be considered during the assessment process. Occupational therapy practitioners are encouraged to think beyond ADLs. The occupational therapy practitioner is strongly encouraged to facilitate a discussion with the client regarding participation in desired occupations, including IADLs, education (i.e., lifelong learning activities), work, leisure, rest and sleep, and social participation.

Performance Skills

The evaluation of a community-living older adult to facilitate productive aging includes overt and subtle factors that may affect performance. The occupational therapist observes and analyzes the *performance skills,* the observable elements of action of an occupation. Performance skills can be subdivided into five categories: motor and praxis, sensory–perceptual, emotional regulation skills, cognitive skills, and communication and social skills (AOTA, 2008b). For example, an older adult may express the desire to increase participation in social activities (e.g., a local gardening club). The occupational therapist evaluates the person's motor skills (e.g., the ability to bend, kneel, and reach in the garden), sensory–perceptual skills (e.g., locate and use appropriate equipment), cognitive skills (e.g., organize and sequence a task), and communication and social skills (e.g., ability to initiate and participate in conversation).

Client Factors

Client factors are the underlying abilities, values, beliefs, and spirituality; body functions; and body structures that affect a person's occupational performance. These underlying client factors can be affected by the presence or absence of illness, disease, deprivation, and disability (AOTA, 2008b). Client factors support a person's performance skills.

Body functions refer to the "physiological function of body systems (including psychological functions)" (WHO; 2001, p. 10). *Body structures* are the "anatomical parts of the body" (WHO, 2001, p. 10). Body structures and body functions are interrelated (e.g., the heart and blood vessels are body structures that support cardiovascular functions such as blood pressure).

In the case of productive aging, occupational therapists are most likely to be interested in the body functions related to the specific areas of occupational performance and the objective of the productive aging intervention (e.g., fall prevention, health promotion, self-management). However, because functions such as attention and memory are very difficult to assess outside of the context of an activity, occupational therapists are more likely to assess performance skills than body functions. Conversely, occupational therapists may assess various factors affecting occupational performance (e.g., loss of balance) or self-efficacy (e.g., fall self-efficacy/fear of falling), which could be considered a psychological body function. When working on an organizational and population level, client factors refer to values and belief, functions, and structures of the organization or the population (AOTA, 2008b).

Performance Patterns

Performance patterns are "behaviors related to daily life activities that are habitual or routine" (AOTA, 2008b); they include habits, routines, rituals, and roles. As a client ages, he or she may experience a loss of social support, career transitions, and mobility limitations that affect the ability to participate in desired occupations (e.g., lifelong learning, religious activities). The resumption or facilitation of continued participation of roles, habits, routines, and rituals is an essential piece of productive aging.

Occupational therapists assess current roles as well as roles that people have held in the past and desired roles for the future. In addition, during the evaluation process, occupational therapists identify habits and routines, often through an assessment of how the individual spends the day. This evaluation is important in determining how a lack of habits or an overly routinized schedule may affect a person's occupational performance, with the objective being to facilitate productive aging. For example, a person who has recently transitioned from being a full-time employee to a retiree may experience a significant shift in his or her schedule from being routinized as a worker to having a schedule void of habits and routine in light of this life transition.

Context and Environment

Occupational therapists acknowledge the influence of cultural, personal, temporal, virtual, physical, and social contextual factors on occupations and activities. *Environmental factors* (physical and social) that support or inhibit occupational performance of community-living older adults should be identified throughout the evaluation and intervention process (AOTA, 2008b). *Contextual factors* (cultural, personal, temporal, and virtual) refer to the "variety of interrelated conditions that are within and surrounding the client" (AOTA, 2008b, p. 642)

Cultural

A person's *cultural context* includes the customs, beliefs, activity patterns, behavior standards, and expectations accepted by the client and his or her cultural group (AOTA, 2008b). Occupational therapists provide culturally responsive care by displaying an awareness of and sensitivity to a client's cultural beliefs about health and how culture may influence the client's typical activity patterns and occupations. By engaging in culturally competent care, the occupational therapist incorporates the individual's values, beliefs, ways of life, and practices into a mutually acceptable treatment plan.

Personal and Temporal

Personal attributes such as gender, socioeconomic status, age, and level of education all factor into the evaluation and intervention process. Patterns of role performance based on culturally and personally defined expectations should be considered. Because people are living longer, there is a greater financial strain to prolong existing financial resources to support the client throughout retirement. In particular, women are living longer than men and are at a greater

risk for poverty (Anzik & Weaver, 2001). In addition, financial limitations and poverty can affect the ability of an older adult to age in place (i.e., remain in the community), access needed caregiving resources, and purchase needed equipment to support occupational performance. On a micro level, the occupational therapy practitioner can examine temporal changes in the client's daily routine to identify how performance skills affect participation in daily activities. Alternatively, a client's financial status may result in the older adult needing to return to the workforce. Therefore, modifications in occupational performance as well as a possible career change may be required to facilitate a return to the workforce.

On a large scale, *temporal context* may refer to the time in a person's lifespan. Temporal context also refers to the phase in which the individual is seeking occupational therapy services. For example, is the client seeking interventions to support current occupational performance while minimizing normative aging changes, or is the client experiencing nonnormative aging changes (e.g., stroke) and is seeking occupational therapy to minimize limitations in occupational performance or regain optimum premorbid function?

Physical

The client's *physical environment* is often the most salient area to address for the community-living older adult. For people to successfully age in place, older adults need to live in an environment that supports their functional abilities. The occupational therapy practitioner can work with the client to facilitate productive aging within the physical environment in which the older adult lives. As clients age and experience normative aging changes, the environment in which they live may no longer meet their needs, or their physical environment may not support their current functional abilities, placing them at risk for a decline in occupational performance. For example, increasing difficulty with self-care (e.g., getting into the tub) and experiencing a fall may increase their risk of institutionalization. As a result, the older adult may seek occupational therapy interventions that address environmental modifications to maximize the person–environment fit for the bathing task (Murphy, Gretebeck, & Alexander, 2007) and or address unsafe strategies used during the bathing task (Murphy, Nyquist, Strasburg, & Alexander, 2006) to facilitate aging in place.

Social

The *social environment* or *context* includes the social network of friends, family, groups, and organizations with which the client has contact (AOTA, 2008b). Older adults experiencing mobility limitations, driving limitations, or limited access to community transportation can contribute to his or her social isolation and experience of loneliness. Alternatively, an older adult whose family is geographically dispersed and has experienced significant loss of local support systems (e.g., death of friends and significant others) may benefit from occupational therapy services to address the risk of social isolation. In addition, with changes in family structures (e.g., geographic dispersion, smaller families, people who never married), family support and opportunities for socialization may be limited for the older adult, placing the person at risk for social isolation or in need of alternate caregiving services to support the older adult in his or her environment.

Virtual

The *virtual environment* is one in which "communication occurs by means of airways (text messaging) or computers (e.g., chat room, e-mail) and an absence of physical contact" (AOTA, 2008b, p. 465). Occupational therapists may need to evaluate the client's previous and current use of technology to interact in the virtual environment (e.g., use of and expertise in e-mailing and text messaging, conversing in chat rooms). The client's comfort level with the tools of the virtual environment may guide the occupational therapist in selecting possible media to support participation in educational activities (e.g., online courses), social participation (e.g., communication with distant family through e-mail or virtual face-to-

face communication or the use of social networking sites), IADL participation (e.g., online bill paying, online grocery shopping), work (e.g., telecommuting), and leisure participation (e.g., playing golf using a gaming system). The occupational therapist considers the age-related changes that may affect the older adult's performance skills and his or her ability to respond to the activity demands associated with using the virtual environment.

Activity Demands

Determining whether a client may be able to complete an activity depends not only on the performance skills, performance patterns, and client factors of a person, but also on the demands the activity itself places on the person. The activity demands include the tools needed to carry out the activity, the space and social demands required by the activity, and the required actions and performance skills needed to take part in the given activity (AOTA, 2008b). Occupational therapy practitioners complete an activity analysis to identify the activity demands on the client and determine what is required to facilitate continued participation in the desired activity (AOTA, 2008b). For older adults faced with primary and secondary aging challenges, the activity demands of a desired occupation may surpass the abilities of the older adult to participate in the desired occupation, therefore limiting productive aging.

Specifically, after the occupational therapist and client identify relevant activities and occupations to address, it becomes necessary to identify activity demands of those activities and occupations that are specific and unique for the client within his or her natural environment. For example, changing activity demands in the bathroom may help community-living older adults improve their independence in bathing or prevent decline in functioning. This individual intervention may include modifying the person's objects and their properties (e.g., soap on a rope, hand-held shower, tub bench), changing the space demands within the physical context (e.g., increasing lighting in bathroom and installing a clear shower curtain to increase illumination in shower area), and modifying the sequence and timing of the bathing routine (e.g., bathing in the morning when the person has more energy; Murphy et al., 2006).

Activity demands at an organizational level may also require modification. For example, a community center may want to increase the safety and accessibility of the activity room for older adults who use wheelchairs. Changing activity demands may include modifying the community center's objects and properties (e.g., height, depth, and firmness of chairs used by participants) and space demands (e.g., number and placement of chairs in the center and minimization of glare on floor surfaces).

Alternatively, occupational therapists may address activity demands at a population level when developing exercise programs for people with low vision who attend senior centers throughout the county. Because of their impaired vision, older adults who want to remain active and fit may have difficulty participating in an exercise program that has not been tailored to meet the needs of someone with low vision. The occupational therapy practitioner may address space demands (e.g., lighting, contrast, glare), sequencing and timing (e.g., coordinating the program schedule to enable people to access public transportation), and objects and materials needed to support exercise participation (e.g., educational materials designed to be readable for an individual with low vision or an alternative format such as recorded/audible).

Occupational therapists, through their use of activity analysis, can identify the activity and context/environment in which the client can perform at his or her best. During the course of occupational therapy intervention, occupational therapy practitioners grade and vary the activity demands of the selected intervention task and the context/environment in which it is performed to provide the client with a "just-right challenge" to be therapeutic and challenging without exceeding his or her current level of skills. Therapists assist the clients in their ability to perform under the current context/environment and activity demands and consider how future changes in the context/environment and activity may challenge the client's skill level.

Considerations in Assessments

Therapists must use their knowledge of assessments and their clinical judgment to decide which standardized or nonstandardized assessments to select for each client at a particular time. When a client is seeking occupational therapy, it is essential to select appropriate assessments to target specified areas of productive aging. Keeping current with the published literature on evaluating community-living older adults provides important information to guide therapists in selecting specific assessments (refer to Table 2). The occupational therapist analyzes and synthesizes the results of the evaluation to create a picture of the strengths and resources that might be used to promote occupational performance as well as to identify barriers that prevent successful participation. These results should be documented not only as required by the setting but also in such a way that they are accessible and meaningful to the client. Documentation of evaluation results typically includes a written report; it also may include oral presentations to relevant team members, particularly if the client is an organization or population.

The client always should be apprised of the evaluation results. When the client is an individual, the family or caregivers may be involved, if the client agrees. Family members or caregivers can provide additional insight into the evaluation, and it may be helpful to include them in the evaluation process. The occupational therapist then uses the evaluation results, along with information from relevant others, to collaborate with the client to develop an intervention plan.

Periodic reevaluations determine the client's progress and need for continued intervention. The incorporation of an occupation-based, top-down approach (Gray, 1998; Trombly, 1993) throughout the evaluation, intervention, and reevaluation process provides the clinician with a more holistic perspective on the client's translation of skills gained during treatment to real-world occupational participation. In addition, scores from standardized assessments, at the time of discharge from occupational therapy services and periodically during the remainder of the client's life, can be used to provide outcome data to assess the effectiveness of intervention and to determine the client's abilities to participate in cognitively and physically challenging occupations (e.g., driving, return to work) or in less-structured and supportive environments.

Intervention

Intervention Process

Occupational therapy intervention for community-living older adults to facilitate productive aging may occur before disability or disease onset, such as health promotion and wellness (i.e., primary prevention phase), after the onset of disability in the health maintenance and management phase (secondary prevention), or in the tertiary prevention stage. The intervention, guided by information about the client gathered during the evaluation, can include a variety of intervention types:

- Using preparatory methods (i.e., therapist-selected methods and techniques that prepare the client for occupational performance)
- Purposeful interventions (i.e., specifically selected activities that allow the client to develop skills that enhance occupational engagement, such as role-playing of social situations or practicing community mobility in a simulated environment)
- Occupation-based interventions (i.e., client-directed occupations within context that match identified goals, such as returning to work, maintaining/retaining participation in desired leisure activities; AOTA, 2008b; Gray, 1998).

The focus of intervention may shift among establishing, restoring, or maintaining occupational performance; modifying the environment or contexts and activity demands or patterns; promoting health; preventing injuries; or preventing further disability and occupational performance problems.

Intervention Plan and Implementation

As a part of the occupational therapy process, the occupational therapist develops an intervention plan that considers the client's goals, values, and beliefs; the client's health and well-being; the client's performance skills and performance patterns; collective influence of the context, environment, activity demands, and client factors related to the client's performance; and the context of service delivery in which the intervention is provided (e.g., caregiver expectations, organization's purpose, payer's requirements, or applicable regulations; AOTA, 2008b). The intervention plan outlines and guides the therapist's actions and is based on the best available evidence to meet the identified outcomes (AOTA, 2008b).

Once the therapist has identified targeted goals in collaboration with the client, the therapist determines the intervention approach that is best suited to address the goals. The intervention approaches used by occupational therapy practitioners include the following (AOTA, 2008b):

- Prevent
- Establish and restore
- Modify
- Create or promote health
- Maintain performance and health.

Occupational therapy practitioners also consider the types of interventions when determining the most effective treatment plan for a given client. The types of interventions include therapeutic use of self; therapeutic use of occupations and activities, which includes preparatory methods, purposeful activity, and occupation-based activity; consultation; and education (AOTA, 2008b). Although all types of occupational therapy interventions are used for all approaches, *therapeutic use of self* (i.e., therapist's use of his or her personality, perception, and judgment; AOTA, 2008b) is an overarching concept that should be considered in each therapeutic interaction. Therapeutic use of self is a vital responsibility of the occupational therapy practitioner, as well as of all members of the health care team.

Intervention Review and Outcome Monitoring

Intervention review is a continuous process of reevaluating and reviewing the intervention plan, the effectiveness of service delivery, and the progress toward targeted outcomes (AOTA, 2008b). Reevaluation may involve readministering assessments or tests used at the time of initial evaluation, having the client complete a satisfaction questionnaire, or answering questions to evaluate each goal. Reevaluation substantiates progress toward goal attainment, indicates any change in functional status, and directs modifications to the intervention plan, if necessary (Moyers & Dale, 2007).

Best Practice and Summaries of Evidence

The following sections include both an overview of specific productive aging interventions and findings from the evidence-based literature of occupational therapy for community-living older adults. A standard process of searching for and reviewing literature related to practice with community-living older adults to facilitate productive aging was used and is summarized in Appendix E.

The research studies presented here include primarily *Level I randomized controlled trials (RCT); Level II studies,* in which assignment to a treatment or a control group was not randomized (cohort study); and *Level III studies,* which did not have a control group. If, however, higher-level evidence was lacking and the best evidence provided for occupational therapy specifically was ranked as Levels IV and V, then those studies were included. *Level IV studies* were experimental single-case studies, and *Level V evidence* included descriptive case reports.

All studies identified by the review, included those not specifically described in this section, were summarized and cited in full in the evidence tables in Appendix F. Readers are encouraged to read the full articles for more details. The summary of evidence highlights the results of four questions pertaining to interventions to support productive aging among community-living older adults, including the areas of IADL performance, the context and environment in which the older adult lives and participates in occupations, the maintenance of health, and the role of occupation in health:

1. What is the evidence for the effect of occupation and activity-based interventions on the performance of selected IADLs for community-dwelling older adults?
2. What is the evidence for the effectiveness of home modification and fall prevention programs on the performance of community-dwelling older adults?
3. What is the evidence for the effect of occupation and activity-based health management and maintenance interventions on the performance of community-dwelling older adults?
4. What is the evidence that participation in occupations and activities supports the health of community-dwelling older adults?

Interventions to Support Performance in IADLs

To age in place, older adults are challenged with navigating an environment that may not support the physical aging changes they experience. Difficulty performing IADLs and ADLs often are associated with these primary and secondary aging changes (Gitlin et al., 2006). IADL participation is essential to enable older adults to remain independent in the community (Baker, 2005; Suchy, Williams, Kraybill, Franchow, & Butner, 2010). When IADL independence declines, the older adult often is faced with relying on others for assistance (formal or informal personal assistance) with the IADLs he or she can no longer complete independently in his or her current context and environment, increasing the risk of institutionalization (Gill & Kurland, 2003). Occupational therapy practitioners have a key role in addressing interventions that affect the older adult's performance and participation within his or her context and environment to maintain or maximize IADL independence to support the older adult's desire to remain in the community.

Forty studies were identified that met the study criteria and addressed IADL participation; of these, 33 were classified as Level I articles, 3 were Level II articles, 3 were Level III articles, and 1 was a Level IV article. These articles were divided into five categories on the basis of type of intervention: (1) occupation-based and client-centered, (2) functional activities, (3) performance skills, (4) home modification and assistive technology, and (5) driving.

Occupation-Based and Client-Centered Interventions

Twelve studies were found that addressed the effectiveness of occupation-based and client-centered

IADL interventions with community-dwelling older adults. Seven were Level I RCTs, 1 was a Level II case control design, 1 a Level III repeated measures within subjects design, and 1 a Level IV single-subject design study. These studies were divided into two areas: multidisciplinary interventions and occupational therapy interventions.

Multidisciplinary Interventions

Among the 12 occupation-based and client-centered interventions, 3 of the 12 were categorized as multidisciplinary interventions (Gitlin et al., 2006; Gitlin, Winter, Dennis, & Hauck, 2008; Ziden, Frandin, & Kreuter, 2008). These studies included interventions that were provided by more than one discipline (e.g., occupational therapy, physical therapy, nursing), and targeted several outcomes, such as ADL and IADL performance and falls efficacy.

There is strong evidence from 2 Level I RCTs reported in 3 articles that multidisciplinary interventions provided to older adults resulted in improved IADL performance. Gitlin and colleagues (2006) studied older adults with chronic conditions, and Ziden and colleagues (2008) studied older adults recovering from hip fractures. In both studies, participants took part in home interventions, and the results indicated a reduction in older adults' perceived functional difficulties, improvement in their confidence and independence in IADLs, and greater improvement in functional activities compared with those who did not receive the interventions. Gitlin and colleagues (2006) found these effects remained 6 months after intervention. In addition, people 80 years or older and those with less education reported greater self-efficacy in managing IADLs than the control group (Gitlin, Winter, et al., 2008). The multidisciplinary interventions reported in these 3 studies were brief (ranging from 5–6 therapy contacts).

Occupational Therapy Inteventions

Eight articles reporting on 6 studies were included in this category. The articles described Lifestyle Redesign interventions, as well as other client-centered and occupation-based occupational therapy interventions provided to community-dwelling older adults. There is mixed evidence that the Lifestyle Redesign 2 program, a lifestyle intervention provided by occupational therapists to slow age-related declines in older adults, improves IADL performance.

The Level I Well Elderly study conducted with 361 older adults found that the Lifestyle Redesign Program was effective in improving physical and role functions related to performance of some IADLs (Clark et al., 1997, 2001; Hay et al., 2002), had a long-term effect on these outcomes (Clark et al., 2001), and was cost-effective (Hay et al., 2002) compared with social activity. Using the Lifestyle Redesign approach with a more ethnically diverse population and under less controlled experimental situations, the Well Elderly II study (Clark et al., 2011; Level I RCT) did not find a difference between groups for improving physical function and role function related to performance of some IADLs. There were, however, significant favorable change scores on bodily pain, vitality, and life satisfaction for the intervention group compared with the control group. Horowitz and Chang (2004), in a Level I RCT of Lifestyle Redesign of 28 older adults in an adult day care program, found no difference between treatment and control groups in role functioning and performance in IADLs.

Other studies found limited to moderate evidence for the effectiveness of client-centered occupational therapy home interventions to improve IADL performance of older adults. Hagsten Svensson, and Gardulf's (2006) Level I RCT conducted in Sweden provided occupational therapy to community-dwelling older adults after surgery for hip fracture. Although most of the intervention was provided in the hospital, a predischarge home visit also was included. There were no differences between the intervention and control groups at discharge and follow-up, but there were significant differences between groups at 2 months. Participants in the occupational therapy group reported significantly more indoor mobility, improved performance of light housework, and increased ease getting in and out of a car than those in the control group.

In a Level II study examining the effectiveness of an intervention for older adults with different functional abilities and with orthopedic, neurological, or chronic impairments, Matteliano, Mann, and Tomita (2002) found that participants who received occupational therapy services through a home care agency improved in the IADLs of food preparation; however, the effect was not significantly different from the group that did not receive the occupational therapy service. One Level IV study examined the effectiveness of an intervention for microwave oven use for meal preparation (Kondo, Mann, Tomita, & Ottenbacher, 1997) and found increased frequency of using cooking appliances, the number of food items prepared, and a reduction on the time spent preparing meals.

Functional Activity Interventions

These studies used targeted exercises or activities that simulated the conditions of daily tasks. Five Level I RCTs and 1 Level III study were identified that addressed the effects of functional activities interventions in the performance of selected IADLs. These 6 studies were divided into two groups: functional tasks exercise programs and simulated IADL programs.

Functional Task Exercise Programs

These studies reported on the effect of functional task exercise programs using exercises such as transporting objects and moving objects from differing height shelves as well as walking. Four studies (de Vreede, et al., 2005; de Vreede et al., 2004; Fisher & Li, 2004; Manini et al., 2007) found moderate evidence for the effectiveness of functional task exercise programs to improve IADLs. Two RCTS compared a functional task exercise program with a resistance exercise program in 122 older women (de Vreede et al., 2004, 2005). de Vreede and colleagues (2004) found that participants in both the functional task and resistance exercise group significantly increased their functional task performance in several IADL tasks ($N = 24$). Although no significant differences between groups were found, effect sizes were greater for the functional task group. However, this study likely was underpowered to detect group effects. A study with a larger sample size ($N = 98$) found that the functional task exercise group had significantly higher physical functional performance in several IADL tasks than did the control and resistance groups (de Vreede et al., 2005). Only changes in the functional task group were sustained after 7 months of intervention.

Similarly, Manini and colleagues (2007) compared the efficacy of three interventions by examining the number of task modifications needed and the timed performance in IADL tasks of 33 lower functioning older adults in a Level I RCT. Task modification can be considered an essential characteristic for identifying older adults at risk of subsequent disablement (Manini et al., 2007; Orellano et al., 2012). After training, all groups showed similar reduction in task modification (Manini et al., 2007). However, only the two functional training groups had a significant reduction in timed performance of functional IADL tasks. In addition, a Level I RCT conducted with 582 community-dwelling senior residents found evidence of the effectiveness of walking programs to increase the IADLs of community mobility by neighborhood walking (Fisher & Li, 2004).

Simulated IADL Programs

Simulated IADL training programs are designed to mimic the performance of daily functional tasks, such as laundry and vacuuming. There is limited evidence for the efficacy of simulated functional IADL programs for improving the IADL performance of older adults. Richardson, Law, Wishart, and Guyatt (2000) conducted a Level I study that compared a program simulating a home and community setting with a traditional clinic treatment setting for patients with compromised functional status. Participants in both groups demonstrated little change in IADL performance during the intervention and the 8 weeks after discharge. A Level II study by Dobek, White, and Gunter (2006) compared the effectiveness of an IADL-based training program with the use of a control timeframe that included no intervention among 14 independently living older adults and found significant improvement in physical fitness and their ability to perform some IADLs.

Performance Skills Interventions

Studies included in this section reported on interventions targeting specific performance skills, such as motor (physical activity), cognitive, and sensory (vision), as well as their impact on IADL performance. Thirteen studies were reviewed related to performance skills interventions and IADL performance of older adults. Eleven studies assessed physical activity interventions, 1 assessed cognitive skills, and 1 examined an intervention that targeted vision.

Physical Activity Interventions

The physical activity intervention studies included 1 systematic review, 1 meta-analysis, 7 RCT Level I studies, 1 Level II study, and 1 Level III study. These studies assessed the effectiveness of general exercise programs, resistance training, aerobics, balance training, flexibility exercises, cardiorespiratory fitness, tai chi, and general physical activity sessions.

The evidence is mixed that physical activity interventions improve IADL performance. In a large Cochrane review of 121 RCTs, Liu and Latham (2007) found evidence supporting the effectiveness of progressive resistance strength training in improving older adults' strength and activity performance. Specifically, they found a positive effect on certain IADLs, such as community mobility and preparing meals. Rejeski and colleagues' (2008) Level I RCT ($N = 424$) determined that participants using a physical activity intervention (400-m walk) had improved satisfaction with physical function and self-efficacy compared with an educational control group. The researchers suggested that among older adults with mobility deficits, physical activity might be effective for improving self-efficacy, satisfaction with physical function, and amount of time spent on activities of moderate or greater intensity.

Ginis, Latimer, Brawley, Jung, and Hicks (2006) compared weight training and weight training plus education and found that both groups showed

improvement at the end of the study in a 16.5-meter walk compared with baseline performance. In a multisite (Level III) study by Wellman, Kamp, Kirk-Sanchez, and Johnson (2007; $N = 620$), significant improvements in tasks related to community mobility (e.g., steps taken per day, number of days walked per week) were found after intervention.

Three of the functional activity interventions studies discussed previously (de Vreede et al., 2004, 2005; Manini et al., 2007) also assessed interventions involving physical activity. These studies further supported the use of physical activities as an effective strategy to improve IADL performance, even though they supported functional activity interventions over physical activities alone. Several studies, however, including a meta-analysis and various RCTs, did not find a direct effect of physical activity interventions (e.g., general exercise programs, strength training) on older adults' IADL performance (Gu & Conn, 2008; Lee & King, 2003; Oida et al., 2003; Pahor et al., 2006; Rejeski et al., 2009; Timonen et al., 2006; Wellman et al., 2007; Wolf et al., 2003).

However, several studies (Level I and Level II) found significant differences between physical activity intervention groups and other interventions or control groups using functional and physical performance measures, which are thought to be relevant constructs related to IADL performance (Gu & Conn, 2008; Pahor et al., 2006; Timonen et al., 2006). Timonen and colleagues (2006), for example, found changes in muscle strength, balance, and walking speed among participants of an exercise group program but did not find changes in IADL performance as assessed by the Joensuu Classification. Pahor and colleagues (2006) determined that after intervention, a physical activity group had significantly higher scores in the Short Physical Performance Battery than a health education control group did.

In summary, some studies found direct evidence of improvement in IADL performance (e.g., community mobility, walking distances, preparing meals), whereas others did not find a direct effect of physical activity interventions (Orellano et al., 2012). Various high-quality studies found improvement in functional performance and physical performance measures, which may or may not be related to IADL performance.

Cognitive Skill Intervention

The effects of training in memory, inductive reasoning, and speed of processing on daily functioning of community-dwelling older adults were studied in a large ($N = 2,832$), multisite Level I RCT (Willis et al., 2006). The study involved three cognitive training groups and a control group. All groups reported less difficulty with performing IADLs 5 years after training. However, the degree of IADL functional decline (e.g., meal preparation, housework, finances, health maintenance, telephone use, shopping) was significantly less among the group targeting inductive reasoning at the 5-year follow-up.

Interventions for Older Adults With Low Vision

There is moderate evidence that vision rehabilitation improves function in older adults with low vision. A Level I RCT (McCabe, Nason, Demers Turco, Friedman, & Seddon, 2000) provided multidisciplinary vision rehabilitation to older adults with low vision and examined whether an individual ($n = 49$) or a family-focused protocol ($n = 49$) increased patients' functional abilities. The vision rehabilitation team included optometry, occupational therapy, and social work. Regardless of group assignment, intervention was offered depending on the patients' level of impairment and capacity. Using the Functional Assessment Questionnaire to determine changes in performance, changes in functional scores (i.e., decrease in dependency and self-reported difficulty performing a task [e.g., preparing a meal, writing a check]) were found in both groups.

Home Modification and Assistive Technology

At the time of this writing, no evidence was identified that interventions related to the external physical environment (e.g., home adaptations) and the objects in them (e.g., assistive technology) supported IADL performance. Mann, Ottenbacher, Fraas,

Tomita, and Granger (1999; Level I RCT) assessed the effects of home modifications and the provision of assistive technology for 52 home-based frail elderly people compared with 52 home-based frail elderly people who received standard care (control group). At 18 months, there were differences in ADL performance between treatment and control groups using the FIM total score and FIM motor score. In addition, the researchers noted a larger percentage of decline in IADL functional independence in the control group; however, this effect was not statistically significant. Fange and Iwarsson (2005), in a Level III single-group study of housing adaptations, found that clients perceived that their housing environment supported daily activities to a greater extent at 2–3 months after intervention than at baseline. However, no significant differences in IADL dependence and in usability of home modifications were found between baseline and 9 months after intervention.

Interventions Supporting Participation in Driving

Seven Level I studies included interventions addressing driving performance skills (e.g., motor and praxis, visual skills) and education (Hunt & Arbesman, 2008; Kua, Korner-Bitensky, Desrosiers, Man-Son-Hing, & Marshall, 2007; Marottoli et al., 2007a, 2007b; Strong, Jutai, Russell-Minda, & Evans, 2008) and context and environment (Arbesman & Pellerito, 2008; Hunt & Arbesman, 2008; Stav, 2008). All were systematic reviews except for Marottoli and colleagues (2007a, 2007b), which was an RCT.

Marottoli and colleagues (2007b) examined the efficacy of a multicomponent physical functioning program addressing motor control and praxis to improve driving performance. Participants included 126 community-dwelling drivers 70 years of age or older who were randomized to an intervention group ($n = 69$) or control group ($n = 57$). The intervention group participated in 8 hours of classroom education and 2 hours of on-the-road training. The control group received two educational sessions in their home: a session (1) on home environmental safety and (2) on vehicle safety. The authors determined participants in the multicomponent physical conditioning program designed to target physical abilities (e.g., axial and extremity flexibility, coordination, speed of movement) relevant to driving safety maintained driving performance, whereas the control group experienced a significant decline in driving performance over a 3-month period (Marottoli et al., 2007b).

Limited evidence exists that vision perception training improves the driving performance of older drivers, as reported by Kua and colleagues (2007). Strong and colleagues (2008) found limited but high-quality evidence that useful field of view training had a significant effect on the driving ability of older adults, with hemianoptic field loss only for those with right-sided lesions.

There is limited-to-moderate evidence documenting the efficacy of driving education on driving performance. A systematic review completed by Hunt and Arbesman (2008) concluded there was evidence supporting driving programs that stressed self-awareness of driving skills. Two additional systematic reviews also found moderate evidence that driving education increased self-awareness and restricted exposure to challenging driving conditions but did not reduce car accidents among older drivers (Kua et al., 2007; Strong et al., 2008).

For more information about the current evidence for occupational therapy interventions related to driving and community mobility for older adults, refer to the *Occupational Therapy Practice Guidelines for Driving and Community Mobility for Older Adults* (Stav et al., 2006). This practice guideline provides a thorough overview of the evidence on driving and interventions for older adults.

Summary of Evidence to Support IADL Participation

Moderate evidence examined occupation and activity-based interventions on IADL performance (e.g., home maintenance, food preparation, shopping, community mobility, caregiving, financial management, communication management) to support productive aging. Specifically, there is strong evidence regarding the effectiveness of multidisciplinary, client-centered and task-specific interventions to address IADL performance (Gitlin et al., 2006; Gitlin, Winter, et al., 2008; Ziden et al., 2008). These interventions were more effective among community-living older adults who were at risk of functional decline (people 80 years or older and those with less education).

The evidence for Lifestyle Design programs is mixed for improving IADL performance. There was limited to moderate evidence that client-centered occupational therapy improves or maintains IADL performance in older adults living in the community. The evidence was moderate for functional task exercise programs and limited for simulated IADL interventions to improve IADL performance.

In the area of performance skills, there was mixed evidence that physical activity programs improve IADLs. Also within the area of performance skills, there was limited evidence that cognitive skills training affects IADL performance. There was moderate evidence that multicomponent vision rehabilitation that includes occupational therapy improves IADL performance in older adults with low vision. There was no difference in the effectiveness, however, between either an individual- or family-focused intervention in this low-vision population. No evidence was identified that home modifications and assistive devices improve IADL performance in community-dwelling older adults.

There is also limited evidence examining interventions targeting improvement of driving performance skills, specifically, the efficacy of simulator-based driver training, visual perception retraining, physical activity interventions, driving educational programs, and automobile adaptations in the context and environment (see Table 3, Case A).

Fall Prevention and Home Modification Interventions to Address Performance

Aging Americans prefer to remain in the community (Mathew Greenwald & Associates, 2003), to live in the least restrictive environment, and to avoid institutionalization as they age (Horgas & Abowd, 2004). As people age, the normative aging process as well as secondary aging changes can affect their ability to remain in their homes safely and to maintain their independence. Occupational therapy practitioners play a pivotal role in addressing the contexts and environments important to older adults' lives and participation in desired occupations (Peterson & Clemson, 2008).

A fall is an example of a significant life event that can limit the client's ability to remain in his or her home. A fall incidence increases the individual's risk for future falls, institutionalization, and death (Stevens et al., 2006; Tinetti, Inouye, Gill, & Doucette, 1995). Falls, which are estimated to occur among 30% of community-living older adults each year (Anderson, Miniño, Fingerhut, Warner, & Heinen, 2004), most often are caused by a combination of intrinsic and extrinsic risk factors. Because of the multifactorial nature of falls, it is important to identify and address the client's multiple fall risk factors (American Geriatrics Society & British Geriatrics Society, 2010).

Thirty-three studies were identified that met the study criteria and addressed fall prevention and home modification interventions to address performance. Thirty-one were RCTs (Level I studies), and 2 were Level II studies. Not all studies included occupational therapy services specifically, but they all involved interventions within occupational therapy's scope of practice. The results were first divided into themes on the basis of the intervention studied: (1) multicomponent or multifactorial studies, (2) studies of physical activity alone, and (3) studies assessing the effectiveness of home assessment and home modifications.

Multicomponent or Multifactorial Interventions

Because of the concomitant nature of a fall event, multicomponent and multifactorial interventions are used to address an individual's risk. The American Geriatrics Society in collaboration with the British Geriatrics Society (2010) defined a *multicomponent intervention* as a group-based intervention that inte-

grates multiple fall risk factors into the group intervention. Multicomponent interventions are not necessarily individually tailored interventions targeting each group members unique fall risk factors. Alternatively, multifactorial approaches to fall prevention are defined as interventions tailored to target an individual's specific risk factors, often combining several interventions in one package (American Geriatrics Society & British Geriatrics Society Guidelines, 2010). The types of interventions included may vary but often incorporate several of the following: home modification, education on health and safety, medication management, vision management, gait and balance training, and exercise. The disciplines providing these services may also vary but often include occupational therapy, internal medicine, physical therapy, nursing, and social services.

Strong evidence suggests approaches that address multiple risk factors reduce falls and difficulties with ADLs and IADLs in at-risk people. Ten Level I RCTs were identified; 3 examined a multicomponent approach (Clemson et. al., 2004; Hornbrook et al., 1994; Shumway-Cook et al., 2007); 6 explored multifactorial approaches (Close et al., 1999; Davison et al., 2005; Gitlin et al., 2006; Hogan et al., 2001; Logan et al., 2010; Nikolaus & Bach, 2003); and 1 RCT compared single interventions, multicomponent, and multifactorial interventions (Day et al., 2002). Clemson and colleagues (2004) reported a 31% reduction in falls at 14-month follow-up for the Stepping On program, which included a 7-week group occupational therapy intervention and incorporated environmental and home safety, balance, strength, vision screening, and medication management. Shumway-Cook and colleagues (2007) provided group exercise, fall prevention education, and falls risk assessment to sedentary older adults. Although there was a 25% decrease in falls for the intervention group at follow-up compared with control group participants, the results were not significant.

Davison and colleagues (2005) reported 36% fewer falls after an intervention that combined occupational therapy, physical therapy, and medical management for older adults presenting to an emergency department after a fall. In addition, participants had shorter duration of hospital admissions during follow-up and better falls efficacy than those in the control group. There was no difference in the proportion of participants falling or the number of hospital admissions between groups. Nickolaus and Bach (2003) reported 31% fewer falls in the year after an intervention that included a diagnostic home visit and home intervention assessing the home for environmental hazards and providing advice for hazard reduction. In addition, training in the use of technical and mobility aids was provided, and a second home visit took place 3 months later. Occupational therapy, physical therapy, nursing, and social work provided the intervention. The authors reported that the intervention was most effective in a subgroup that fell two or more times before study recruitment. The results indicated that the rate of falls and proportion of frequent fallers was significantly reduced in this subgroup.

Close and colleagues (1999) found that an occupational therapy home assessment and a medical visit with referrals, as appropriate, led to a reduction in falls and fall risk, a decrease in the chance of hospital admission, and a slower decline in ADL function at 1-year follow-up. All participants were recruited to the study after presenting to the emergency department after a fall. Participants in the intervention group were provided with equipment (e.g., handrails) and referred to social services for additional adaptations. All participants in the Logan and colleagues (2010) study were recruited after calling an ambulance after a fall. The multifactorial interventions incorporated in this study included strength and balance exercises, home assessment of hazards, and review of medications and blood pressure as provided by occupational therapy, physical therapy, and nursing. Referrals were made to other agencies as needed. The results indicated that there were fewer calls for an ambulance, fewer falls, better performance in ADLs and IADLs, and a significant decrease in fear of falling at follow-up.

Gitlin and colleagues (2006) evaluated the effectiveness of an individualized program to reduce difficulties in ADLs and IADLs, improve self-efficacy, and reduce fear of falling in community-dwelling older adults over the age of 70 who had difficulty in one or more ADLs. Five sessions provided by an occupational therapist examined environmental hazards and incorporated problem solving to identify behavioral and environmental contributors to performance difficulties. A single visit by a physical therapist focused on balance and muscle strengthening and fall recovery techniques. Results of the study indicated that participants in the intervention group had less difficulty with ADLs and IADLs, improved self-efficacy, and decreased fear of falling compared with control group participants. In addition, those in the intervention group had fewer home hazards and greater use of adaptive strategies, with significant improvements persisting at 1-year follow-up.

Hogan and colleagues (2001) found no difference in falls and emergency department visits between groups for an intervention providing an individualized treatment plan plus exercise for older adults who fell within 3 months before study recruitment. The authors reported, however, that there was a significantly longer time frame between falls and fewer falls were noted for those participants reporting two or more falls during the prerecruitment period.

Day and colleagues (2002) studied falls for older adults living at home with good to excellent self-reported health. Using an intervention that incorporated group-based exercise, home hazard management, and vision in various combinations, the authors reported that exercise alone provided the strongest evidence for a single intervention approach. The addition of home hazard management, vision management, or both further reduced falls.

Physical Activity Interventions

Studies of physical activity interventions in the productive aging systematic review comprised both group and individual sessions and included balance retraining, walking, general exercise in sitting and standing, lower-extremity strengthening, use of a workstation format, and tai chi. Mixed but overall positive results were found from studies that measured the effect of physical activity programs on the performance of community-dwelling older adults. Six RCTs reported a significant decrease in falls and fall risk after physical activity, regardless of the type of exercise incorporated into each study (Buchner et al., 1997; Faber, Bosscher, China Paw, & van Wieringen, 2006; Gardner, 1997; Means, Rodell, & O'Sullivan, 2005; Skelton et al., 2005; Voukelatos, Cumming, Lord, & Rissel, 2007). Exercise programs in these studies included functional walking, tai chi, balance, flexibility, lower-limb strengthening, and gait training. Voukelatos and colleagues (2007) also reported a reduction in fear of falling in a study using tai chi with community-dwelling older adults.

Lin, Wolf, Hwang, Gong, and Chen (2007) examined the effect of several fall prevention programs; the group participating in an exercise program showed improved functional reach, improved balance scores, and decreased fear of falling compared with either an education group or a home safety assessment and modification group. In a Level I RCT of Finnish older adults living in the community, Luukinen and colleagues (2007) found no significant difference in fall rates after exercise between control and intervention groups; however, results indicated a significant decrease in the decline of balance skills over a 6-month period. Lord, Ward, Williams, and Strudwick (1995) compared three intervention approaches: (1) an extensive intervention combining exercise with strategies for maximizing vision and sensation, (2) a minimal intervention providing brief advice, and (3) a no-intervention control group in a Level I RCT. Although researchers found no difference in fall rates, the participants receiving the most extensive intervention had a decrease in some physiological risk factors related to falls, such as knee flexion and sit-to-stand time but no improvement in balance.

Nitz and Choy (2004), in a Level I RCT, compared control participants who received a fall prevention pamphlet with those participating in a series of workstations consisting of balance activities in addition to receiving the educational pamphlet. Participants in the workstation group showed improvement in functional motor ability, lateral reach, and functional step com-

pared with control group participants, but there was no difference in falls between groups at follow-up.

In Hauer and colleagues' study (2001), older adults in a geriatric rehabilitation unit were randomized to either an exercise program emphasizing strength, balance, and functional performance or a placebo control group before discharge to the community. Both groups received physical therapy twice a week that did not emphasize strength and balance. The results indicated that those in the exercise intervention group had improved strength, functional motor performance, and balance, as well as a reduced fear of falling compared with control group participants. There was no difference between groups for falls.

In several Level I RCTs included in the productive aging systematic review, results varied with the participants' age, fall history, and activity level. For those people ages 80 years or older, strengthening, balance retraining that progressed in difficulty, and a walking plan led to fewer falls and fewer injuries when falls did occur (Campbell et al., 1997; Robertson, Devlin, Gardner, & Campbell, 2001). Campbell and colleagues (1997) determined that there was no difference in ADL performance at follow-up. Means and colleagues (2005) reported that participants in an exercise intervention group with a history of multiple falls had fewer falls in follow-up than the control group with a similar fall history. Morgan, Virnig, Duque, Abdel-Moty, and DeVito (2004), reported falls in higher functioning adults increased after an exercise program that focused on improving muscle strength, joint flexibility, balance, and gait, while lower functioning elders had a decrease in the risk of falls.

Home Assessment and Home Modification

The home assessment and home modification interventions included hazard identification, home modifications that included structural changes to the inside and outside of the home, assistive technology, and assistive devices. A Level II prospective cohort study (Liu & Lapane, 2009) surveyed older adults at baseline and during a 2-year follow-up period as part of the second Longitudinal Study of Aging. The researchers found that older adults with residential modification at baseline (e.g., railings, bathroom modifications) were less likely to experience a decline in physical functioning (Liu & Lapane, 2009). Cumming and colleagues (1999), in a Level I RCT, compared occupational therapy home visits for home modifications for older adults before hospital discharge to a no intervention control. The occupational therapist facilitated the implementation of the home modifications. Although there was no difference in falls at follow-up for both groups, there was a significant difference at follow-up between groups for those participants reporting one or more falls in the year before recruitment.

In a Level II nonrandomized controlled trial in Sweden (Petersson, Kottorp, Bergström, & Lilja, 2009), occupational therapists provided assessments for home modifications for older adults with disabilities reporting difficulty in at least one of the following areas: getting in and out of the home, mobility indoors, or self-care in the bathroom. The local government provided grants to install the home modifications. Participants in the intervention group reported significantly less difficulty in everyday tasks at follow-up compared with the comparison group.

The Level I RCT conducted by Campbell and colleagues (2005) studied targeted falls prevention provided to older adults at least 75 years of age with severe visual impairment. There were four intervention arms to this RCT: (1) home safety assessment and modification provided by an occupational therapist, (2) vitamin D supplementation and a home exercise program provided by a physical therapist, (3) a combination of both interventions, or (4) a social visit. Although there were significantly fewer falls in the home safety group versus exercise condition, strict adherence to exercise also was associated with fewer falls. When comparing just these two arms of the RCT, neither group reported reduced injuries as a result of the falls.

In a Level I RCT by Mann and colleagues (1999), an occupational therapist provided a functional assessment, environmental interventions, and assistive technology to frail elderly adults living alone. Although

both intervention and control groups had a functional decline at 18-month follow-up, the control group declined significantly more than the control group.

Tomita, Mann, Stanton, Tomita, and Sundar (2007; Level I RCT) evaluated the effectiveness of commercially available smart home technology to operate lights, appliances, doors, and windows for frail elderly living alone. Although there was no difference in IADL performance between groups at follow-up, those in the intervention group reported a high degree of satisfaction with the technology. Stevens, Holman, Bennett, and deKlerk (2001; Level I RCT) reported no differences between groups when a home modification assessment and information on hazard reduction was provided to healthy older adults in the intervention group by a research nurse compared with a control group (i.e., no education on hazard reduction or home assessment).

A Level I RCT (Pighills, Torgerson, Sheldon, Drummond, & Bland, 2011) compared the effectiveness of a home modification assessment by an occupational therapist to that of a nonprofessional assessor. The study also included a no-treatment control group. Both the occupational therapists and the nonprofessional assessors received training in home modification assessment. Outside agencies provided the home modifications for the older adults. Although there was no effect on fear of falling, those in the occupational therapy assessment group had fewer falls than control group participants 12 months after assessment. There was no difference when comparing falls for the trained assessor and control groups. There was no difference in ADLs at follow-up between either occupational therapy or assessor groups versus control group participants.

Summary of Fall Prevention and Home Modification Evidence to Support Performance

The evidence supports the efficacy of multifactorial or multicomponent interventions to address fall risk and facilitate maximum independence among community-dwelling older adults. Specifically, strong evidence exists supporting the role of occupational therapy in individual and group sessions when targeting educational strategies to remain safe and independent, recommending assistive technology, recommending and using home modifications to support aging in place, providing fall risk reduction, and maximizing independence (see Table 3, Cases B1 and B2).

Health Management and Maintenance Interventions to Support Performance

Primary and secondary aging changes experienced by older adults can impair their occupational performance. Occupational therapy practitioners play a pivotal role in providing interventions to facilitate and maintain older adults' performance in the areas of occupation after a change in health status. Health management and maintenance, one of the IADLs, targets the development, restoration, maintenance, or modification of routines to promote health (AOTA, 2008b). The older adult's ability to manage his or her own health and to participate in health managing and health promoting activities can positively influence health, mortality, and quality of life (Arbesman & Mosley, 2012).

Twenty-eight articles were identified as studies examining the effect of occupation and activity-based health management and maintenance interventions to support productive aging. Twenty-four articles were Level I RCT, systematic reviews, or meta-analyses. Three articles were Level II non-RCTs, and 1 article was a Level III pretest–posttest design. Four programmatic themes resulted from the review of the literature: (1) client-centered occupational therapy programs, (2) health education programs, (3) self-management programs, and (4) programs devoted to specific skills.

Client-Centered Occupational Therapy Programs

There was moderate to strong evidence from 6 articles (Clark et al., 1997, 2001; Dahlin Ivanoff, Sonn, & Svensson, 2002; Eklund, Sonn, & Dahlin-Ivanoff, 2004; Murphy et al., 2010; Murphy et al., 2008) based on 4 Level I RCTs that

client-centered occupational therapy interventions among community-dwelling older adults improved health management (Arbesman & Mosley, 2012).

Dahlin Ivanoff and colleagues (2002) conducted a RCT examining the efficacy of an occupational therapy health education program for community-dwelling older adults with macular degeneration. People attending a vision clinic were randomized to the standard care intervention ($n = 94$) or a health education program ($n = 93$) and then were broken into smaller respective groups. The health education program was conducted for 2 hours weekly over an 8-week period. Each group consisted of 4–6 participants, was led by an occupational therapist, and included education and skill training strategies for older adults with macular degeneration. Other disciplines involved in the group program included an ophthalmologist, an optometrist, a low vision therapist, and a lighting or illumination expert. Compared with the standard care intervention group, community-dwelling older adults who participated in the health education program had higher reported confidence in performing daily occupations (Dahlin Ivanoff et al., 2002).

After a 9-month community-based occupational therapy program, the treatment group participants in the Lifestyle Redesign RCT reported an increase in physical function and mental health as measured by the RAND SF–36 (Hays, Sherbourne, & Mazel, 1993; e.g., pain, physical functioning, role limitations associated with health conditions or emotional problems, social functioning, general mental health), and role function domains associated with health management (Clark et al., 1997, 2001).

Murphy and colleagues (2008, 2010) conducted 2 RCTs examining client-centered occupational therapy interventions for older adults with hip and knee osteoarthritis. The initial study compared the efficacy of an exercise and activity strategy training program, led by an occupational therapist, with an exercise and health education program from the Arthritis Foundation led by health education interventionists. Murphy and colleagues (2008) found the occupational therapy intervention, which included educating participants and having them actively practice joint protection as well as behavioral strategies (e.g., activity pacing) and incorporating meaningful activities into daily routines, resulted in statistically significant greater peak physical activity than the control group did.

Health Education Programs

Moderate evidence from 3 RCTs supports the use of a group health education program to improve the health and function of community-living older adults. Alp, Kanat, and Yurtkuran (2007) examined the efficacy of a group health education program for older adults with osteoporosis, targeting pain, balance as measured with the Sensitized Romberg Test and Timed Sit to Stand (Cheng et al., 1998), and quality of life measured with the RAND SF–36 (Hays et al., 1993). The intervention group ($n = 25$) participated in five sessions that included osteoporosis education and medication management, diet, living safely, and exercise (Alp et al., 2007). The study concluded that participants in the treatment group of the RCT had significantly lower pain levels and improved balance and quality of life compared with the control group.

Self-Management Programs

Among 2 Level I RCTs, there was moderate evidence examining the efficacy of individualized health education programs. In these studies, people worked collaboratively with a health care professional to develop an individualized plan to address the participant's health on the basis of his or her goals and preferences (Holland et al., 2005; Phelan et al., 2004). While occupational therapy practitioners were not consistently involved in the self-management programs in the identified studies, the interventions falls within the scope of occupational therapy practice (Arbesman & Mosley, 2012).

Holland and colleagues (2005) randomized 504 Medicare–managed care participants in the California Public Employees Retirement system to a treatment group ($n = 255$) or control group ($n = 249$). The intervention group participated in the Health

Matters Program, which included an individualized health action plan, health coach, and patient education. The control group received no intervention in the first 12 months but was able to participate in the intervention after 12 months. Holland and colleagues (2005) concluded the treatment group participants had lower rates of depressive symptoms and higher participation in aerobic and stretching exercises than the control group. Phelan and colleagues (2004) examined the efficacy of a health enhancement program on participation in physical activity and depression. The treatment group of the RCT ($n = 101$) included the collaborative development of a health action plan with the participant. The control group ($n = 100$) participants were provided with information regarding community-based programs and given a tour of the local senior center. The authors concluded that individuals in the treatment group had significantly greater improvement in ADL function than participants in the control group did (Phelan et al., 2004).

Specific Performance Skill Interventions

Several studies were categorized as interventions targeting performance skills, specifically the efficacy of cognitive–behavioral interventions to address physical activity and sleep on community-living older adults (Brawley, Rejeski, & Lutes, 2000; Montgomery & Dennis, 2003), the efficacy of cardiac rehabilitation program (Rejeski et al., 2003), and habit training for older adults with incontinence (Ostaszkiewicz, Chestney, & Roe, 2004). Evidence was limited, and the existing evidence was weak regarding the efficacy of cognitive–behavioral interventions to improve physical activity adherence (Brawley et al., 2000; Rejeski et al., 2003), sleep (Montgomery & Dennis, 2003), and habit training interventions to improve incontinence (Ostaszkiewicz et al., 2004). Bartels, et al. 2004 (Level I RCT) found better functional outcomes for independent living skills and health management for community-dwelling older adults with severe mental illness in a combined health management and skills training program.

Summary of Evidence for Health Management and Maintenance Interventions to Support Performance

Studies analyzing the effectiveness of interventions targeting health routines reflect the importance of individualized interventions that can be adjusted as the older adult's needs change. The evidence emphasizes that one-on-one encounters have a greater effect than those interventions that do not include a one-on-one component. In addition, it appears that effectiveness is higher for client-centered programs that are tailored to the preferences of the program participant compared with the provision of general materials educating the individual on available resources (e.g., list of existing community-based programs). These practice approaches form the foundation of client-centered occupational therapy practice. Six articles, describing 4 RCTs, provide strong evidence supporting the effectiveness of individual and group client-centered occupational therapy interventions to improve occupational performance in community-dwelling older adults (Clark et al., 2001; Gitlin et al., 2006; see Table 3, Cases C1 and C2).

Evidence Related to Occupational Engagement and Health Outcomes

Ninety-eight studies examining occupational engagement and health outcomes among community-dwelling older adults were identified, including 3 Level I studies and 95 Level II studies. The literature and findings exploring occupational engagement and the relationship to health among older adults are discussed here. Literature is presented within the following seven categories: IADLs; work; sleep; and physical, social, leisure, and religious activities.

Participation in IADLs

Twelve Level II studies were examined that met the criteria for the productive aging evidence-based review and related to participation in IADLs. Studies examining caregiving as an occupation and its relationship to the health of the older adult care-giver found poorer health outcomes among older adult caregivers, including depressive symptoms and increased health care use (Bookwala et al., 2004). Similarly, dependence in any IADL has been associated with increased mortality (Ginsberg, Hammerman-Rozenberg, Cohen, & Stessman, 1999). Living in restrictive environments, including those environments where the older adult is not able to leave his or her home or neighborhood (Xue, Fried, Glass, Laffan, & Chaves, 2008) and not participating in outdoor activities (Inoue, Shono, & Matsumoto, 2006), has been associated with limitations in IADLs, frailty, and increased mortality. Alternatively, lower mortality has been associated with IADL participation outside the home (Kono, Kai, Sakato, & Rubenstein, 2004).

Participation in Work

Consistent with the early conceptualizations of productive aging, the health effects of participation in work was examined (Caro et al., 1993; Hinterlong, 2008; Hinterlong & Williamson, 2006/2007). Thirteen Level II articles were categorized during the literature review that examined participation in work, including volunteer work (Stav et al., 2012). Herzog and colleagues (1989) emphasized the importance of work, either paid or unpaid, as a core concept of productive aging. Moderate evidence was found that supports the relationship between work and positive health outcomes. Specifically, working either for pay or volunteering has been associated with improved mortality (Ayalon, 2008; Harris & Thoreson, 2005; Hsu, 2007; Luoh & Herzog, 2002; Oman, Thoreson, & McMahon, 1999), ADL independence (Hammerman-Rozenberg, Maaravi, Cohen, & Stessman, 2005), better mental health outcomes (e.g., lower depression levels), a more positive view on life (Hao, 2008; Lum & Lightfoot, 2005; Shmotkin, Blumstein, & Modan, 2003), and greater life satisfaction (Van Willigen, 2000).

Participation in Sleep

Rest and sleep, an area of occupation in the *Occupational Therapy Practice Framework: Domain and Process*

(AOTA, 2008b), has facilitated the identification of literature examining the health outcomes associated with sleep. There is limited literature examining the effect of sleep and health on older adults (Stav et al., 2012). Four research studies, including 1 Level I study and 3 Level II studies, met the criteria for the systematic review (Stav et al., 2012). A study conducted by Goldman et al., (2007) found too much or too little sleep was associated with functional limitations in women. For older adults to function optimally, they require approximately 6 to just over 7 hours of sleep (Goldman et al., 2007).

Participation in Physical Activity

Twenty-one studies (1 Level I and 20 Level II), met the criteria for the systematic review (Stav et al., 2012). There was strong evidence examining the relationship between participation in physical activity and positive health outcomes among community-living older adults (Stav et al., 2012). Specifically, the health benefits of physical activity for older adults include reducing mortality (Glass et al., 1999; Gregg et al., 2003), staying active (Burton, Shapiro, & German, 1999), improving ADL/IADL independence (Keysor, 2003; Seeman, & Chen, 2002; Stessman, Hammerman-Rosenberg, Maaravi, & Cohen, 2002), preventing cognitive decline (Yaffe, Barnes, Nevitt, Lui, & Covinsky, 2001), and reducing the effect of diseases (Laukkanen, Kauppinen, & Heikkinen, 1998; Miller, Rejeski, Reboussin, Ten Have, & Ettinger, 2000).

Physical activity definitions varied among the identified studies and included functional mobility (e.g., walking; Gregg et al., 2003), home management and maintenance tasks (e.g., shopping, meal preparation, home maintenance; Miller et al., 2000; Stessman et al., 2002), and leisure activities (e.g., swimming, dancing, gardening; Gregg et al., 2003). Older adults may want to participate in physical activity to help maximize their function and minimize disability as they age. Occupational therapy practitioners play an essential role in supporting occupational engagement by means of activity participation to facilitate productive aging.

Participation in Social Activity

Thirty-two research studies (1 Level I and 31 Level II) that met the criteria for the systematic review were categorized into the social activity category (Stav et al., 2012). Social activities included social groups outside the home, whether a spouse was present, consistent contact with a friend, religious service attendance, and social network participation. Bass and Caro (2001) emphasized the importance of social engagement among older adults in their definition of productive aging. There was strong evidence supporting engagement in social activities and participation in social networks as a strategy to limit cognitive and physical decline (Avlund, Damsgaard, & Holstein, 1998; Barnes et al., 2004; Bassuk, Glass, & Berkman, 1999; Ertel, Glymour, & Berkman, 2008; Giles, Glonek, Luszcz, & Andrews, 2005; Mendes de Leon et al., 1999; Seeman, Lusingnolo, Albert, & Berkman, 2001). Alternatively, the lack of social activity participation has been associated with a negative effect on an older adult's health (Ayis, Gooberman-Hill, Bowling, & Ebrahim, 2006; Crooks et al., 2008; Fratiglioni, Wang, Ericsson, Maytan, & Winblad, 2000).

Social activity and social network engagement have been associated with mediating the functional cognitive decline among older adults as they age (Barnes et al., 2004; Bassuk et al., 1999; Ertel et al., 2008; Seeman et al., 2001). In addition, social activity participation has been associated with improvement in a person's ability to perform ADLs (Mendes de Leon et al., 1999) and with improved longevity (Avlund et al., 1998; Giles et al., 2005). Research also revealed older adults who participated in social activities had a higher quality of life (Dahan-Oliel et al., 2008; Silverstein & Parker, 2002; Stav et al., 2012).

Participation in Leisure Activity

Twelve Level II studies were identified that met the criteria for the productive aging evidence-based review. These were categorized in the leisure activity category (Stav et al., 2012). Butler and Gleason (1985) include societal engagement and community participation in their definition of productive aging. This is consistent with the *Occupational Therapy Practice Framework* (AOTA, 2008b), which identifies leisure activities as important areas of occupation. Engagement in leisure activity may help improve an older adult's health by extending one's lifespan and overall well-being (Jacobs, Hammerman-Rozenberg, Cohen, & Stessman, 2008) and reducing the risk of dementia or improving cognition (Ghisletta, Bickel, & Lövdén, 2006; Scarmeas, Levy, Tang, Manly, & Stern, 2001; Verghese et al., 2003; Wang et al., 2002; Wilson et al., 2002). Participation in leisure, which has been positively associated with beneficial health outcomes (e.g., improved survival) among older adults, includes games, crossword puzzles, reading, sports, visiting people or participating in clubs, going on outings, taking trips to museums, and gardening, (Jacobs et al., 2008; Scarmeas et al., 2001; Wilson et al., 2002).

Participation in Religious Activity

Fourteen studies (1 Level I and 13 Level II) were identified that met the criteria for inclusion in the productive aging systematic review and focused on religious activity (Stav et al., 2012). There is moderate evidence supporting the relationship between participation in religious activities and health of older adults (Stav et al., 2012). McCullough and colleagues (2000) conducted a meta-analysis and concluded that participation in religious activity is associated with reduced mortality. The studies examining the means for religious participation (e.g., listening to religious media vs. attending religious activity in the community) were mixed with respect to their relationship on mortality. la Cour, Avlund, and Schultz-Larsen (2006) concluded only those attending religious services in the community benefited from religious participation with respect to lower mortality, whereas Helm, Hays, Flint, Koenig, and Blazer (2000) found private religious participation in the home also had a positive relationship with lower mortality. Religious participation has been associated with fewer depressive symptoms (Greenfield & Marks, 2007; Hebert, Dang, & Schulz, 2006) and fewer ADL and IADL limitations (Park et al., 2008).

Summary of Evidence Related to Occupational Engagement and Health Outcomes

Studies examining the relationship between participation in occupations and health outcomes concluded that IADLs; work; and physical, social, leisure and religious activities are positively associated with health and quality of life for older adults (Stav et al., 2012). Although there is limited evidence on the relationship between sleep and health, the limited research does find sleep to be an important occupation associated with the health of older adults. These studies provide evidence supporting the foundation of occupational therapy, which has postulated that participation in desired occupations can support and improve the health of the client (AOTA, 2008b). Clinicians developing interventions for older adult clients should strive to facilitate participation in preferred occupations as a strategy to positively affect health (Stav et al., 2012; see Table 3, Cases D1 and D2).

Discontinuation, Discharge Planning, and Follow-up

Like all components of the occupational therapy process, the client (individual, organization, population) should be involved in decisions related to discontinuation, discharge planning, and follow-up. Discharge planning should commence at the time the therapist develops the intervention plan (AOTA, 2008b). Performing appropriate and timely intervention reassessments and determining the client's progress toward the established goals and desired outcomes will help determine whether occupational therapy services should continue or whether the client has reached maximal benefits from occupational therapy and should be discharged (AOTA, 2008b). Discontinuing therapy at the individual level may occur for a variety of reasons, such as achievement of goals, preference not to participate in the intervention, transfer to a different setting, inability to participate in intervention, or status change caused by a new acute condition or other illnesses or injury requiring development of a new evaluation and related treatment plan (AOTA, 2010d). Discontinuing therapy at the organizational and population level may occur for many reasons, such as the inability or unwillingness to participate in the suggested intervention, possibly because of changes in financial status, or administrative changes (e.g., changes in the organization or population's goals/focus).

Regardless of the reason for discontinuation of services, it is important that a discharge plan be developed and initiated at the beginning of care. Occupational therapists should develop the discharge plan in collaboration with the client or significant others, transition site staff, and other team members/personnel (AOTA, 2010d). The therapist should develop the discharge or transition plan on the basis of the "client's needs, goals, performance, and appropriate follow up resources" (AOTA, 2010d, p. 419). Outcomes of occupational therapy to facilitate productive aging at the individual, organizational, and population level may include prevention, quality of life, role competence, self-advocacy, occupational justice, occupational performance, adaptation, health and wellness, and participation (AOTA, 2008b). The occupational therapist may schedule a follow-up phone call or screening with the individual, organization, or population to reassess the client's status and to determine whether occupational therapy services should be reinstated. Occupational therapy services may be reinitiated if the client needs a refresher to maintain and retain skills or the client or therapist identifies new concerns. Clinicians need to be cognizant of federal-, state-, and setting-specific regulations regarding reassessment requirements.

An important part of the discharge planning process is retaining the skills gained from the occupational therapy intervention. Strategies to retain skills may include the use of written home programs to prevent decline in functioning after therapy discharge and recommendations or referrals to other services such as community-based programs (e.g., aquatic classes, yoga, tai chi, Matter of Balance; Tennstedt et al., 1998). Another important component of discharge planning with older adults is ensuring a smooth transition of occupational therapy services when someone is transferred to a different setting by effectively communicating with pertinent team members and transition sites in collaboration with the older adult and his or her significant others.

An additional key facet of discharge planning is respecting and facilitating the older adult's autonomy (Atwal & Caldwell, 2003) by ensuring that discharge decisions are made collaboratively with the client and significant others. Occupational therapy practitioners may occasionally incur ethical issues, especially regarding how to facilitate autonomy while ensuring nonmaleficence and beneficence (AOTA, 2010b; Durocher & Gibson, 2010). Therapists should consider the capacity of the older adult client to make autonomous decisions (Darzins, 2010) when weighing the ethical concerns of various discharge settings (e.g., home setting vs. a long-term care setting).

Facilitating adherence to recommendations, home/follow-up programs, and equipment usage/modifications after discharge is an important consideration during the discharge planning process. Suggestions for facilitating adherence to recommendations/equipment usage include collaborating with clients and relevant others on discharge recommendations or possible equipment needs, investigating the discharge contexts and environments to determine whether recommendations are feasible, instructing the client and significant others in equipment usage, incorporating recommendations or equipment into the client's previously learned habits, routines, roles, and rituals, and following up on recommendations/equipment usage after discharge (AOTA, 2008b; Cumming et al., 2001; DeForge et al., 2008; Hoffman & McKenna, 2004).

Barriers to adherence of recommendations include lack of transportation for community-based appointments or referral sites, unwillingness to make recommended changes or use recommended equipment, limited understanding of the purpose of the recommendations and equipment, equipment design and appearance, space constraints (related to equipment), financial issues, or the belief that the recommendation or equipment was unnecessary (Cumming et al., 2001; DeForge et al., 2008; Scherer, 2000, as cited in Hoffman & McKenna, 2004; Hoffman & McKenna, 2004).

Documentation

Occupational therapy practitioners carefully document their services in the areas of evaluation, intervention, and outcomes (AOTA, 2008b). Occupational therapy practitioners document their intervention and discharge recommendations and communicate them to the other team members, the client, and relevant others. This documentation should be completed "within the time frames, format, and standards established by the practice settings, agencies, external accreditations programs, payers and AOTA documents" (AOTA, 2010d, p. 417). "The purpose of occupational therapy documentation is to

1. Articulate the rationale for the provision of occupational therapy services and the relationship of this service to the client's desired outcomes

2. Reflect the therapist's clinical reasoning and professional judgment

3. Communicate information about the client from an occupational therapy perspective

4. Create a chronological record of client status, occupational therapy services provided, and client outcomes." (AOTA, 2008b, p. 684).

The following types of documentation may be completed for each client (person, organization, or population), as required by legal requirements, the practice setting, third-party payers, or some combination of these:

- Evaluation or screening or consultation report
- Occupational therapy service contacts
- Occupational therapy intervention plan
- Progress report(s)
- Recommendation for adaptive or other equipment or modification
- Reevaluation report
- Discharge or discontinuation report (AOTA, 2008b).

Documentation must disclose all sources of information used to formulate the conclusions (assessment tools, methods, observations, client's perceptions and feedback, family input). The *Guidelines for Documentation of Occupational Therapy* (AOTA, 2008a) outline specific report contents and fundamental elements of documentation.

Coding and Billing

Diagnosis *(ICD–9–CM)* and procedure codes *(CPT)* should be chosen to reflect the condition(s) for which the patient was treated and the therapist's intervention(s), respectively. Documentation should support the selected codes. Appendix B provides a list of diagnosis codes that may frequently be used for this population; however, care should be taken to identify the most precise code(s) for each patient. The chart in Appendix C defines the most commonly used *CPT* codes and provides some examples of occupational therapy treatment that could be billed using each code. The therapist should determine the code or codes that best describe the treatment provided. Coverage and payment for specific services and codes vary among payers, and each insurance plan should be reviewed before determining proper coding.

Implications for Occupational Therapy Practice

Occupational therapy practice with community-dwelling older adults includes not only traditional practice using the medical model but also practice in nontraditional settings. The wealth of opportunities are endless.

The evidence-based literature review examined how involvement in occupations and activities supports health of older adults and facilitates productive aging. Potential areas of growth for occupational therapy practice to enhance productive aging fell into the following categories: physical activity, social activity, leisure activity, religious activity, general activity, work/volunteering, sleep, and IADL participation (AOTA, 2011a; Stav et al., 2012). Examples of emerging types of employment related to productive aging and the evidence-based literature review are presented in Table 4.

Table 4. Nontraditional/Emerging Employment for Productive Aging*

Type of Employment	Brief Description
Accessibility consultant	Provides services related to accessibility issues in the community (e.g., churches, museums, stores, organizations)
Administrator of a nursing home, assisted living facility, adult day health center, senior center, Area Agency on Aging, or similar organizations	Oversees or manages facility's operations; could include overseeing a particular health care department or the entire operations of the facility
Aging-in-place specialist	Consults about home or other modifications for aging in place
Occupational therapist specializing in low vision services	Evaluates functional vision; trains in eye exercises, adaptive equipment, and compensatory strategies for people with low vision
Consultant to Area Agencies on Aging, senior centers, or other organizations that assist older adults	Provides expert advice or consultation to organizations
Health or wellness coach	Helps clients achieve their personal health and wellness goals using a coaching model/method
Job coach	Assists with prospective or new retirees; help older adults reach their desired goals
Ergonomics consultant	Provides work site and home site evaluations; provides work site accommodations
Geriatric care manager/geriatric case manager	Helps provide assistance to families and significant others who care for older adult relatives by providing expertise, resources, assistance, and coordination of care
Gerotechnology developer/consultant	Consults/develops gerotechnology for aging in place or other areas
Housing consultant/employment in a housing department	Advises housing department on accessibility issues, home modifications and adaptations for a variety of clients (e.g., older adults, people with mental illness), advocates for appropriate housing public policies, assists in the design development of housing
Livable communities consultant/specialist	Educates and advises community planning boards about livable communities; advocates for livable communities; helps with assessing livability of communities; makes suggestions for making the community more inclusive
Lobbyist	Advocates for appropriate public policy for older adults
Naturally occurring retirement community consultant	Assists to develop or implement programs and services within a naturally occurring retirement community that would benefit its members
Older driver evaluations, training, consultant	Works with older adults and transportation authorities in areas such as older driver evaluations, transportation safety, and recommendations to automobile manufacturers regarding car designs to meet the needs of the growing aging population
Work site consultant	Works with the client to support health and wellness, including job modifications for older workers (e.g., to address age-associated changes, facilitate employment of older workers, recommend work site accommodations)
Retirement transition planner	Helps older adults understand how to plan as well as implement activities to take the place of work when they retire

*Some of the jobs in the table require additional certifications or training.
Note. From Academy for Certification of Vision Rehabilitation and Education Professionals, n.d.; Brachtesende, 2005a, 2005b; Elbert & Neufeld, 2010; Evans et al., 2008; Grisbrooke, & Scott, 2009; Hewitt, Howie, & Feldman, 2010; National Association of Professional Geriatric Care Managers, n.d.; Parry & Coleman, 2010; Rizza, 2010; Stav et al., 2008; Waldron, & Layton, 2008; Wright, 2006.

The systematic review on productive aging identified evidence for the effectiveness of occupation and activities on occupational performance and health and the effect of fall prevention interventions and home modifications on occupational performance (Arbesman & Mosley, 2012; Chase et al., 2012; Orellano et al., 2012; Stav et al., 2012). Occupational therapy practitioners must be "knowledgeable about evidence-based research and [apply] it ethically and appropriately to provide occupational therapy services consistent with best practice approaches" (AOTA, 2010d, p. 3). The following general recommendations are based on the evidence described previously mentioned (see Table 5).

- Consistently use standardized assessment tools and outcome measures for evaluating occupational performance, home safety (Chase et al., 2012), and IADLs whenever possible to facilitate reimbursement and enhance outcome data collection (Orellano et al., 2012).
- Discuss sleep and sleep patterns as a part of the occupational profile because a lack of, too much, or poor quality sleep can affect older adults' occupational performance (Bursztyn, Ginsberg, Hammerman-Rozenberg, & Stessman, 1999; Bursztyn & Stessman, 2005; Goldman et al., 2007).
- Use client-centered intervention plans that include a "mix of exercise, education, home modifications or assistive technology [to provide] the best results in fall prevention and performance support for community-dwelling older adults" (Chase et al., 2012).
- Use occupation-based interventions that are individualized for the specific needs of the client (individual, organization, or population) and promote health (Stav et al., 2012).
- Identify how occupational therapy interventions will affect each older adult client's participation and performance of meaningful occupations (Orellano et al., 2012).
- Assimilate the use of functional and occupation-based activities within the older adults' relevant contexts to facilitate IADL performance (Orellano et al., 2012).

- Use a holistic intervention approach focusing on each older adult's engagement in meaningful IADLS, in addition to ADLs and other areas to promote health and well-being (Orellano et al., 2012; Stav et al., 2012).
- Encourage community-dwelling older adults' involvement or participation in a variety of occupations and activities to support their health, such as physical activity, social activity, leisure activity, religious activity, work/volunteer work, general activity, and IADLs (Stav et al., 2012).
- Use evidence-based interventions to facilitate the development of health routines and habits among community-dwelling older adults (Arbesman & Mosley, 2012).
- Incorporate successful health management approaches within the evaluation, intervention planning, and intervention implementation process (Arbesman & Mosley, 2012).
- Inform older adults about health education programs, including self-management programs, which may help lessen pain, improve physical activity levels, and improve participation and functioning (Arbesman & Mosley, 2012).
- Integrate diverse driving interventions to positively affect the driving performance of community-dwelling older adults (Orellano et al., 2012).
- Consult with aging organizations to develop and implement primary, secondary, and tertiary preventive educational and intervention programs and to develop resources for community-dwelling older adults (AOTA, 2011a; Stav et al., 2012).
- Consider alternative funding sources to help pay for preventive and health promotion services or equipment not currently reimbursable under Medicare or private insurance (AOTA, 2011a; Stav et al., 2012).

Implications for Occupational Therapy Research

There is a growing body of research supporting occupational therapy's role in productive aging. The

Table 5. Recommendations for Occupational Therapy Interventions for Productive Aging

Recommended*	No Recommendation	Not Recommended

IADLs

Home-based multicomponent program (including occupational therapy) in adults with differing functional abilities (A)
Client-centered occupational therapy program, such as Lifestyle Redesign program (B)
Exercise involving functional activities for older adults (B)
Progressive resistance strength training to improve community mobility and meal preparation (B)
Physical activity for improving self-efficacy and increasing satisfaction with physical function and increasing time spent on activities of moderate or greater intensity in older adults with mobility deficits (B)
Physical conditioning to improve driving performance for older adults (B)
Short-term classroom and on-road instruction to improve driving knowledge (B)
Multidisciplinary vision rehabilitation to improve function in older adults with low vision (B)
Occupation-centered interventions in the home setting for community-dwelling older adults (C)
Long-term physical exercise program to improve community mobility (C)
Cognitive skill training for community-dwelling older adults (C)
Simulated IADL programs for older adults (C)
Visual skills training, community mobility programs, and vehicle adaptations to improve driving performance in older adults (C)
Physical activity programs to improve IADL performance (I)
Home modifications to improve IADL performance in older adults (I)
Weight training to improve walking performance (I)

Fall Prevention and Home Modification

Home modification and adaptive equipment provided by occupational therapy practitioners to reduce functional decline and improve safety (A)
Multicomponent or multifactorial intervention approach addressing multiple risk factors to reduce falls (A)
Physical activity (regardless of type) to reduce falls and decrease fall risk (B)
Strengthening, balance retraining, and a walking plan to reduce falls and injuries for those > 80 years (B)
Occupational therapy assessment followed by home modifications for those with a history of falls (B)
Home modification for older adults aging with a disability reduced perceived difficulty with ADLs and IADLs (B)
Home safety assessment for older adults with visual impairment (B)

Health Management

Client-centered occupational therapy to improve physical functioning and occupational performance related to health management in frail older adults, and older adults with osteoarthritis and macular degeneration (A)
Group health education programs led by educators and other health professionals (A or B)
Self-management health programs individually tailored in conjunction with health professionals (B)
Peer-led self-management programs that include diagnosis-specific information, medication management, and problem-solving skills (B)
Cognitive–behavioral intervention for improving adherence to a physical-activity program (C)
Cognitive–behavioral intervention for improving sleep of older adult with insomnia (C)
Community-based health management program combined with skills training for community-dwelling older adults with severe mental illness (C)

*The terminology used for the recommendations was language used in the article(s) from which the evidence was derived.

Note. Criteria for level of evidence (A, B, C, I, D) are based on standard language (Agency for Healthcare Research and Quality, 2008). Suggested recommendations (recommended, no recommendation, not recommended) are based on the available evidence and content experts' clinical expertise regarding the value of using the intervention in practice. ADLs = activities of daily living; IADLs = instrumental activities of daily living.

A—There is strong evidence that occupational therapy practitioners should routinely provide the intervention to eligible clients. Good evidence was found that the intervention improves important outcomes and concludes that benefits substantially outweigh harm.

B—There is moderate evidence that occupational therapy practitioners should routinely provide the intervention to eligible clients. At least fair evidence was found that the intervention improves important outcomes and concludes that benefits outweigh harm.

C—There is weak evidence that the intervention can improve outcomes, and the balance of the benefits and harms may result either in a recommendation that occupational therapy practitioners routinely provide the intervention to eligible clients or in no recommendation as the balance of the benefits and harm is too close to justify a general recommendation.

I—Evidence is insufficient to determine whether occupational therapy practitioners should be routinely providing the intervention. Evidence that the intervention is effective is lacking, of poor quality, or conflicting and the balance of benefits and harm cannot be determined.

D—Recommend that occupational therapy practitioners do not provide the intervention to eligible clients. At least fair evidence was found that the intervention is ineffective or that harm outweighs benefits.

evidence-based literature review on productive aging illuminates some of the current evidence justifying practice as well as areas where additional research is needed. As a profession, occupational therapy must continually strive to enhance our research efforts in the area of productive aging to encompass not only traditional occupational therapy interventions but also emerging trends and areas of practice. On the basis of the results of the literature review, the following are general suggestions where additional research is needed:

- Explore the relationship between home modifications and ADL or IADL performance (Chase et al., 2012).
- Determine the effectiveness of occupational therapy interventions to reduce functional deficits and improve functioning and participation of community-dwelling older adults (AOTA, 2011b).
- Examine the effect of functional activities and occupation-based interventions on IADL performance (Orellano et al., 2012).
- Investigate the effect of client-centered and activity-specific occupational therapy interventions on IADLs such as "financial management, caregiving, care of pets, child rearing, communication management, and safety and emergency maintenance" (Orellano et al., 2012).
- Develop and encourage use of sensitive IADL outcome measures to help document the efficacy of intervention (Orellano et al., 2012).
- Investigate the effectiveness of occupational therapy interventions addressing aspects of cognition and IADL performance among community-dwelling older adults (Orellano et al., 2012).
- Explore the relationship and effectiveness of rehabilitation directed at vision loss to address IADL performance among community-dwelling older adults (Orellano et al., 2012).
- Explore the relationship between IADL performance and assistive technology and environmental modifications (Orellano et al., 2012).

- Study the relationship of occupational therapy intervention, which includes participation in occupations/activities, on the health of community-dwelling older adults (Stav et al., 2012).
- Examine the effectiveness of health management and maintenance interventions on occupational performance of older adults (Arbesman & Mosley et al., 2012).
- Explore the effectiveness of cognitive–behavioral interventions on health management and maintenance habits and routines (Arbesman & Mosley, 2012).
- Examine the effectiveness of occupational therapy to improve and retain exercise/physical activity routines of community-dwelling older adults.

Implications for Occupational Therapy Education

Gerontology education is crucial for occupational therapy students, especially over the next 20 years, when a majority of the baby boomers will have reached older adulthood (Institute of Medicine, 2008). Occupational therapy practitioners, in particular, need to become knowledgeable about working with community-dwelling older adults to facilitate productive aging, because this age group will require a larger proportion of health care services in the near future (Institute of Medicine, 2008). In addition, the Institute on Medicine (2008) stresses the importance of revising the current genre of care to address the unique needs of this escalating elderly population.

In addition to understanding older adults, current and future students are required by the Accreditation Council for Occupational Therapy Education (2012) to "articulate and apply occupational therapy theory and evidence-based evaluations" and to "keep current with evidence-based professional practice" (p. 1). This practice guideline and systematic reviews can serve as classroom resources to facilitate student learning about available evidence for practice with community-dwelling older adults to facilitate productive aging. Additional suggestions for incorporating the results of the systematic reviews are as follows:

- Educate students on the importance of health management and maintenance routines and habits for promoting wellness among community-dwelling older adults and specific benefits of occupational therapy intervention (Arbesman & Mosley, 2012).
- Teach students strategies to address the diverse needs of community-dwelling older adults within public health, health care, and community settings.
- Use fieldwork sites that serve community-dwelling older adults across a variety of settings, such as adult day health, senior centers, Area Agencies on Aging, and home-based practices (AOTA, 2011b).
- Provide fieldwork experiences that use occupational engagement to improve the health and well-being of community-dwelling older adult clients (Stav et al., 2012).
- Educate students about evidence-based interventions that reduce mortality rates and improve the health of older adults (Stav et al., 2012).

- Instruct students in using evidence-based resources, such as practice guidelines, to enhance practice decisions.
- Infuse evidence about the relationship of occupational engagement to health of older adults into the curriculum (Stav et al., 2012).

Summary

In summary, facilitating productive aging to support engagement in occupation can occur within the traditional medical model or through new and emerging practice areas. The growing body of evidence supporting the effectiveness of productive aging interventions among community-living older adults encompasses the philosophy and practice of occupational therapy. Occupational therapists need to collaborate with the client, families, and colleagues from other professions to facilitate productive aging, regardless of the setting. The overarching goal of occupational therapy interventions targeting productive aging for community-dwelling older adults is to provide client-centered, occupation-based, evidence-supported intervention to promote health and participation in meaningful occupations.

Appendix A.
Preparation and Qualifications of Occupational Therapists and Occupational Therapy Assistants

Who Are Occupational Therapists?

To practice as an occupational therapist, the individual trained in the United States

- Has graduated from an occupational therapy program accredited by the Accreditation Council for Occupational Therapy Education (ACOTE®) or predecessor organizations;
- Has successfully completed a period of supervised fieldwork experience required by the recognized educational institution where the applicant met the academic requirements of an educational program for occupational therapists that is accredited by ACOTE or predecessor organizations;
- Has passed a nationally recognized entry-level examination for occupational therapists; and
- Fulfills state requirements for licensure, certification, or registration.

Educational Programs for the Occupational Therapist

These include the following:

- Biological, physical, social, and behavioral sciences
- Basic tenets of occupational therapy
- Occupational therapy theoretical perspectives
- Screening evaluation
- Formulation and implementation of an intervention plan
- Context of service delivery
- Management of occupational therapy services (master's level)

- Leadership and management (doctoral level)
- Professional ethics, values, and responsibilities.

The fieldwork component of the program is designed to develop competent, entry-level, generalist occupational therapists by providing experience with a variety of clients across the lifespan and in a variety of settings. Fieldwork is integral to the program's curriculum design and includes an in-depth experience in delivering occupational therapy services to clients, focusing on the application of purposeful and meaningful occupation and/or research, administration, and management of occupational therapy services. The fieldwork experience is designed to promote clinical reasoning and reflective practice, to transmit the values and beliefs that enable ethical practice, and to develop professionalism and competence in career responsibilities. Doctoral-level students also must complete a doctoral experiential component designed to develop advanced skills beyond a generalist level.

Who Are Occupational Therapy Assistants?

To practice as an occupational therapy assistant, the individual trained in the United States

- Has graduated from an occupational therapy assistant program accredited by ACOTE or predecessor organizations;
- Has successfully completed a period of supervised fieldwork experience required by the recognized educational institution where the applicant met

the academic requirements of an educational program for occupational therapy assistants that is accredited by ACOTE or predecessor organizations;

- Has passed a nationally recognized entry-level examination for occupational therapy assistants; and

- Fulfills state requirements for licensure, certification, or registration.

Educational Programs for the Occupational Therapy Assistant

These include the following:
- Biological, physical, social, and behavioral sciences
- Basic tenets of occupational therapy
- Screening and assessment
- Intervention and implementation
- Context of service delivery
- Assistance in management of occupational therapy services
- Professional ethics, values, and responsibilities.

The fieldwork component of the program is designed to develop competent, entry-level, generalist occupational therapy assistants by providing experience with a variety of clients across the lifespan and in a variety of settings. Fieldwork is integral to the program's curriculum design and includes an in-depth experience in delivering occupational therapy services to clients, focusing on the application of purposeful and meaningful occupation. The fieldwork experience is designed to promote clinical reasoning appropriate to the occupational therapy assistant role, to transmit the values and beliefs that enable ethical practice, and to develop professionalism and competence in career responsibilities.

Regulation of Occupational Therapy Practice

All occupational therapists and occupational therapy assistants must practice under federal and state law. Currently, 50 states, the District of Columbia, Puerto Rico, and Guam have enacted laws regulating the practice of occupational therapy.

Note. The majority of this information is taken from the *Accreditation Standards for a Doctoral-Degree-Level Educational Program for the Occupational Therapist* (ACOTE, 2012a), *Accreditation Standards for a Master's-Degree-Level Educational Program for the Occupational Therapist* (ACOTE, 2012b), and *Accreditation Standards for an Educational Program for the Occupational Therapy Assistant* (ACOTE, 2012c).

Appendix B.
2010 Selected *ICD–9–CM* Codes

Abnormal involuntary movements	781.0
Alzheimer's disease	331.0
Amyotrophic lateral sclerosis	355.20
Blindness and low vision	369.00–369.9
Bursitis, elbow	726.33
Bursitis, hand/wrist	726.4
Carpal tunnel syndrome	354.0
Cataract	366.10
Cerebrovascular disease	430.0–438.9
Chronic obstructive pulmonary disease and allied conditions	490–496
Chronic pain	338.2
Congestive heart failure	428.00–428.40
Contracture of joint	718.0–718.9
Cerebrovascular accident, acute	436
Cerebrovascular accident, late effects	438
Dementias	290.0–290.9
Diabetes without mention of complication	250.0 (250.00–250.03)
Diabetic retinopathy	362.01–362.07
Diseases of pulmonary circulation	415.0–417.9
Falls, risk for	V15.88 (used with ICD code)
Fatigue	780.7
Fractures	800.00–828.1
Glaucoma	365.00–365.9
Head injury	959.01
Hemiplegia/hemiparesis	342.0
Hereditary and degenerative diseases of the central nervous system	330.0–337.9
Hypertension	401.0 (401.0–404.9)
Hypotension	458.0–458.2

(continued)

Ischemic heart disease	410.0–414.9
Macular degeneration, dry	362.51
Macular degeneration, wet	362.52
Memory loss	780.93
Muscle atrophy	728.2
Muscle incoordination	781.3
Muscle weakness	728.87
Myocardial infarction, acute	410.0
Osteoarthritis and allied disorders	715.00–715.98
Osteoporosis	733.00
Other disorders of the central nervous system	340–345.91 and 348–349.9
Other respiratory diseases	510.0–519.9
Pain, back	724.5
Pain, joint(s)	719.4
Parkinson's disease	332.0
Rheumatoid arthritis and other polyarthropathies (Inflammatory)	714.0–714.9
Rotator cuff disorder and allied conditions	725.10–726.19
Tendon inflammation	726.90

Note: Other *ICD–9* codes may be used in occupational therapy practice. For additional coding information, see www.cms.hhs.gov/ICD9ProviderDiagnosticCodes.

Appendix C.
Selected *Current Procedural Terminology*™ *(CPT)* Codes for Occupational Therapy Evaluations and Interventions for Older Adults

The following chart can guide occupational therapists in making clinically appropriate decisions in selecting the most relevant *CPT* code to describe occupational therapy evaluation and intervention for older adults. Occupational therapy practitioners should use the most appropriate code from the current *CPT* manual based on specific services provided, individual patient goals, payer coding and billing policy, and common usage.

Examples of Occupational Therapy Evaluation and Intervention	Suggested *CPT* Code(s)
Evaluation	
Comprises the initial evaluation of the older adult's status and performance in areas of occupation, performance skills, performance patterns, context and environment, activity demands, and client factors ■ Functional evaluation using standardized and non-standardized assessments. ■ Evaluate/assess older adult's overall functioning in ADL and IADL activities using standardized and non-standardized assessments, and gather data from various other sources (e.g., medical record, occupational profile, interview, caregivers, significant others). Develop individual goals to address performance deficits.	**97003**—Occupational therapy evaluation
Formal reassessment of changes in performance due to changes in status, diagnosis, or if intervention plans needs significant revisions ■ Re-assessment of an older adult's status and progress, usually after a change in patient status, using standardized and non-standardized assessments.	**97004**—Occupational therapy reevaluation
Evaluation of neurocognition, including global cognitive functions, executive function, memory, learning, problem solving, constructional praxis, language, attention, and other neural substrates for occupational performance ■ Qualified health professional time for administration and interpretation of standardized cognitive assessments and preparation of the report. ■ Examples of common assessments used by occupational therapists for this population can be found on Table 2.	**96125**—Standardized cognitive performance testing (e.g., Ross Information Processing Assessment) per hour of a qualified health care professional's time, both face-to-face time administering tests to the patient and time interpreting these test results and preparing the report

(continued)

Examples of Occupational Therapy Evaluation and Intervention	Suggested *CPT* Code(s)
Evaluation *(continued)*	
▪ Administer, interpret, and report findings from assistive technology assessment to identify technology to improve an older adult's specific area of function, such as the use of a portable magnification system for a person with low vision.	**97755**—Assistive technology assessment (e.g., to restore, augment or compensate for existing function, optimize functional tasks, and/or maximize environmental accessibility), direct one-on-one contact by provider, with written report, each 15 minutes
▪ Participate in a medical team conference as part of a diagnostic/evaluation team whereby the team discusses the evaluation findings, diagnoses, and recommendations with a client and his/her family.	**99366**—Medical team conference with interdisciplinary team of health care professionals, face-to-face with patient and/or family, 30 minutes or more, participation by non-physician qualified health care professional
▪ Participate in a medical team conference as part of a diagnostic/evaluation team whereby the team reviews evaluation findings and clarifies diagnostic considerations and recommendations prior to meeting with a client and his/her family.	**99368**—Medical team conference with interdisciplinary team of health care professionals, patient and/or family not present, 30 minutes or more; participation by non-physician qualified health care professional
Intervention	
Intervene to restore client factors including strength, endurance, flexibility, and active, assistive, and passive range of motion using exercises such as progressive resistive; prolonged stretch; or isokinetic, isotonic, or isometric strengthening; or closed kinetic chain ▪ Individualized exercise program for physical skill development to be able to return to work and instruction in a home exercise program to maintain strength and range of motion gained during skilled therapy. ▪ Design and train an older adult in an individualized exercise program, such as to improve strength and range of motion in order to participate in desired occupations (e.g., gardening).	**97110**—Therapeutic procedure, one or more areas, each 15 minutes; therapeutic exercises to develop strength and endurance, range of motion and flexibility
Intervene through modulation (facilitation and inhibition) of sensory input and stimulation of motor responses using neuromuscular reeducation and neurorehabilitation approaches ▪ Application of neurorehabilitation techniques to facilitate motor and sensory processing and promote adaptive responses to sitting, standing, and posturing to facilitate participation in desired occupation after a stroke (e.g., using a computer or playing catch with grandchildren). ▪ Develop and train in use of motor responses to effect change in functional performance and limit risk of fall (e.g., toileting, toilet transfers, bathing, tub transfers).	**97112**—Therapeutic procedure, one or more areas, each 15 minutes; neuromuscular reeducation of movement, balance, coordination, kinesthetic sense, posture, and/or proprioception for sitting and/or standing activities
▪ Design and train in a daily arthritis aquatic exercise program to improve functioning. ▪ Train older adult in an aquatic exercise maintenance program to be completed at home or other venue (e.g., senior center, assisted living facility).	**97113**—Therapeutic procedure, one or more areas, each 15 minutes; aquatic therapy with therapeutic exercises
▪ Use of selected individualized therapeutic activities as an intervention to improve performance of specific functional tasks. ▪ Develop and train older adult in the use of specific activities (e.g., hobbies, guided imagery, progressive muscle relaxation) to reduce stress and increase ability to function in his/her usual home and community environment.	**97530**—Therapeutic activities, direct (one-on-one) patient contact by the provider (use of dynamic activities to improve functional performance), each 15 minutes
▪ Individualized intervention focusing on improvement of cognitive skills. Train in the use of memory compensation and/or memory retrieval techniques to enhance the older adult's ability to remember important emergency telephone numbers.	**97532**—Development of cognitive skills to improve attention, memory, problem solving, (includes compensatory training), direct (one-on-one) patient contact by the provider, each 15 minutes

Examples of Occupational Therapy Evaluation and Intervention	Suggested *CPT* Code(s)
Intervention *(continued)*	
• Develop compensatory methods (e.g., medication timer/planner) to provide cueing to take medication. • Develop and instruct older adult in compensatory strategies for completion of daily home management activities such as meal preparation, clothes washing. • Train in methods of adapting bathroom, bathing routine, and habits to improve safety and independence for bathing task.	**97535**—Self care/home management training (e.g., ADL and compensatory training, meal preparation, safety procedures, and instructions in use of assistive technology devices/adaptive equipment), direct one-on-one contact by provider, each 15 minutes
• Individualized intervention focusing on community/work integration. • Teach community mobility skills using public or alternative transportation methods. • Instruct an older adult in driving re-training skills to help compensate for paralyzed arm after a stroke.	**97537**—Community/work reintegration training (e.g., shopping, transportation, money management, avocational activities and/or work environment/modification analysis, work task analysis, use of assistive technology device/adaptive equipment), direct one-on-one contact by provider, each 15 minutes
• Direct group activities for 2 or more clients to support a common goal. • Group intervention focusing on arthritis self-management techniques.	**97150**—Therapeutic procedure(s), group (2 or more individuals) (Group therapy procedures involve constant attendance of the physician or therapist, but by definition do not require one-on-one patient contact by the physician or therapist)
• Assess and fit an older adult with a hand splint for a beginning hand contracture.	**97760**—Orthotic(s) management and training (including assessment and fitting when not otherwise reported), upper extremity(s), lower extremity(s) and/or trunk, each 15 minutes

Note. The *CPT 2012* codes referenced in this document do not represent all of the possible codes that may be used in occupational therapy evaluation and intervention. Not all payers will reimburse for all codes. Refer to *CPT 2012* for the complete list of available codes.

CPT™ is a trademark of the American Medical Association (AMA). All rights reserved.

Codes shown refer to *CPT 2012. CPT* codes are updated annually. New and revised codes become effective January 1. Always refer to annual updated *CPT* publication for most current codes.

ADL = activities of daily living; IADL = instrumental activties of daily living.

Appendix D.
Alternative Funding Sources
for Productive Aging

Innovative occupational therapy interventions in emerging areas (e.g., prevention and wellness) may require novel thinking by occupational therapy practitioners to garner reimbursement for their services (Merryman, 2002). Traditional funding sources such as Medicare or private insurance may not cover some of the services needed to facilitate productive aging (Kaminsky, 2010), and older adults may be unable to afford to pay privately for the services (Doll, 2010). Therefore, occupational therapy practitioners should consider outside funding sources, including grants, because most alternative funding involve grants (Kaminsky, 2010; Nishimura & Myers, 2007).

Many types of grants exist (e.g., foundation-funded grants, government-funded grants), and practitioners will need to determine what type of grant would best support the program or services they want to provide (Doll, 2010). Because many grants are designed specifically for nonprofit agencies and public institutions (e.g., universities) rather than for-profit agencies or individuals (Doll, 2010), occupational therapy practitioners may have to work collaboratively or partner with an aging agency or educational institution to seek or secure funding (Nishimura & Myers, 2007). Local, state, and national foundations also may have grant funding available for the development of novel community programs (Doll, 2010; Nishimura & Myers, 2007). Foundation grant applications are often shorter and less stringent than government grant applications and may have less competition than large federal government grants (Doll, 2010).

Although every grant application varies depending on the funding source, most program development grants have typical items required for each application (Center for Participatory Change, n.d.; Doll, 2010; Grantwritersonline, 2006; Non-Profit Guides, n.d.; see Table D1). It is beneficial to gain some foundational grant-writing skills before completing a grant application. Occupational therapy practitioners can gain grant-writing knowledge and expertise from a variety of sources. Many communities and universities offer grant-writing classes or continuing education for health care providers who have never previously applied for grant funding. Occupational therapy clinicians may also be able to collaborate with local university faculty or staff at a local aging agency to complete a request for funding. Numerous resources exist to help you get started in your quest for funding (see Table D2).

In addition to grants, occupational therapy practitioners should be aware of the Program of All-Inclusive Care for the Elderly (PACE), which was authorized by the Balanced Budget Act of 1997 (Centers for Medicare and Medicaid Services, 2011). To qualify for the program "participants must be at least 55 years old, live in the PACE service area, and be certified as eligible for nursing home care by the appropriate State agency. The PACE program becomes the sole source of services for Medicare and Medicaid eligible enrollees" (Centers for Medicare and Medicaid Services, 2011, p. 1). An interdisciplinary team (including occupational therapy) assesses eligible seniors to determine seniors' needs and the services they can benefit from and provides services as appropriate (Centers for Medicare and Medicaid Services, 2011). The "PACE programs provide social and medical services primarily in an adult day health center, supplemented by in-home and referral services in accordance with the participant's needs" (Centers for Medicare and Medicaid Services, 2011). For more information, or to determine the location of PACE service areas near you, please, refer to the Centers for Medicare and Medicaid Services Web site (www.cms.gov/pace).

Table D1. Typical Items Requested in Program Development Grant Applications

Item	Description of Item
Project Summary/Abstract	Brief overview of project
Organizational Profile	Information about organization requesting funds
Purpose/Statement of Need/Needs Assessment	Rationale/evidence of need for the project and the purpose and scope of project for which you are requesting funds
Goals/Objectives/Outcomes/Timeline	Discussion of project goals and timelines to meet goals
Methods/Activities/Implementation plan	Description of activities/strategies that will be conducted to meet goals within set timeline
Program Evaluation Plan/Strategies	Process/strategies for conducting evaluation to determine progress/achievement of goals
Budget	Amount of funds requested and a breakdown of funding to be spent on various parts of project
Future Funding/Sustainability	Strategies for sustaining funding of the project after the grant funds are depleted
Attachments/Addendums	If you are working with a nonprofit agency, a letter of proof about tax-exempt (501c3) status may be required. A list of the board of directors of the agency, letters of support or commitment, and biographical sketches of key personnel also may be requested. Other typical items include copies of evaluation or other forms that will be used for the project.

Note. Center for Participatory Change, n.d.; Doll, 2010; Grantwritersonline, 2006; Non-Profit Guides, n.d.

Table D2. Resources for Alternative Funding

Name	Information	Web Site
Foundation Center	Grant proposal writing tips, foundation search	http://foundationcenter.org/
Grants.gov	Granting opportunities, writing tips	http://www.grants.gov/
The Grantsmanshipcenter	Grant-writing training	http://www.tgci.com/
Corporation for Public Broadcasting	Grant proposal writing tips	http://www.cpb.org/grants/grantwriting.html
Grant Professionals Association	Consultants and grant resources	http://www.grantprofessionals.org/
U.S. Dept of Health and Human Services: Office of Extramural Research	Grant-writing tips	http://grants.nih.gov/grants/grant_tips.htm
Non-Profit Guides	Tips for grant writing for nonprofits	http://www.npguides.org/
Grant Writers online	Tips for writing grants	http://www.grantwritersonline.com/

Note. Kaminsky, 2010; Nishimura & Myers, 2007

Appendix E.
Evidence-Based Practice

One of the greatest challenges facing health care systems, service providers, public education, and policy-makers is ensuring that scarce resources are used efficiently. The growing interest in outcomes research and evidence-based medicine over the past 30 years, and the more recent interest in evidence-based education, can in part be explained by these system-level challenges in the United States and internationally. In response to the demands of the cost-oriented health care system in which occupational therapy practice is often embedded, occupational therapists and occupational therapy assistants are routinely asked to justify the value of the services they provide on the basis of scientific evidence. The scientific literature provides an important source of legitimacy and authority for demonstrating the value of health care and education services. Thus, occupational therapy practitioners, other health care practitioners, and educators are increasingly called on to use the literature to demonstrate the value of the interventions and instruction they provide to clients and students.

According to Law and Baum (1998), *evidence-based occupational therapy practice* "uses research evidence together with clinical knowledge and reasoning to make decisions about interventions that are effective for a specific client" (p. 131). An evidence-based perspective is founded on the assumption that scientific evidence of the effectiveness of occupational therapy intervention can be judged to be more or less strong and valid according to a hierarchy of research designs or an assessment of the quality of the research. AOTA uses standards of evidence modeled on those developed in evidence-based medicine. This model standardizes and ranks the value of scientific evidence

for biomedical practice using the grading system in Table E1 (Sackett, Rosenberg, Muir Gray, Haynes, & Richardson, 1996). In this system, the highest levels of evidence include systematic reviews of the literature, meta-analyses, and randomized controlled trials. In randomized controlled trials, the outcomes of an intervention are compared with the outcomes of a control group, and participation in either group is allocated randomly. The systematic reviews presented here include *Level I randomized controlled trials; Level II studies,* in which assignment to a treatment or a control group is not randomized (cohort study); and *Level III studies,* which do not have a control group. *Level IV studies,* which are single-case experimental design, sometimes reported over several participants, were included in one systematic review.

The systematic reviews were initiated and supported by AOTA as part of the Evidence-Based Practice (EBP) project. In 2006, an Ad Hoc Work Group on Implementing Occupation-Based Practice reported to the AOTA Board of Directors to "fund and disseminate the results of disciplinary and interdisciplinary research that supports the effectiveness of occupation based practice" (downloaded from www.aota.org/News/Centennial/Background/AdHoc/41327/41346.aspx, p. 6). As a result of the Ad Hoc Workgroup's report, then-President Carolyn Baum's report to the Representative Assembly included a motion to "charge the President to integrate an evidence-based literature review on the effectiveness of occupation and activity-based intervention into the AOTA Evidence-Based Practice initiative" (www.aota.org/Governance/RA/PastMeetings/Minutes/36039.asp, p. 9). To select an appropriate population for

Table E1. Levels of Evidence for Occupational Therapy Outcomes Research

Levels of Evidence	Definitions
Level I	Systematic reviews, meta-analyses, randomized controlled trials
Level II	Two groups, nonrandomized studies (e.g., cohort, case-control)
Level III	One group, nonrandomized (e.g., before and after, pretest and posttest)
Level IV	Descriptive studies that include analysis of outcomes (e.g., single-subject design, case series)
Level V	Case reports and expert opinion that include narrative literature reviews and consensus statements

Note. Adapted from "Evidence-Based Medicine: What It Is and What It Isn't," by D. L. Sackett, W. M. Rosenberg, J. A. Muir Gray, R. B. Haynes, & W. S. Richardson, 1996, *British Medical Journal, 312,* pp. 71–72. Copyright © 1996 by the British Medical Association. Adapted with permission.

the review, AOTA staff and the EBP project consultant reviewed the evidence-based literature reviews completed by 2008 and categorized them by the six practice areas identified in AOTA's *Centennial Vision:* productive aging; children and youth; rehabilitation, disability, and participation; work and industry; mental health; and health and wellness. Input on the selection of a potential target population was requested from occupational therapy practitioners, researchers, and educators. In addition, AOTA and the American Occupational Therapy Foundation staff were asked for input. As a result of these discussions, the focus of the review was narrowed to the study of occupation and activity-based interventions in community-dwelling older adults. A series of focused questions were developed in conjunction with a group of content experts in productive aging and EBP on the basis of all components of the areas of occupation (ADLs, IADLs, education, work, play, leisure, social participation, rest, and sleep). The content experts included occupational therapy practitioners, researchers, and educators in this area. Content experts prioritized the questions on the basis of the types of evidence occupational therapy practitioners need to inform and guide their practice with community-dwelling older adults.

The following focused questions were included in the review:

1. What is the evidence for the effect of occupation and activity-based interventions on the performance of selected IADLs for community-dwelling older adults?

2. What is the evidence for the effectiveness of home modification and fall prevention programs on the performance of community-dwelling older adults?
3. What is the evidence for the effect of occupation and activity-based health management and maintenance interventions on the performance of community-dwelling older adults?
4. What is the evidence that participation in occupations and activities supports the health of community-dwelling older adults?

Methodology

Databases and sites searched included Medline, PsycInfo, the Cumulative Index to Nursing and Allied Health Literature/CINAHL, AgeLine, and OTseeker. In addition, consolidated information sources, such as the Cochrane Database of Systematic Reviews and the Campbell Collaboration, were included in the search. These databases are peer-reviewed summaries of journal articles and provide a system for clinicians and scientists to conduct evidence-based reviews of selected clinical questions and topics. Moreover, reference lists from articles included in the systematic reviews were examined for additional potentially relevant articles, and selected journals were hand searched to ensure that all appropriate articles were included. Search terms for the reviews were developed by the consultant to the AOTA EBP project and AOTA staff in consultation with the authors of each systematic review and reviewed by the advisory group. The search terms were developed not only to capture pertinent articles but also to ensure that the terms relevant to the specific thesaurus of each database were included. Table E2 lists the search terms related to populations and interventions included in each systematic review. A medical research librarian with experience in completing systematic review searches conducted all searches and confirmed and improved the search strategies. In addition, a filter based on one developed by McMaster University was used to narrow the search.

A total of 5,021 citations and abstracts were included in the reviews. The question on the relationship of occupation and health yielded 1,555 references, the IADL question resulted in 1,830, the health management question had 808, and the falls and home modification question yielded 828 citations and abstracts. The consultant to the EBP project completed the first step of eliminating citations on the basis of titles and abstracts. Review authors and their team of students completed the next steps of eliminating citations on the basis of titles and abstracts. The full-text versions of potential articles were retrieved. Then the review teams determined final inclusion in the review on the basis of predetermined inclusion and exclusion criteria, which were critical to providing a structure for the quality, type, and years of publication of the literature incorporated into the reviews.

The review of all four questions was limited to the peer-reviewed scientific literature published in English. Literature published in Spanish also was included in the IADL review. The review included consolidated information sources such as the Cochrane Collaboration. Except as described here, the literature included in the review was published between January 1990 and October 2008.

All studies in the review included interventions that were within the scope of practice of occupational therapy (AOTA, 2010c). Participants for studies in the review were community-dwelling older adults and included those living at home or with family, in retirement communities, and in assisted living facilities. Except for one Level IV study included in the IADL review, all studies incorporated in the reviews were Level I, II, and III evidence.

The review excluded data from presentations, conference proceedings, non–peer-reviewed research literature, research reports, dissertations, and theses. In addition, studies of participants in the hospital, skilled nursing facilities, and hospice were excluded from the review because they were not considered to be community-dwelling older adults. Also excluded from the review were studies of participants with major diagnoses such as stroke, dementia, and Parkinson's disease. Level IV and V evidence as well as studies outside the scope of practice of occupational therapy were excluded from the review. In addition to these general steps, procedures specific to each question are described in the following paragraphs.

For Question 3 (the effect of occupation and activity-based health management interventions), a second search was performed to include articles more current (through November 2010) than those published by October 2008. A total of 187 citations and abstracts were found.

The systematic review for Question 4 (participation in occupation and activities supporting health) was structured slightly differently from the other questions. The question examined how occupation and activities can affect a variety of outcomes related to health (e.g., mortality, depression, dementia). The studies included in the review were primarily longitudinal studies—large follow-up studies of older adults. One-time surveys of older adults that examined the relationship between occupation and health were not included in the review because they lack the longitudinal perspective that strengthens the ability to determine potential causation.

Table E3 presents the number and levels of evidence for articles included in each review question. A total of 192 articles were included in the review. The teams working on each focused question reviewed the articles according to their quality and levels of evidence. Each article included in the review was then abstracted using an evidence table that provides a summary of the methods and findings of the article and an appraisal of the strengths and weaknesses of the study based on design and methodology. Review authors also completed a Critically Appraised

Table E2. Search Terms for Systematic Reviews for Productive Aging

Category	Key Search Terms
Population	Aged (includes ages 80 or older and frail elderly), aging, aged (80 or older), 65+, gerontology, frail elderly
Intervention: IADLs	Instrumental activities of daily living, activities of daily living, activity participation, instrumental activities, home maintenance, household management, household maintenance, housekeeping, home management, shopping, cooking, food preparation, menu planning, driving, automobile driving, highway safety, bicycles, bicycling, walking, pedestrians, habits, pets, bonding (human-pet), child rearing, grandparents, caregivers, caregiver burden, elder care, financial strain, economic security, financial management, financial skills, money management, habits, emergency medical service communication services, security measures (electronic), equipment alarm systems, alarm systems, safety devices, household security, safety, assistive technology, assistive devices, assistive devices and communication, communication, communication aids for the disabled, communication assistive devices, communication devices, communication skills training, optical aids, eyeglasses lenses, hearing aids, religion, religion and religions, activities, religious service attendance, religiosity, spirituality, spiritual well-being, healthy aging, productive aging, successful aging, wellness programs
Intervention: Home Modification and Fall Prevention Programs	Falls, accidental falls, accidents (home), home accident, accident proneness, home accidents, fractures, hip injuries, fear of falling, fall prevention, accident prevention, architectural accessibility, aging in place, independent living, naturally occurring retirement communities, community-dwelling, home safety, home environment, home evaluation, home assessment, environmental modifications, environmental interventions, environmental hazards, housing adaptation, environmental barriers, environment design, universal design, person environment fit, housing for the elderly, home maintenance, home modification, housing improvement, assisted living facilities, retirement communities, retirement housing, homes for the aged, interior design, interior design and furnishings, furnishings, floor and floor coverings, activities of daily living, instrumental activities of daily living, occupational performance, personal care, self-care skills, self-help devices, hip protectors, equipment design, assistive technology, adaptive equipment
Intervention: Health Management	Health promotion, health education, health behavior (includes patient compliance, self-examination, and treatment refusal), health management, health maintenance, patient education, client education, disease management, lifestyle, health behavior, healthy attitudes, diet, nutrition education/aging, weight control, diets, dental health education, diet therapy, menu planning, diabetic diet, tobacco use cessation, smoking cessation, substance-related disorders, substance dependence, drug rehabilitation, relapse, drug use, alcoholism, rehabilitation (psychosocial), psychosocial rehabilitation, exercise, therapeutic exercise, yoga, tai chi, physical activity, physical fitness, exercise movement techniques, bicycling, exercise adherence, strength training, hydrotherapy, swimming, sports, activity participation, activity patterns, habits, rigidity (habit rigidity) sleep, relaxation, relaxation therapy, rest
Intervention: Occupation and Health	Healthy aging, productive aging, successful aging, activity participation, activity patterns, work, job satisfaction, retirement, employment, postretirement work, reemployment, volunteerism, voluntary workers, volunteer experiences, volunteer services, activism, leisure, leisure time, leisure activities, hobbies, holidays, recreation, social participation, friends, friendship, interpersonal relations, family, intergenerational relations, grandparents, grandparents as parents, peer group, social support, community involvement, involvement, lifestyle, daily activities, activities of daily living, physical mobility, mobility aids, toileting, bowel and bladder management, instrumental activities of daily living, financial management, financial strain, economic security, economic resources, caregivers, caregiver burden, elder care, child rearing, automobile driving, highway safety, automobiles, education, adult education, learning (in adulthood), education (continuing), sleep, relaxation, relaxation techniques, relaxation therapy, rest, work rest cycles, habits, walking, pedestrians, health promotion, health education, health behavior, healthy attitudes, preventive medicine, patient education, food preparation, diet, nutrition education, weight control, smoking cessation programs, tobacco use cessation, diet, menu planning, exercise, physical activity, physical fitness, therapeutic exercise, bicycling, sports, yoga, tai chi, exercise movement techniques, hydrotherapy, swimming, early ambulation, sexual behavior, psychosexual behavior, urinary incontinence, constipation, pets, bonding (human-pet), communication, communication skills, communication skills training, communication aids for the disabled, religion, religiosity, religious practices, religious activities, religious service attendance, spirituality, spiritual well-being, rehabilitation (psychosocial), psychosocial rehabilitation, disease management, treatment compliance

Table E3. Number and Levels of Evidence for Articles Included in Each Systematic Review

Review Question	Number of Articles Included in Review				
	Level I	Level II	Level III	Level IV	Total in Each Review
IADLs	31	3	3	1	38
Home Modification and Fall Prevention Programs	27	2	0	0	29
Health Management	23	3	1	0	27
Occupation and Health	3	95	0	0	98
Total for Each Level	84	103	4	1	
				Total in All Reviews	192

Topic (CAT), a summary and appraisal of the key findings, clinical bottom line, and implications for occupational therapy of the articles included in the review for each question. AOTA staff and the EBP project consultant reviewed the evidence tables and CATs to ensure quality control.

The systematic reviews presented in this issue cover many aspects of occupational therapy practice for community-dwelling older adults and have many strengths. Four focused questions were included in the reviews, covering information on a variety of aspects of the *Occupational Therapy Practice Framework: Domain and Process* (AOTA, 2008b). A total of 192 articles were included in the reviews, with 96% of them being Level I and II evidence. The reviews involved systematic methodologies and incorporated quality control measures.

Limitations of selected studies incorporated in the reviews include the following: small sample size, lack of blinding, wide variation of interventions included in reviews, high rates of attrition during follow-up, or the use of imprecise or outdated measures. Depending on the level of evidence, there may have been a lack of randomization, lack of control group, and limited statistical reporting. Some studies were conducted in simulated settings, and it may be difficult to generalize the findings to real-life daily activities. It is difficult to separate the effects of a single intervention that is part of a multifactorial intervention. Studies included in the fall prevention and home modification review had different or unreported definitions of falls. A wide range of diagnoses and clinical conditions may have been included in meta-analyses and systematic reviews incorporated in these reviews.

Appendix F.
Evidence Tables

Table F1. Instrumental Activities of Daily Living (IADLs)

Author/Year	Study Objectives	Level/Design/Participants	Intervention and Outcome Measures	Results	Study Limitations
Clark et al. (1997)	The article evaluated the effectiveness of preventive occupational therapy services tailored for multiethnic, independent-living older adults.	I—Randomized controlled trial $N = 361$ community-living older adults ≥ 60 yr; occupational therapy intervention group ($n = 122$); social control group ($n = 120$); no intervention control group ($n = 119$) Mean age: 74.4	Intervention group: 9-mo treatment period, occupational therapy—2 hr/wk of group occupational therapy and 9 hr/week of individual occupational therapy Social group: 9-mo treatment period—2.25 hr/wk, focused on activities intended to promote social interaction Control group: No intervention for the 9-mo period Outcome Measures: • Functional Status Questionnaire (FSQ) • RAND 36-item Short Form Health Survey (SF–36)	Significant differences between occupational therapy group and 2 other groups were found on the RAND SF–36, including role limitations in the performance of some IADLs. No difference was found on the FSQ physical function subscales of IADL.	Self-report measures were used. IADL outcomes were not comprehensively measured. Results may not generalize to other living situations.
Clark et al. (2001)	The objective was to assess whether the long-term health of participants of the Lifestyle Redesign Program Study improved compared with the control group.	I—Randomized controlled trial $N = 285$ independent-living older adults 95 intervention; 186 control participants Mean age: 74	Group 1: occupational therapy treatment group (Lifestyle Redesign Program)—2 hr/wk of group occupational therapy and 9 hr of individual occupational therapy across 9 mo Group 2: Generalized social activity control group received sessions of 2.25 hr/wk over the treatment period Group 3: No-treatment control group Outcome Measures: • FSQ: A self-report measure of difficulty and functional independence in activities of daily living and social activities. It addresses some IADLs, such as prepare foods, take public transportation, houseclean, and shopping. • RAND 36-item Short Form Health Survey (RAND SF–36): A self-report measure that addresses physical functioning and role functioning items related to the performance of some IADLs.	No statistically significant benefit was seen in the IADL scale as measured by the FSQ 6-mo postintervention. Significant benefit was seen from occupational therapy for physical functioning and role functioning.	Self-report measures were used. IADL outcomes were not comprehensively measured.

(continued)

Table F1. Instrumental Activities of Daily Living (IADLs) *(continued)*

Author/Year	Study Objectives	Level/Design/Participants	Intervention and Outcome Measures	Results	Study Limitations
Clark et al. (2011)	The objective was to determine the effectiveness of lifestyle-intervention in improving mental and physical well-being in ethnically diverse community-living older people.	I—Randomized controlled trial N = 460 community living older adults ≥ 60 yr; occupational therapy intervention (n = 232); control group (n = 228) Mean age: 74.9	Intervention by occupational therapists Intervention group: 6-mo treatment period, 2 hr/wk of group occupational therapy and up to 10 hr of individual occupational therapy Control group: No intervention for the 6-mo period Outcome Measure: ■ RAND 36-item Short Form Health Survey (SF-36)	No significant differences between the occupational therapy group and the control group were found in physical function and role limitations related to IADL on the RAND SF-36.	Self-report measures used. IADL performances were not comprehensively measured. Results may not generalize to other living situations.
de Vreede et al. (2004)	The article evaluated the feasibility of a functional tasks exercise program designed to improve functional performance of community-dwelling older women by comparing it with a resistance exercise program.	I—Randomized controlled trial N = 24 community-dwelling, medically stable women n = 12 function group (FG) n = 12 resistance group	Intervention both groups: 3 times weekly for 12 wk, 1-hr sessions Functional task program: Practice phase (2 wk), variation phase (4 wk), daily task, (6 wk); weight transported and repetitions of functional exercise. The aim of the exercises was to improve daily tasks on the domains affected in older adults. Resistance group: exercise aimed at strengthening muscle groups (e.g., dumbbells, elastic bands, raising body) Outcome Measure: ■ Assessment of Daily Activity Performance (ADAP; 16 common tasks; transferring laundry, boarding a bus, carrying groceries, making a bed, etc., and other not IADLs like pouring water, reaching forward, putting and removing a jacket, getting down and up from the floor, etc.)	Total ADAP scores increased for both groups (p = .001); also for functional upper-body strength, functional lower-body strength, upper-body flexibility, balance, and coordination, and endurance at 3 mo. FG changed 7.5U (points) for total ADAP. No significant differences between groups, except for effect sizes (small for upper-body strength [.34], moderate for lower-body strength [.54], and large [.83] for endurance in favor of the functional task group). Comparable drop-out rate (17% functional task group vs. 8% resistance group)	No control group without exercise program; small sample size; unknown clinical relevance of change. ADAP scores are given such as upper-body strength, lower-body strength flexibility, balance, coordination, endurance, and total score (outcome measure include IADLs and other activities together).

Author/Year	Objective	Design and Sample	Intervention and Outcome Measures	Results	Limitations
de Vreede et al. (2005)	The objective was to determine whether a functional-task exercise program and a resistance exercise program have different effects on the ability of community-living older people to perform daily tasks.	I—Randomized control trial, single blind $N = 98$ healthy community-living women aged ≥ 70 yr Functional-task intervention ($n = 33$); resistance intervention ($n = 34$); control group ($n = 31$) Mean age: 74; range: 70–84	Control group: No intervention was provided during the 12-wk intervention period. Functional-task exercise group: Task-specific exercises were performed 3x/wk in 40-minute sessions for 12 wk to improve ability in daily tasks. Motor, environmental, and cognitive aspects of the tasks were graded in increased challenges. Resistance exercise program: Exercises were performed 3x/wk in 1-hr sessions for 12 wk to strengthen the muscle groups important for daily tasks performance. Outcome Measure: ■ ADAP, which assesses physical functional performance through 16 common tasks, such as transferring laundry and boarding a bus scored in five domains: upper-body strength, lower-body strength, flexibility, endurance, and balance and coordination.	At the end of a 12-wk training period, the functional-task exercise group had significantly higher ADAP total score and individual scores in 3 of its domains than the control group and the resistance group. Nine mo after baseline, the changes in ADAP total score and all of its domains of the control group were significantly different from those of the function group, but not the resistance group.	Men were not included in the study. Limitations included the learning effect. The ADAP tasks were used as a training as well as assessment tool in the functional training group.
Dobek, White, & Gunter (2006)	The objective was to determine the degree an activity of daily living program would affect performance on ADLs and IADLs as well as the fitness of older adults.	II—Nonrandomized controlled design $N = 14$ independent-living older adults age ≥ 70 yr with different functional abilities Mean age: 82	Control period: First 10-wk period in which participants did not receive ADL training. Training period: Second 10-wk period in which the same participants took part in a ADL-based training program that consisted of a multistation circuit with 9 different activity stations, mimicking daily household activities, 2/wk. Outcome Measures: ■ Physical-Performance Test (PPT): Measures ability to perform daily functional abilities, including some components of IADLs ■ Physical-Functional Performance–10 (PFP–10): Measure functional IADLs tasks ■ Senior Fitness Test (SFT): Assess the domains of physical fitness, specifically strength, endurance, balance, and flexibility	No significant changes in the overall test scores on the PPT, PFP–10 and SFT were seen during the control period. After the training period, improvements ranging from 7% to 31% were seen on the PPT and the PFP–10. Improvements ranging from 11% to 33% were seen only on 3 of the 6 components of the SFT. The magnitudes of change in the IADLs scores were significantly greater than the magnitude of change for the SFT.	Small sample size could limit applicability of results. Because the study was conducted in a simulated setting, generalization to real life daily activities routines is limited.

(continued)

Table F1. Instrumental Activities of Daily Living (IADLs) *(continued)*

Author/Year	Study Objectives	Level/Design/Participants	Intervention and Outcome Measures	Results	Study Limitations
Fange & Iwarsson (2005)	The article investigated longitudinal changes in ADL dependence and aspects of usability of housing among Swedish clients receiving housing adaptation grants.	III—Pretest–posttest *N* = 131 clients; [88 women (67%), 43 men (33%)] Mean age: 71; median age: 74 Took place in Swedish municipalities	Housing adaptation—Initial evaluation (A) made by occupational therapist through home visits. Follow-ups were evaluated by project leader and occupational therapists [first follow-up 2–3 mo after adaptation (B) and second follow-up 6–7 mo after adaptation (C)]. Outcome Measures: ■ ADL Staircase-Revised Version (Sonn & Hulter-Asberg, 1991; Iwarsson 1997, 1998): comprises 5 PADLs and 4 IADLs: cooking, shopping, cleaning, and transportation (observation and interview) ■ Usability in My Home Instrument (Fange, 2002; Fange & Iwarsson, 2003) comprises self-administered measures of activity, personal, and social aspects.	A: 48% of the sample was dependent on IADL (only; 37 were dependent in IADL and PADL). There were no significant differences in B or C after housing adaptations in IADL activities. Activity aspects included meal preparation, cleaning, ironing, managing repair of clothes (home establishment and management). No significant improvements in clients' perception was found between A and C; clients perceived that their housing environment supported daily activities to a greater extent at B than at A; however, no changes were found further along in the process (C) [i.e., improvement seen (A–B) not statistically significant].	One group (no control group). Different house adaptations (not a systematic intervention) and clients' needs (not a homogenous group of clients), might need to use different outcome measures. Clients can decline rapidly, needing additional or different house adaptations. IADL: shopping and transportation are done out of the house.
Fisher, Atler, & Potts (2007)	The objective was to examine the effectiveness of short-term, home-based occupational therapy intervention program for ADLs of community-living, frail, older people.	III—Repeated-measures within-subjects designs *N* = 8 community-living frail older adults between 74 and 90 yr Mean age: 80.1	Control phase: No intervention was provided for 2–4 wk after the initial pretest. Intervention phase: Four 45-min sessions for 2–4 wk after the second pretest of Occupational Therapy Intervention Process Model (OTIPM) using a compensatory approach (adaptive occupation) for ADL and IADL performance. Outcome Measures: ■ Assessment of Motor and Process Skills (AMPS): a standardized observational tool used to evaluate the quality of 16 ADLs motor and 20 ADLs process skills observed when a person performs ADL tasks. ■ Clinical records: included (a) summary information of the client-centered performance context and the participant's baseline strengths and problems of occupational performance; (b) the participant's goals; (c) the therapist's intervention plan; (d) a summary of what interventions were implemented during each visit; and (e) documentation as to whether the participant met his or her goals.	ADL motor ability for the posttest was significantly higher than for either of the pretests. There were no significant differences between the control and intervention phases for ADL process ability. Qualitative analysis revealed that 78% (17/22) of the goals with documented outcomes exhibited some type of improvement.	Increased threat to internal validity secondary to the study design. Small sample size. No control group. Results limited secondary to ineffective occupational therapy documentation data.

Fisher & Li (2004)	The objective was to evaluate the effects of a neighborhood walking program on quality of life and neighborhood walking activity among older adults.	I—Randomized controlled trial *N* = 582 community-dwelling senior residents ≥ 65 yr; intervention (*n* = 224); control (*n* = 358) Mean age: 74	Intervention group: Leader-guided neighborhood walking program 3x/wk for 6 mo. Control group: Received a health education and information program, mailed regularly during the 6-mo intervention period. Outcome Measures: ■ Short Form (SF–12) Mental and Physical Summary Scores from the scale of the RAND 36–Item Short Form ■ Satisfaction with Life Scale ■ Neighborhood walking activity: It measured the frequency of neighborhood walking activity during the 6-mo intervention.	Compared with the control group, the neighborhood walking group significantly improved the physical and mental functioning as measured by scores on the SF–12. The intervention group significantly increased levels of walking in comparison with the control group.	Small sample size within neighborhood participants (5 to 17). The intervention group received differential attention from those in the control group.
Ginis et al. (2006)	The article compared a weight training alone treatment (WT) to an WT plus education treatment (WT + ED) about the use of strength-training gains when performing activities of daily living.	I—Randomized controlled trial *N* = 64 healthy community-dwelling older adults 68–85 yr of age Mean age: 74.4	Interventions: WT: Weight training for 12 wk (2 sessions/wk) targeting 8 major muscle groups. This group received a placebo educational intervention. WT + ED: Received the weight training plus behavioral training and associated written materials emphasizing the link between WT and ADL. Baseline and posttest measures were collected for self-efficacy measure for performing 8 lab-based ADL physical tasks and performance of the 8 ADL tasks. Outcome Measure: ■ IADL Outcome measure was a 16.5-m walk crossing a street at a traffic signal.	The WT + ED treatment had greater posttest self-efficacy for performing the ADL lab tasks than the WT treatment. Greater ADL self-efficacy did not translate into better ADL performance. Both groups showed improvement in 16.5-m walk (IADL outcome measured) at end of study compared with baseline.	Both groups received weight training. No pure control group was used. Small sample size. Short training exercise program.

(continued)

Table F1. Instrumental Activities of Daily Living (IADLs) *(continued)*

Author/Year	Study Objectives	Level/Design/Participants	Intervention and Outcome Measures	Results	Study Limitations
Gitlin et al. (2006)	The objective was to test the efficacy of a multicomponent intervention to reduce functional difficulties and home hazards and to enhance self-efficacy and adaptive coping in older adults with chronic conditions.	I—Randomized control trial *N* = 319 community-living older adults ages ≥ 70 yr with functional difficulties; intervention (*n* = 160); controls (*n* = 159) Mean age: 79	Intervention group: 6 mo of client-centered occupational therapy/physical therapy home intervention of education and problem solving; home modifications; energy-conserving techniques; and balance, muscle strengthening, and fall-recovery techniques for specific targeted functional areas. This program consisted of 5 occupational therapy contacts (4 90-minute visits and 1 20-minute telephone contact) and 1 physical therapy visit (90 minutes). Control group: This group did not receive any intervention. Outcome Measures: ■ IADL index: Assess self-perceived difficulty in light housework, shopping, preparing meals, managing money, telephone use, and taking medications ■ Functional self-efficacy index: Assessment of one's ability to perform a particular activity and achieve a desired outcome in ADLs, IADLs, and mobility ■ Home hazard index: Assesses the presence of potential tripping and falling hazards ■ Control-oriented strategy index: An investigator-developed measure to assess adaptive behavioral, cognitive, and environmental strategies	After 6 mo intervention, participants had less difficulty with IADLs, greater confidence in managing daily functional activities, greater use of control-oriented strategies, and greater improvement in functional activities than control participants. A greater proportion of intervention participants showed significant improvement in preparing meals. The magnitude of 12-mo effects was similar to those at 6 mo for IADL functional difficulty, home hazards, and control-oriented strategy use with minimal therapy contact.	Study outcomes were subjective self-reports, and performance-based measures were not included. Attention bias as the intervention group received attention from the health professionals, which could have an effect on the results.
Gitlin, Winter, et al. (2008)	The objective was to examine whether specific demographic groups benefited more from participating in a 6-mo in-home intervention previously found to effectively reduce functional difficulties.	I—Randomized controlled trial *N* = 319 community-living older adults ages ≥ 70 with functional difficulties; intervention (*n* = 160); controls (*n* = 159) Mean age: 74	Same as study described above.	At 6 mo, estimates of interaction effects of intervention by gender, age, race, and education for IADL difficulty were not statistically significant. At 12 mo, Whites reported significantly less IADL difficulty than did non-Whites (mostly African American). At 6 mo, women demonstrated greater self-efficacy than did men. At 12 mo, older and less-educated participants reported greater self-efficacy than their counterparts.	Study outcomes were subjective self-reports, and performance-based measures were not included. Attention bias because the intervention group received attention from the health professionals, which could have an impact on the results

	Author/Year	Level/Design/Sample	Intervention and Outcome Measures	Results	Study Limitations
Gu & Conn (2008)	The article synthesized the results of primary studies and quantified the effect of exercise interventions on the functional status of older adults of the general population.	I—Meta-analysis 19 randomized controlled trial studies of exercise interventions for older adults ≥ 65 yr; overall sample size of 2,201 participants. Sample size of studies ranged from 21–486 participants. Mean ages of the studies ranged from 65 to 88 yr (median 75 yr).	30 exercise interventions: aerobic, strength or resistance (included in 76% of the interventions), flexibility, balance, functional, and other exercises Interventions involving multiple behaviors were excluded (e.g., diet plus exercise) and studies of people with specific diseases (e.g, arthritis). 73% of the interventions were center-based (e.g., community center, training facility, gymnasium). Half the interventions were delivered 3–5x/wk. Outcome Measures: Functional status variables— ■ Capacity to carry out ADLs and IADLs ■ Functional performance measures ■ Physical performance measures (chair-rise, walk speed, walk endurance, balance)	An effect size (ES) of .04 was found for measures of ADL and IADL. This is a very modest ES and not significantly different from zero. ES for functional performance was .37 and for physical performance were from .24 to .30; all significantly different from zero.	Group ADL and IADL performance measures. Does not identify the ADL and IADL measures used in the studies. No information on control groups.
Hay et al. (2002)	The objective was to evaluate the cost-effectiveness of a 9-mo preventive occupational therapy program in the Well-Elderly Study.	I—Randomized controlled trial N = 163 culturally diverse adults aged ≥ 60 yr (use of health care services was collected only on Cohort II of the Well Elderly Study); intervention (n = 51); control participants (n = 112) Mean age: 74	Group 1: Occupational therapy treatment group (Lifestyle Redesign Program). 2 hr/wk of group occupational therapy and 9 hr of individual occupational therapy across 9 mo. Group 2: Generalized social activity control group Group 3: Nontreatment control group Outcome Measures: ■ Program costs ■ Caregiving and health care costs ■ Cost-effectiveness analysis through a cost-effectiveness ratio calculation	Although the health care and caregiver costs of the occupational therapy group were substantially lower than that for the combined control groups, no significant differences were detected across treatment groups. The occupational therapy groups were very cost-effective on the basis of the cost-effectiveness ratio analysis.	Small sample size of the intervention group. Focus on healthy people may have imposed a ceiling on potential cost-effectiveness.
Horowitz, & Chang (2004)	The authors studied whether a 16-week lifestyle redesign pilot study program conducted within a medical model adult day program would improve the health and well-being of frail, older adults.	I—Randomized controlled N = 28 participants [n = 12 occupational therapy group (CG) of which 4 dropped out] Ages ≥ 60 yr (mean age 74.3 yr; range 60–84 yr) Some participants had chronic conditions; others were caregivers.	Intervention: 16-wk occupational therapy lifestyle redesign program of 1.5 hr weekly (at center) plus some monthly home visits (sessions). All services were offered and facilitated by occupational therapists. Each weekly session had a specific topic and outline focus on daily routines, physical and mental activity, nutrition and dining, medication management, home and community safety, and assistive technology. CG participated only in the typical medical model day program. Outcome Measures: ■ FSQ; amended version ■ Short Form–36 (SF–36)	No statistically significant differences were noted between groups on posttest after adjusting for covariates. No differences before and after intervention were noted on the ADL FSQ.	Small sample size. Short time period.

(continued)

Table F1. Instrumental Activities of Daily Living (IADLs) (continued)

Author/Year	Study Objectives	Level/Design/Participants	Intervention and Outcome Measures	Results	Study Limitations
Hunt & Arbesman (2008)	The objective was to assess the effectiveness of person-related interventions on driving ability in older adults.	I—Systematic review N = 19 studies reviewed: • 10 Level I • 6 Level II • 3 Level III	Studies critically appraised in the systematic review addressed interventions in the visual, cognitive, and motor areas; education; passengers; and medical interventions Outcome Measure: • Driving performance	The systematic review revealed inclusive evidence concerning the efficacy of the Useful Field of View (UFOV) training for older adult driving performance. Conclusive evidence demonstrated that older adults respond positively to programs stressing self-awareness of driving skills. Limited evidence exists suggesting that training in a driving simulator results in better on-road performance than watching driving educational videos. Insufficient evidence exists for the effect of Dynavision, home exercise program, educational programs, and role of passengers had on driving skills and performance effectiveness.	Individual study limitations include lack of randomization, lack of control group, small sample size, learning effect, and use of self-report measures. The results should be interpreted with caution because of the scarcity of evidence in each intervention area.
Kondo et al. (1997)	The article examined the effectiveness of microwave ovens in assisting elderly people with disabilities with cooking food.	IV—Single-subject design (ABAB) N = 5 community-dwelling older adults with physical and sensory disability, ages ≥ 62 yr	Twelve-wk study (each phase lasted 3 wk) Training in the use of microwave oven 2 or 3x/wk for 3 wk during phase A of no intervention Outcome Measures: • Frequency of using cooking appliances • Number of food items prepared • Time spent preparing meal	The mean of frequency of using cooking appliances increased in all participants (10.6% minimum; 19.3% maximum). The number of food items prepared increased by an average of 13.9% per day at the intervention phase. The mean for time spent preparing meal decreased by an average of 38% in cooking time.	This study used a single-participant design, and generalizability of findings is limited. Data collection included self-report, which may be less accurate than direct observation. Illness and special events of some of the participants had an impact on the results.

Lee & King (2003)	The objective was to investigate whether exposure to a specific physical activity intervention would increase the time that initially inactive older adults spend engaged in physical activities that were not specifically prescribed by the intervention.	I—Combined results from two randomized controlled trials Study one: $N = 103$ community-dwelling older adults ≥ 65 yr, initially sedentary Study two: $N = 93$ community-dwelling women ≥ 49 yr, initially sedentary Study one mean age: 70 Study two mean age: 63, range 49–82	Study one: 1 hr, 4x/wk. ■ Fit & Firm intervention group: Home and group-based aerobic fitness, and muscle strength exercises program and phone calls follow-ups to enhance behavioral adherence. ■ Flexibility intervention group: Home-based stretching sessions program to enhance (falta terminar) Study two: ■ Physical activity group: 40 minutes, 4x/wk of brisk walking in or around the home ■ Nutrition instruction group: Monthly instruction to meet national dietary recommendations. Outcome Measures: ■ Community Health Activities Model Program for Seniors Questionnaire (CHAMPS PA): Assesses changes in time and frequency of physical activity undertaken by older adults over time	The time spent in household activities remained unchanged from baseline to 12-mo post-intervention in both studies.	No control group. The CHAMP instrument included self-report, which may be less accurate than direct observation. This tool does not address the complete universe of activities of discretionary time use in older adults.
Liu & Latham (2007)	The objective was to assess the effects of progressive resistance strength training (PRT) on older people and to identify adverse events.	I—Systematic review $N = 121$ randomized control trials studies reviewed	Studies critically appraised in the systematic review addressed progressive resistance strength training (PRT) exercises 2 to 3x/wk and at a high intensity. Outcome Measures: ■ Physical function ■ Muscle strength	The systematic review revealed that PRT had a large positive effect on muscle strength. PRT resulted in small but significant improvements in older adults' performance of simple activities, such as walking, as well as their physical abilities in more complex daily activities such as preparing a meal.	Adverse events were poorly recorded. No information is provided in relation to IADL outcome measures used in the reviewed studies.
McCabe et al. (2000)	The objective was to test the hypothesis that vision rehabilitation using optometry, occupational therapy, and social work services increase patients' functional ability and to assess whether involving families in the intervention results in more successful outcomes.	I—Randomized controlled trial 97 participants with visual impairments ≥ 19 yr Intervention 1 ($n = 49$); Intervention 2 ($n = 49$) Mean age: 69	Vision rehabilitation program involving optometry, occupational therapy, and social work services administered to two groups: ■ Individual protocol ■ Family-focused group Regardless of group assignment, intensity of intervention depended on the patient's level of impairment and capacity to learn new techniques. Outcome Measures: ■ Functional Assessment Questionnaire (FAQ): A self-report measure of difficulty and functional independence in activities of daily living and social activities. It includes IADLs such as prepare foods, take public transportation, and house clean.	Change in functional scores for the total population from baseline to completion of treatment showed a significant decrease in dependency (FAQ) and a decrease in self-reported difficulty performing tasks (FAQ). Change scores showed no statistically significant differences between the individual and family intervention groups at the end of the treatment.	Did not include a no-treatment control group. Used self-report measure. Modification of the FAQ for this study could have an effect in the findings. A small sample size did not reach the necessary power to show a significant group difference. IADLs measurement was not comprehensive.

(continued)

Table F1. Instrumental Activities of Daily Living (IADLs) (continued)

Author/Year	Study Objectives	Level/Design/Participants	Intervention and Outcome Measures	Results	Study Limitations
Manini et al. (2007)	The objective was to determine the efficacy of 10 wk of resistance, functional, or functional plus resistance training in older adults who modify tasks of everyday life and are at risks of subsequent disability.	I—Randomized controlled trial $N = 32$ independent-living older adults ages ≥ 70 with different functional abilities ■ Resistance intervention ($n = 11$) ■ Functional and resistance intervention ($n = 11$) ■ Functional training ($n = 10$) Mean age: 82	Control period: First 10-wk period in which participants did not participate in any intervention Resistance training (RT) intervention: 10-wk intervention period, 2x/wk, 30–45 min each session of graded resistance exercises Functional training (FT) intervention: 10-wk intervention period, 2x/wk, 30–45 min each session of functional exercises: chair rise, stair ascent and descent, laundry basket lift and carry, vacuuming carpet, kneel rise and supine to stand Functional and Resistance Training (FRT) intervention: 10-wk intervention period, 2x/wk, 30–45 min each session of resistance and functional training. Outcome Measures: ■ Task Modification and Timed Performance Scale: Valid measure that quantifies how individuals complete functional tasks (chair rise, stair ascent and descent, laundry basket lift and carry, vacuuming, kneel rise and supine to stand) ■ Muscle strength	Those who performed only FT improved in both components of functional ability (task modification and time performance), but did not have consistent increase in muscle strength. Those who performed only RT increased muscle strength, but only reduced task modification. Those who performed the FRT had less dramatic changes in muscle strength and function ability than the other two groups, but had consistent improvement in both component of functional ability (task modifications and timed performance) and muscle strength.	Small sample size. Possibility of seasonal effect on results because interventions and control periods were not conducted concurrently.
Mann et al. (1999)	The objective was to evaluate the effectiveness of a system of assistive technology devices and environmental interventions services to promote independence and reduce health care costs for physically frail elderly people.	I—Randomized controlled trial $N = 104$ home-based frail elderly people Intervention ($n = 52$); control participants ($n = 52$) Mean age: 73	Group 1: Assistive technology and environmental intervention services every 6 mo for 18 mo Group 2: Control group received standard care services Outcome Measures: ■ Older Americans Research and Service Center Instrument (OARS–IADL): Measures level of functioning of elders. It addresses 7 IADLs items. ■ Functional Independence Measure (FIM™): Measures the ■ Craig Handicap Assessment and Reporting Technique (CHART): Measures the degree of impairment resulting in handicap. It addresses community mobility and some IADLs.	After the 18-mo intervention period, both groups had reduced FIM total and motor scores. A greater percentage of participants in the control group, however, declined on the areas of IADL, mobility, and occupation than for the intervention group participants. The control group also incurred significantly greater expenses for health services than the control group.	Small sample size could limit generalizability of results. Lack of control of variables in the control group. IADL measurement was not comprehensive.

Author	Objective	Study Design/Participants	Intervention and Outcome Measures	Results	Study Limitations
Marottoli et al. (2007b)	The objective was to determine whether an education program consisting of classroom and on-road training could enhance driving performance of individuals with driving difficulties at baseline.	I—Randomized control trial *N* = 126 community-living drivers ≥ 70 yr Intervention (*n* = 69); control participants (*n* = 57) Mean age: 80	Intervention group: Participants received a combination of 8 hr of classroom and 2 hr of on-road instruction. The classroom instruction was based on the AAA Driver Improvement Program, the literature, and common on-road errors encountered in an earlier study. On-road instruction was based on the literature and common errors encountered in an earlier study. Control group: Two modules were presented to participants: a home environment safety and a vehicle safety module at the participants' home. Outcome Measures: ■ Driving performance: A road test based on the Connecticut Department of Motor Vehicles test: Parameters assessed included speed, lane changes, merging, observance of signs and signals, interaction with traffic, and operation of vehicle ■ Knowledge test: The test included 20 road knowledge questions from the AAA Driver Improvement Program and 8 road sign questions	At 8 wk, the intervention group scored significantly higher in the road and knowledge test than the control group.	Clinical relevance of the difference between two groups on driving performance is unknown. Lack of psychometric properties of outcome measures.
Matteliano, et al. (2002)	The objective was to explore the relationship of receipt of community-based occupational therapy services to changes in instrumental activities of daily living.	II—Case–control *N* = 81 older patients who received home-health care services with orthopedic, neurological, or chronic impairments Occupational therapy and physical therapy (*n* = 42); physical therapy (*n* = 39) Mean age: 78	Group 1: Patients received occupational therapy services through a home care agency. Group 2: Patients who did not receive occupational therapy services. Outcome Measures: ■ IADLs: It measures the level of independence in meal preparation, household management, laundry, and money management. IADLs were scored using the 7 point scale based on level of caregiver assistance used with the FIM. ■ FIM–ADL performance	Participants receiving occupational therapy improved on ADL function, including grooming, bathing, dressing, and toileting. Study participants receiving occupational therapy demonstrated improvement in the IADLs of food preparation, but this was not significantly different from the group that did not receive occupational therapy.	Use of a nonstandardized instrument for measuring IADL could minimize the applicability of the results to the overall population of elderly people. Only food preparation outcomes were reported for IADL. Retrospective design does not control for extraneous variables. Study participants were not equally represented in the diagnostic groups. Data were collected for clinical and not research purposes.

(continued)

Table F1. Instrumental Activities of Daily Living (IADLs) (continued)

Author/Year	Study Objectives	Level/Design/Participants	Intervention and Outcome Measures	Results	Study Limitations
Oida et al. (2003)	The objective was to evaluate the effects of regular exercise over 5 yr on mortality and ADL impairments in elderly people.	II—Nonrandomized cohort study N = 245 home-based older adults ≥ 70 yr Intervention (n = 155); control participants (n = 90) Mean age: 73	Intervention group: Received a 5-yr program that consisted of a combination of a home-based exercise program (walking, stretching, and strengthening) and a support program based on health education theories. The latter consisted of a group-based health class given 6x/yr, a community-based social support of voluntary walking or recreational activities with classmates, and individual self-monitoring and counseling. Control group: This group did not receive any intervention. Outcome Measures: ■ State of independence: A standardized sheet for assessment of independence published by the Ministry of Health and Welfare. It classifies participants as independent, mobility impairment, and ADL impairment (which include domestic activities). ■ Mortality	Mortality was significantly lower for women participating in the intervention group. Although the women showed lower adjusted relative risk for ADL impairment, it approached significance.	Nonrandom allocation of participants to groups may have introduced some variables bias. Small number of men in study.
Pahor et al. (2006)	The objective was to assess the effect of a comprehensive physical activity (PA) intervention on the Short Physical Performance Battery (SPPB) and other physical performance measures.	I—Randomized control trial N = 424 community-living older adults between 70 and 89 yr Intervention (n = 213); control participants (n = 211) Mean age: 76.8	Control group (SA): Participants received successful aging health intervention sessions weekly for the first 26 wk and monthly the next 6 mo. Session topics included nutrition, medication, foot care, and basic physical activity education. PA group: A combination of balance, aerobic, strength, and flexibility exercises. The first 2 mo, 3 sessions per week were conducted in a center. During the next 4 mo, 2 sessions were conducted in a center and 3 sessions were performed at participants' home. The next 6 mo consisted of home-based interventions and optional center-based sessions. This intervention included group-based behavioral counseling sessions. Outcome Measures: ■ SPPB: Standardized time measure of lower extremity physical performance, which includes standing, balance, walking speed, and ability to rise from a chair.	At 8 weeks, the SPPB scores for the PA group were significantly higher compared to the SA (successful aging) group. The 400-m walk speed declined in the SA group and remained stable in the PA group. Both results were uniform over a follow-up duration of 1.2 yr; 12.2% of participants in the PA group and 15.6% of participants in the SA group experienced major mobility disability.	No control group without intervention. Measures community mobility (IADL) indirectly by 400-m walk speed.

			■ 400-m timed walk CHAMPS PA questionnaire: It assesses changes in PA over time. It derives average minutes and frequency of both moderate and overall PA performed across an average week in the past month.		
Rejeski et al. (2008)	The objective was to investigate the effect of physical activity on self-efficacy and satisfaction with physical functioning in older adults ≥ 70 yr who have deficits in mobility.	I—Randomized controlled trial N = 424 community-dwelling older adults ≥ 70 yr with lower extremity mobility impairment Intervention (n = 213); 211 control participants (n = 211) Mean age: 77	Physical activity intervention (PA) group: 12 mo of aerobic, strength, balance, and flexibility exercises, primary walking 5x/wk. Control group: Received health education for successful aging (SA) once a month during 12 mo. Outcome Measures: ■ Community Health Activities Model Program for Seniors Questionnaire (CHAMPS PA): Assesses changes in time and frequency of physical activity undertaken by older adults over time. ■ Self-efficacy for the 400-m walk ■ Satisfaction with physical function	Both groups increased the weekly time of physical activities of moderate intensity or greater from baseline to 12 mo (SA group 5.76 minutes; PA group 63.23 minutes). However, the PA group reported a significant greater increase in time spent in physical activities ($p < .001$). Participants in PA compared with participants in SA had significantly better profiles for satisfaction with physical function ($p = .006$) and self-efficacy for the 400-m walk ($p = .005$) at 12 mo.	Use of self-report, which may be less accurate than direct observation. The study did not provide specific scores of each domain assessed by the CHAMP. There was variability in PA goals for each participant in response to a wide range of physical disabilities.
Rejeski et al. (2009)	The objective was to examine the functional status of older adults who participated in the LIFE–P study at 2 yr after the participants had completed the original 12-mo assessment.	I—Randomized control trial N = 79 community-living older adults ages 70 to 89 yr Intervention (n = 41); control participants (n = 38) Mean age: 76.8	Control group: Participants received successful aging (SA) health intervention sessions weekly for the first 26 weeks and monthly the next 6 mo. Session topics included nutrition, medication, foot care, basic physical activity education. Physical activity (PA) group: Group received a combination of balance, aerobic, strength, and flexibility exercises. The first 2 mo, 3 sessions per week were conducted in a center. During the next 4 mo, 2 sessions were conducted in a center and 3 sessions were performed at participants' homes. The next 6 mo consisted of home-based interventions and optional center-based sessions. This intervention included group based behavioral counseling sessions. Outcome Measures: ■ SPPB: Standardized time measure of lower-extremity physical performance, which includes standing, balance, walking speed, and ability to rise from a chair ■ 400-m walk ■ CHAMPS PA questionnaire: It assesses changes in PA over time. It derives average minutes and frequency of both moderate and overall PA performed across an average week in the past month.	At 2 yr after completing the 12-mo LIFE–P intervention, participants in the PA group continued to self-report marginal statistical significant higher SPPB scores than those in the SA group. The results for gait speed in the 400-m walk did not reach statistical significance. 12% of the participants in the PA group failed the 400-m walk at 36 mo compared with 22% in the SA group.	Small sample size. Data were obtained from participants of only 1 of the 3 participating centers at the beginning of the intervention. No control group without intervention. Measures community mobility (IADL) indirectly by 400-m walk speed.

(continued)

Table F1. Instrumental Activities of Daily Living (IADLs) *(continued)*

Author/Year	Study Objectives	Level/Design/Participants	Intervention and Outcome Measures	Results	Study Limitations
Richardson et al. (2000)	The study determined whether improvement in ADL and IADL skills was greater when elderly patients with compromised functional status receive rehabilitation therapy in EASY Street (ES; several modules that mimic indoor and outdoor environments that challenge frail elderly persons, simulated home and community settings) than a traditional treatment setting.	I—Randomized control trial

$N = 88$ patients stratified by age 55–75 yr, 76–90 yr, and by IADL scores

ES ($n = 44$); treatment ($n = 44$) | Intervention: three 1-hr treatment sessions per week for the first 2 mo and 2/wk for the 3rd and 4th month.

ES: Simulated environment with 13 modules: bank, grocery store, bus, restaurant, theater, pharmacy, post office, putting green, car, department store, kitchen, apartment with living room and others

Treatment: Received therapy in a gymnasium or therapy room that did not resemble their living environment

Outcome Measure:
■ SAILS (Structure Assessment of Instrumental Living Skills): measured self-care, instrumental and communication areas

Assessed at baseline, within 1 wk, intervention, 16 wk after commencement of therapy, discharge, and 8 wk following discharge | No differences at baseline

No statistically significant change was found by group, time of assessment, and group time interaction, for overall SAILS or any SAILS domain. | Small sample size.

Loss of participants.

It is possible that the instrument may have been insufficiently responsive to detect small but important changes. |
| Stav (2008) | The objective was to investigate the effects of drivers' license policies and community mobility programs on older adult participation. | I—Systematic review

$N = 7$ studies reviewed 6 Level II, 1 Level III | Studies critically appraised in the systematic review addressed policy interventions related to licensure restrictions, relicensing criteria, and retesting and community mobility interventions related to program effectiveness and program evaluation.

Outcome Measure:
■ Older driver traffic accidents and fatalities rates | The systematic review revealed inclusive evidence suggesting that relicensing policies requiring in-person renewal and vision testing may lower fatality rates and that licensing and driving restrictions can decrease crashes and traffic violations. Increase in fatalities rates is greater in unprotected nondrivers (pedestrians and bicyclists).

Results from assessments used in driving rehabilitation are valuable in predicting long- and short-term crashes of older adults.

Limited evidence suggests that transportation programs for nondrivers may increase community mobility. | Lack of randomization, lack of control groups, small sample size, learning effect, confounding variables, and use of self-reported measures. |

| Timonen et al. (2006) | The authors studied whether a multi-component exercise program consisting of strength, balance, and functional exercises could improve ADL/IADL functions in very old frail patients recuperating from an acute illness. | I—Randomized controlled trial

Participants: 68 women, ≥ 75 yr (m = 83 y, SD = 3.9)

Exercise treatment group (n = 34); control group (n = 34) | Exercise group intervention: group exercise program, for 10 wk, 2 sessions/wk (progressive resistance training, functional exercises such as raising from chair, rising to tip-toe, cool-down or relaxation period, and stretching at home)

Control group: Participants received 1 visit per week after discharge, were taught an exercise program including functional exercises, and were advised to perform it 2–3x/wk.

Outcome Measure:
■ Joensuu Classification | No change over time in ADLs or IADLs was observed in either group. No intervention effects were identified in either group for ADLs or IADLs.

Changes were observed in muscle strength, balance, walking speed, and mood (physiological aspects). | Scale (outcome measure) might not be sensitive to modest change. |
| Wellman et al. (2007) | The authors assessed the Eat Better & Move More (EBMM) Program effectiveness in a variety of community sites nationwide that serve older populations. | III—Pretest–posttest

Participants: from 10 nationwide OAA (Older Americans Act) nutrition programs with no physical activity program.

≥ 60 yr (50 yr for Native Americans)

N = 999 enrolled; 620 completed the program (35% to 85% completed in each site)

Mean age 74.6 (range: 53–101) yr; 82% were women; 41% ethnic minority groups)

Program completers had significantly fewer health conditions than noncompleters. | Intervention EBMM: 12 weekly sessions of mini-talks and activities for group nutrition (emphasize benefits of eating more fruits and vegetables, calcium-rich foods and dietary fiber; sensible portions and deficiencies and excesses) and physical activity sessions (emphasize benefits of walking, learned to use a step counter, performed simple stretching exercises, walk more at home and away, dress for all weather walking and stay hydrated—using EBMM guidebook).

Measure:
■ Physical activity questionnaire included Modified Baecke Questionnaire for Older Adults—measures household and leisure activity
■ Walking: Steps and blocks walked, days walking, stairs climbed
■ State of change questionnaire | Significant increase in steps taken per day, stairs climbed, average blocks walked, and number of days walked per week. | No control group.

Wide variation in completion rate.

Does not report on outcomes for household activities. |

(continued)

Table F1. Instrumental Activities of Daily Living (IADLs) *(continued)*

Author/Year	Study Objectives	Level/Design/Participants	Intervention and Outcome Measures	Results	Study Limitations
Willis et al. (2006)	The objective was to determine the effects of cognitive training on daily function and durability of training of cognitive abilities.	I—Randomized controlled single-blind trial, 5-yr follow-up and 4 groups. N = 2,832 participants ■ Memory (n = 711) ■ Reasoning (n = 705) ■ Speed training (n = 712) ■ Control participants (n = 704)	Interventions: 1. Reasoning training group 2. Memory training group 3. Speed training group 4. Control group (CG) Independent variable: Type of training, time, booster. 10 training sessions of 60–75 min; booster at 11 and 35 mo (4 75-min sessions to a subsample) Outcome Measure: ■ Participant's self-ratings of difficulty (IADL difficulty from the minimum Data Set-Home Care [meal preparation, housework, finances, health maintenance, telephone used, and shopping]) Measured at baseline, 1, 2, 3, and 5 yr	Participants who received cognitive training reported less difficulty with IADLs 5 yr after training compared with CG. Participants in the 3 training groups reported and IADL decline of at least .20 SD less than CG participants. The effect size reached statistical significance only for the reasoning group. Lower declines in function (less difficulty in IADL) compared with the CG (5 yr).	Use of self-report. Participants were not blind that they were receiving the intervention. No use of placebo for control group.
Wolf et al. (2003)	The objective was to evaluate the effects of 2 exercise approaches, tai chi (TC) and computerized balance training (BT), on specify primary outcomes (biomedical, functional, and psychosocial indicators of frailty) and secondary outcomes (occurrences of falls).	I—Randomized controlled trial N = 200 participants (162 women), ages 70 and over (mean age 76.2) living in the community and ambulatory. ■ TC (n = 72) ■ BT (n = 64) ■ Education control (ED) (n = 64)	Intervention: TC: Synthesis of 108 forms into to 10, emphasized all components of movement that typically become limited with aging (encourage home practice twice a day but not monitored); group intervention 2x/wk. BT: Balance system, view of moving cursor representing the center of body mass, instructed to move the cursor into specific targets that can be placed anywhere on the monitor; individual intervention once a week ED: Instructed not to change their exercise level throughout the study, met weekly with gerontological nurse/researcher to discuss topics of interest; group intervention once a week Outcome Measure: ■ IADL with the Lawton and Brody IADL scale	No significant changes were observed across the 3 groups and the 3 assessments of participants for IADL performance.	Short study time (4 mo). Changes were observed in falls and biomedical variables.

| Ziden et al. (2008) | The objective was to investigate whether home rehabilitation can improve balance confidence, physical function, and daily activity level compared with conventional care in the early phase after hip fracture. | I—Randomized controlled trial

$N = 102$ community dwelling elderly, ≥ 65 yr, hip fracture, speaks Swedish

Mean age: 81.9 yr ($SD = 6.8$)

Home Rehabilitation (HR) and Conventional Care Group (CG) | Intervention: Multiprofessional Home Rehabilitation (HR) focused on supported discharge, independence in daily activities and enhancing physical activity and confidence. At discharge, patient was accompanied home by a physical therapist and occupational therapist, brief intervention periods for a maximum of 3 wk after discharge by occupational therapy, physical therapy, and nurse in some occasions.

Physical therapy: Encourage and support self-efficacy, meaning confidence in locomotion and physical activity, special attention to outdoor ambulation; learning by doing

Occupational therapy: Activity safety and independence in ADL home rehabilitation intervention based on individual needs and goals

Outcome Measures:
■ Instrumental Activity Measure (IAM; walking 300m, cooking a simple meal/dinner, using public transportation, simple shopping, major shopping, cleaning and washing; domestic activities and outdoor activities)
■ Frenchay Activity Index (FAI): Domestic and outdoor activities. | Most of the HR (88%) took outdoor walks compared with less than half (46%) of the CG ($p < .001$).

IAM: Significant difference at 1 mo follow-up in outdoor activities ($p = .0014$) and domestic activities ($p = .0292$)

FAI: Also domestic and outdoor difference (0.0119 and 0.0007, respectively)

HR demonstrated a higher degree of recovery. | 6 patients of HR did not participate in the intervention program.

Some (20; 37%) of the CG participated in other care and rehab actions.

Not well-structured program.

Not all patients received exactly same services (different number of home visits). |

Note. IADL = instrumental activities of daily living; ADL = activities of daily living; PADL = personal activities of daily living; SD = standard deviation.

Table F2. Home Modifications and Fall Prevention Programs

Author/Year	Study Objectives	Level/Design/Participants	Intervention and Outcome Measures	Results	Study Limitations
Buchner et al. (1997)	To evaluate the effect of strength and endurance training on balance, fall risk, and health services use	I—Randomized controlled trial $N = 105$ older adults	Supervised endurance and/or strengthening exercise, followed by self-supervised exercise. Outcome Measures: General health status, IADL status, falls	Greater time before first fall. Control group had more falls during follow-up and had longer hospitalizations. No difference in IADL status.	▪ Self-report bias ▪ Groups not blinded to intervention ▪ Assessment ceiling effect
Campbell et al. (1997)	To evaluate the effect of a home-based exercise program on falls	I—Randomized controlled trial $N = 116$ women ≥ 80 yr	Home visits for strengthening and balance Outcome Measures: Balance, falls, physical activity scale, IADL status	Improved balance, fewer falls after 1 yr Control group became less active over time at a faster rate. No difference in IADL	▪ Study participants did not include representation from a more fit, healthy group. ▪ Self-report of falls
Campbell et al. (2005)	To evaluate the efficacy of home safety and exercise programs to reduce falls in older people with low vision	I—Randomized controlled trial $N = 391$ older adults with low vision	Home safety and assessment delivered by an occupational therapist and an exercise program prescribed by physical therapist, both, or social visit only Outcome Measures: Number of fall and injuries resulting from falls	Fewer falls occurred in the home safety program but not in the exercise program. Those adhering more strictly to exercise had fewer falls. Neither program was effective in reducing injuries from falls.	▪ Recruitment through primary care may have provided a more generalizable population. ▪ Self-report bias
Clemson et al. (2004)	To evaluate the effectiveness of a multifactorial small group intervention on fall reduction	I—Randomized controlled trial (stratified blocks of 4) $N = 310$ adults ≥ 70 yr	Occupational therapist-led small-group learning, exercise, cognitive–behavioral fall prevention program. Outcome Measure: Number of falls	31% reduction in falls, with men having slightly better results than women	▪ Self-report bias ▪ Possible contamination ▪ Evaluated as a multifactorial program
Close et al. (1999)	To evaluate the effectiveness of an occupational therapy assessment and referral process on falls	I—Randomized controlled trial $N = 184$ adults ≥ 65 yr seen in emergency department	Detailed medical and occupational therapy assessment (home visit) and referral as needed Outcome Measures: Falls, ADL status, hospital admissions	Fall and recurrent fall risk were reduced. Lower odds of admission to hospital Slower decline in ADL function	▪ Contamination may have occurred. ▪ Small sample size, more frail elders not included ▪ Self-report bias possible
Cumming et al. (1999)	To evaluate the effect of occupational therapy assessment and environmental modifications on the risk of falls	I—Randomized controlled trial $N = 530$ older adults after a hospital stay	Home visit by an occupational therapist to make recommendations for home modifications for safety Outcome Measure: Falls	Those with history of falls had a reduced number of falls during follow-up.	▪ Difficult to separate the impact of the overall occupational therapy home visit from home modifications specifically ▪ Self-report bias possible

Study	Design	Intervention/Outcome Measures	Results	Limitations
Davison et al. (2005)	To evaluate a multifactorial intervention on fall prevention	I—Randomized controlled trial N = 313 older adults with fall history	Referral and recommendation as needed to in-home modifications and medical management Outcome Measures: Falls, number of fallers, hospital stays	Falls were reduced by 36% and significantly shorter hospital stays. No difference in the proportion who continued to fall, number of fall-related visits; and hospital admissions during follow-up.	▪ Contamination possible ▪ Evaluated as an intervention package ▪ Lack of comparison related ▪ Self-report bias possible
Day et al. (2002)	To evaluate the effectiveness of 1 or more of 3 interventions (group exercise, home hazard reduction, and vision help) on falls	I—Randomized controlled trial N = 1,090 adults ≥ 70 yr	After an assessment, participants were assigned to 1 or more of these interventions: strength and balance, home hazard removal, vision assistance Outcome Measure: Falls	Group exercise intervention provided positive results; however, the addition of either home hazard reduction or vision recommendations, or both, provided the best results.	▪ Group exercise participants not blinded ▪ Self-report bias possible ▪ Participants reported good overall health
Faber et al. (2006)	To evaluate the effectiveness of an exercise program on fall prevention	I—Randomized controlled trial N = 278 frail and pre-frail older adults	Either 1 of 2 exercise programs incorporating balance and functional strength Outcome Measure: Falls	Pre-frail participants had a small but significant reduction in fall-risk, especially after 11 weeks of the program.	▪ Some participants were in the nursing home part of the facility. ▪ Individuals not randomized ▪ Self-report bias possible
Gardner (1997)	To evaluate the effectiveness of home-based exercises on fall prevention	I—Randomized controlled trial N = 233 elder women	Lower-limb strengthening and balance retraining 4x/wk for 2 mo Outcome Measures: Falls	Fewer number of falls reported by the intervention at 1 yr.	▪ Self-report bias possible
Gitlin et al. (2006)	To evaluate the effectiveness of a multicomponent home intervention on level of functional difficulties	I—Randomized controlled trial N = 319 older adults ≥ 70 yr who report difficulty with ADLs	5 occupational therapy visits (for evaluation, recommendations, education, home modifications) and 1 physical therapy visit (for balance and strengthening exercise training) Outcome Measures: Self-report of functional level, fear of falling, self-efficacy	At 6 mo, intervention group reported less difficulty with ADLs and IADLs (especially in bathing), less fear of falling, and greater confidence in their abilities.	▪ Attention bias possible ▪ Limited generalizability to vulnerable older adults ▪ Self-report bias possible
Hauer et al. (2001)	To evaluate the effectiveness of strengthening exercises and progressive functional-balance activities on falls	I—Randomized controlled trial N = 57 women 75–90 yr with fall history who were admitted to rehab	Resistance training with progressive resistance and progressive functional balance tasks Outcome Measures: Falls, leg strength	Incidence of falls between groups was not significantly different. Significantly improved leg strength was reported in all areas addressed. Walking, stepping, standing up, and balance performance improved.	▪ Small number of participants ▪ Self-report of falls ▪ Not clear if clients lived in assistive living facility or independently
Hogan et al. (2001)	To evaluate the effectiveness of a community-based consultation service on fall prevention	I—Randomized controlled trial N = 163 adults ≥ 65 yr with fall history	Assessment was completed, then an interdisciplinary team designed an individualized plan and provided a written for exercise or modifications or education. Outcome Measure: Number of falls	Time between falls was longer for intervention group, but results unclear overall.	▪ Intervention programs not clearly described ▪ Self-report of falls (recall over a 3-mo time frame)

(continued)

Table F2. Home Modifications and Fall Prevention Programs (continued)

Author/Year	Study Objectives	Level/Design/Participants	Intervention and Outcome Measures	Results	Study Limitations
Hornbrook et al. (1994)	To evaluate the effectiveness of a home hazard reduction, exercise, and education on fall prevention	I—Randomized controlled trial N = 3,182 HMO members ≥ 65 yr, independent	Home hazard reduction, group educational sessions, exercises, with quarterly maintenance sessions Outcome Measure: Number of falls	Lower fall rates for intervention participants but no significant effect on probability of medical care from a fall.	▪ Self-report bias ▪ Low intensity of interventions ▪ Cannot generalize about severe falls
Lin et al. (2007)	To compare the effectiveness of fall prevention programs in improving quality of life in older adults	I—Randomized controlled trial N = 150 adults (mean age = 76.8 yr) who had had a recent fall	Exercise training group, education group, or Home Safety Assessment and Modification (HSAM) group Outcome Measures: Quality of life, falls, balance and gait, fear of falling, functional reach, and balance	Fall rates between groups were not significantly different. The exercise group had greater improvements in functional reach, balance, gait, and fear of falling than the education group. The HSAM group improved significantly in ADL score. The education group improved significantly on ADL and physical quality of life score.	▪ Low generalizability to frail elderly ▪ Use of different therapists to provide intervention ▪ Participants may have experienced improvements from simply recovering from their fall. ▪ Self-report bias ▪ Not all home modifications were implemented.
Liu & Lapane (2009)	To quantify the effect of home modifications on decreasing the risk of physical function decline	II—Cohort study N = 9,447 participants of the Second Longitudinal Study on Aging	Modifications to the home or assistive technology used in the home Outcome Measure: Functional ability status	Those who had some type of modifications or equipment at baseline had a reduction in risk of functional decline.	▪ Definitions of modifications and assistive equipment varied ▪ Clients self-reported functional abilities and presence of modifications
Logan et al. (2010)	To evaluate whether a program to prevent falls in the community would reduce the rate of falls in older people	I—Randomized controlled trial N = 204 adults ≥ 60 yr with fall history	Assessments and individualized plans for group sessions, home evaluations, or hazard reduction/home modification recommendations Outcome Measures: Falls over 1 year, ADL status, fear of falling	Those in the intervention group had a lower rate of falls per year, higher ADL scores, and less fear of falling; they called for an ambulance less frequently.	▪ Self-report bias ▪ Length of intervention varied per participant. ▪ Unable to identify which intervention impacted each individual outcome.
Lord et al. (1995)	To evaluate the effect of a 12-mo exercise program on balance, strength, and falls	I—Randomized controlled trial N = 197 women ages 60–85	Twice weekly exercise class that was part of a community-based program Outcome Measures: Falls, postural sway, reaction time, leg strength neuromuscular control	Those who attended > 75% of the classes during the year had fewer falls and improvement in most physiological measures	▪ Participants not blinded ▪ Self-report bias

Study	Design	Intervention	Results	Limitations
Lord et al. (2005)	To evaluate the effect of exercise, visual training, and counseling on fall risk and falls	I—Randomized controlled trial N = 620 people ≥ 75 yr	One group of extensive intervention level, 1 minimal level, and 1 control group Outcome Measures: Falls, fall risk	No significant difference in rate of falls Extensive intervention group had a reduction in physiological fall risk factors.	■ Group not blinded ■ Possible contamination
Luukinen et al. (2007)	To evaluate the effect of an individualized, exercise-oriented program effective on falls for frail elders	I—Randomized controlled trial N = 486 adults, mean age = 88 yr	Individualized intervention plan that may include home exercise, group exercises, self-care exercises, walking exercise, or any combination thereof Participants took the intervention plan to their physicians for approval before beginning exercise. Outcome Measure: Falls	No significant difference in overall number of falls but after the study, it took the intervention group longer to start falling.	■ Limited adherence to recommendations ■ Self-report of falls (study included those with cognitive impairments)
Mann et al. (1999)	To evaluate the effect of assistive technology (AT) and home environment on the independence and health care costs of frail older adults	I—Randomized controlled trial N = 104 older adults with mean age = 73 yr	A comprehensive functional assessment by an occupational therapist, recommendations for AT, and environmental interventions and a follow-up assessment Outcome Measures: Functional status, pain, health care costs	Although both groups demonstrated a decline in overall functional status, the control group had a significantly greater decline and showed a significant increase in pain. The control group also had higher health care use.	■ Frail elders not defined ■ Compared with standard care ■ Potential volunteer bias ■ Self-report of issues ■ Intervention group not blinded
Means et al. (2005)	To evaluate the effect of a rehabilitation exercise program effective on falls, balance, and mobility	I—Randomized controlled trial N = 338 ≥ 65 yr who can walk ≥ 30 ft	6-wk group program of active stretching, postural control, endurance walking, and repetitive muscle coordination exercises Outcome Measures: Time to complete functional obstacle course, falls	Completion time of the functional obstacle course improved. Those with history of falls from intervention group had fewer falls.	■ Functional obstacle course is not a standardized tool. ■ Attention bias not addressed
Morgan et al. (2004)	To evaluate the effectiveness of a low-intensity exercise program on reducing risk of falls among at-risk elders	I—Randomized controlled trial N = 294 men and women ≥ 60 yr	Small group exercise sessions 3x/wk for 8 wk Outcome Measures: Risk of fall and falls	Participating elders with low physical functioning had a decreased risk of falls. It increased risk of falls for higher functioning older adults.	This study included some participants who lived in an assisted living facility. This population may be more frail and in poorer health. ■ Possible contamination
Nikolaus & Bach (2003)	To evaluate the effectiveness of a multidisciplinary home intervention team on falls	I—Randomized controlled trial N = 360 older adults with mean age = 81.5 yrs	Home visit with individualized package of interventions as needed to include hazard identification, education, or recommendations for new or modified techniques Outcome Measure: Falls	31% fewer falls in the intervention group	■ Self-report bias ■ Not clear which intervention had largest impact or how the exact intervention was determined.

(continued)

Table F2. Home Modifications and Fall Prevention Programs (continued)

Author/Year	Study Objectives	Level/Design/Participants	Intervention and Outcome Measures	Results	Study Limitations
Nitz & Choy (2004)	To compare the effectiveness of a workstation format and a community-based traditional exercise class program in reducing falls	I—Randomized controlled trial N = 73 adults ≥ 60 yr	All received a falls risk education booklet and completed an incident calendar. Workstation format sessions of functional balance tasks or traditional group exercise format sessions Outcome Measures: Number of falls, balance	Both groups had significantly fewer falls at the end of the study. Intervention group showed significantly more improvement in functional motor ability and balance, lateral reach, and functional step test.	▪ High dropout rate, due in part to location or transportation issues (48% attendance) ▪ Not blinded ▪ Self-report bias
Petersson et al. (2009)	To investigate the long-term effect of home modification on the ability of people aging with disabilities to perform everyday life tasks	II—Quasi-experimental pretest–posttest N = 103 adults with disabilities ≥ 40 yr	Home modifications provided as needed Outcome Measure: Performance of everyday life tasks	Participants in the intervention group reported a significantly lower level of difficulty in everyday life tasks, with small to moderate effects continuing at both 2 and 6-mo follow-up.	▪ Lack of randomization ▪ Relatively small control group compared with intervention group
Pighills et al. (2011)	To assess the effectiveness of an environmental assessment and modification provided either by occupational therapists or nonprofessional assessors to prevent falls	I—Randomized controlled trial N = 238 adults ≥ 70 yr with a history of falls in the previous year	Intervention was the assessment and modification of home environment. Assessment and training were provided by occupational therapist (n = 73), nonprofessional assessor (n = 87). Control group—usual care (n = 78). Outcome Measures: Fear of falling, falls, quality of life, and ADLs	Although there was no effect on fear of falling, those in the occupational therapy assessment group had fewer falls than control group. There was no difference when comparing falls for the trained assessor and control groups. There was no difference in ADLs at follow-up between either occupational therapy or assessor groups versus controls.	Authors reported that it may be difficult to generalize to other populations because community-dwelling older adults in only 1 center in England were included.
Robertson et al. (2001)	To evaluate the effectiveness of a home-delivered exercise program on falls	I—Randomized controlled trial N = 240 adults ≥ 75 yr	Set of muscle strengthening and balance retraining that progressed in difficulty and a walking plan Outcome Measure: Falls	Those ≥ 80 yr in the intervention group had fewer falls and less injury from falls that did occur. Not effective for those taking psychotropic meds.	▪ Self-report of both doing the home program AND falls ▪ Not blinded
Shumway-Cook et al. (2007)	To evaluate the effectiveness of group exercise and fall prevention education classes in preventing falls	I—Randomized controlled trial N = 453 adults, mean age = 75.6 yr	Group exercise and fall prevention classes Control group received educational brochures only Outcome Measures: Number of falls, balance	Not significantly different in number of falls Intervention group had small but significant improvements in balance, leg strength, and general mobility.	▪ Possible contamination ▪ Different locations may have impacted attendance ▪ Not blinded ▪ Self-reported falls

Study	Level/Design	Intervention and Outcome Measures	Results	Limitations
Skelton et al. (2005)	I—Randomized controlled trial *N* = 100 women; mean age = 72.8 yr	Assessment followed by classes targeting dynamic balance, flexibility, gait and functional skills Outcome Measures: Falls; fall-related injuries	Significantly fewer falls than those in the control group, especially during the follow-up period	▪ Not blinded ▪ Relatively low number of participants ▪ Attention bias ▪ Self-report
Stevens et al. (2001)	I—Randomized controlled trial *N* = 1,737 adults ≥ 70 yr	Home visit with hazard assessment, free installation of devices, and education Outcome Measure: Falls	No differences in falls between intervention and control group	May not have eliminated enough or the correct home hazards
Tomita et al. (2007)	I—Randomized controlled trial *N* = 113 adults ≥ 60 yr	Both groups received a 2.5-hr in-home assessment by an occupational therapist or nurse Installation and training on a computer and smart home technology Outcome Measures: Living situation, functional status	Significantly higher on the Functional Independence Measure™ cognitive level The intervention group remained the same in IADL scores whereas the control significantly declined. Significantly higher rate of lively independently	▪ High attrition rate ▪ Attention bias ▪ Lack of standardization ▪ Lack of reliability between outcome tools ▪ Statistical difference in age between groups
Voukelatos et al. (2007)	I—Randomized controlled trial *N* = 702 adults ≥ 60 yr	16-wk community-based tai chi classes Outcome Measures: Number of falls, balance	Fall rate was significantly lower fall rate and better balance.	▪ Self-reported falls ▪ Attention bias not addressed ▪ Variety of instructors and types of tai chi classes

Note. IADL = instrumental activities of daily living; ADL = activities of daily living; HMO = health maintenance organization.

Table F3. Health Management and Maintenance Interventions

Author/Year	Study Objectives	Level/Design/Participants	Intervention and Outcome Measures	Results	Study Limitations
Alp et al. (2007)	To evaluate whether the self-management program *Choices for Better Bone Health* is effective to promote behavioral strategies for improving bone health, life quality, pain perception, physical function, and balance in osteoporotic subjects	I—Randomized controlled study $N = 50$ postmenopausal sedentary women with a diagnosis of idiopathic osteoporosis $n = 25$ Choices group $n = 25$ Control group	Interventions: *Choices for Better Bone Health*—5 sessions that incorporate education regarding osteoporosis and medication management, diet, living safely, and exercise Control: Compliance with sedentary lifestyle Outcome Measures: Visual Analogue Scale (VAS), Short Form–36– quality of life (SF–36) Sensitized Romberg Test (SRT), Timed Sit to Stand (TSS)	Participants in the intervention group scored significantly better at 6-mo follow-up on pain intensity (VAS), balance assessment (SRT), TSS, and the following subscales of the SF–36 quality-of-life measures: physical function, physical role limitations, social function, mental health, vitality, pain, general health perceptions, and emotional role limitations.	Sample was from only 1 hospital
Bartels et al. (2004)	To assess the effectiveness of a combined skills training (ST) and health management intervention (HM) for older adults with severe mental illness	II—Nonrandomized controlled trial $N = 24 \geq 60$ yr with a diagnosis of schizophrenia, schizoaffective disorder, bipolar disorder, other psychotic disorder or treatment refractory depression and persistent functional impairment requiring ongoing support $n = 12$ HM + ST (intervention) $n = 12$ HM only (control)	Interventions: ST = Hour-long group skills training twice a week. HM = Assessment and monitoring of routine and chronic health care needs and promotion of preventive health care Intervention Group: HM + ST Control Group: HM Outcome Measures: ■ Independent Living Skills Survey ■ Social Behavior Schedule ■ Brief Psychiatric Rating Scale ■ Scale for the Assessment of Negative Symptoms ■ Preventive health care	After 1 yr, the HM+ST group had better functional outcomes with medium to large effect sizes with respect to independent living skills, social skill, and health management, compared to those receiving HM alone. After 2 years, both groups had improved preventive health care.	· Lack of randomization Pilot study had a small sample size
Brawley et al. (2000)	To determine the effectiveness of a group-mediated cognitive–behavioral intervention (GMCB) on adherence rates to physical activity in older adults	I—Randomized controlled trials $N = 60$ apparently healthy, sedentary adults —50 at follow-up $n = 20$ GMCB $n = 20$ standard physical activity (SPA) $n = 20$ waiting list controls (WLC)	Interventions: WLC = weekly 1-hr lecture discussion plus phone calls SPA = center-based and home-based physical activity GMCB = physical activity plus weekly cognitive-behavioral intervention Outcome Measures: Physical Activity Recall Health Related Quality of Life (HRQOL)	At 6 mo, the GMCB and SPA groups were more active, had higher aerobic power, and had improved HRQOL compared with WLC. At 9-mo follow-up, GMCB group had a higher frequency of weekly physical activity than the SPA group.	Small sample size Authors report that physiological data were not included

Study	Purpose	Design/Sample	Interventions and Outcome Measures	Results	Quality
Chodosh et al. (2005)	To assess the effectiveness of self-management programs for hypertension, osteoarthritis, and diabetes	I—Meta-analysis Databases searched through September 2004 include Cochrane Library, MEDLINE, PsycINFO, and Nursing and Allied Health Also searched bibliographies of reviews	Interventions: 53 studies included in the meta-analysis were randomized controlled trials of self-management programs for osteoarthritis (14), diabetes mellitus (26), and hypertension (13) compared with a control or usual care Outcome Measures: Function, pain, weight, blood pressure, fasting blood glucose level, and hemoglobin A_{1c}	Participation in self-management interventions resulted in a minimal but statistically significant difference in pain and function. In addition, the self-management programs resulted in lowered systolic blood pressure and a reduction in hemoglobin A_{1c}. It is not known what components of the program are most responsible for benefits.	Studies included in the meta-analysis were of variable quality. Outcomes for osteoarthritis such as mood and quality of life were not included in the analysis.
Clark et al. (2001)	To evaluate the efficacy of preventive occupational therapy intended to reduce health-related declines among urban, multiethnic, independent-living older adults	I—Randomized controlled trial $N = 361$ participants recruited from 2 federally subsidized apartment complexes for older adults, located in or near Los Angeles Cohort I ($n = 143$) Cohort II ($n = 218$) Inclusion: Living independently in their communities and without marked dementia	Interventions: Group 1 = Participants received occupational therapy treatment that focused on helping the older adults incorporate positive changes within their ongoing lifestyles Group 2 = Participated in activities Group 3 = No intervention Outcome Measures: At completion of program and 6-mo follow-up RAND SF–36 Functional Status Questionnaire (FSQ) Life Satisfaction Index Medical Outcomes Study Health Perception Scale	The results indicate statistically significant differences between the intervention and control groups on the FSQ quality of interaction and 6 of 8 subscales of the SF–36 (physical functioning, role functioning, vitality, social functioning, role emotional, and general mental health). There were no differences between groups on all other outcome measures.	Study is of good quality.
Clark et al. (1997)	To evaluate the efficacy of preventive occupational therapy intended to reduce health-related declines among urban, multiethnic, independent-living older adults	I—Randomized controlled trial $N = 361$ participants recruited from 2 federally subsidized apartment complexes for older adults, located in or near Los Angeles Cohort I ($n = 143$) Cohort II ($n = 218$) Inclusion: Living independently in their communities and without marked dementia	Interventions: Group 1 = Participants received occupational therapy treatment that focused on helping the older adults incorporate positive changes within their ongoing lifestyles Group 2 = Participated in activities Group 3 = No intervention Outcome Measures: At completion of program and 6-mo follow-up RAND SF–36 Functional Status Questionnaire (FSQ) Life Satisfaction Index Medical Outcomes Study Health Perception Scale	Compared with the 2 control groups, the occupational therapy group showed a significant benefit in quality of interaction, life satisfaction, self-perception of health, and seven dimensions of SF–36 for physical and mental health (bodily pain, physical functioning, role limitations attributable to health problems, vitality, social functioning, role limitations attributable to emotional problems, and general mental health).	Study is of good quality.

(continued)

Table F3. Health Management and Maintenance Interventions (continued)

Author/Year	Study Objectives	Level/Design/Participants	Intervention and Outcome Measures	Results	Study Limitations
Dahlin-Ivanoff et al. (2002)	To investigate the effect of a health education program on perceived security in the performance of daily occupations 4 mo after the intervention period	I—Randomized controlled study $N = 253$ people attending a low-vision clinic in Sweden > 65 yr with diagnosed age-related macular degeneration At 4-mo follow-up, 184 participants remained (93 in intervention, 94 in control group).	Interventions: Group Health Education = Medical information and instruction on glasses, optical aids, and lighting in areas of occupation included self-care, meals, communication, orientation and mobility, food preparation, shopping, financial management, and cleaning Control: Standard intervention for the target groups at the low vision clinics Outcome Measures: Perceived security in performing daily occupations	The study showed significant differences in systematic change in perceived security between the health education group and the control group in several occupations at the 4-mo evaluation for 13 of 28 occupations. The health education group showed changes toward an improved level of perceive security in 22 daily occupations, whereas those in the control group declined in 22 specific daily occupations.	High dropout rate
Eklund et al. (2004)	To investigate the effect of a health education program on perceived security in the performance of daily occupations 28 mo after the intervention	I—Randomized controlled study $N = 253$ people attending a low-vision clinic in Sweden > 65 yr with diagnosed age-related macular degeneration At 28-mo follow-up, 184 participants remained (62 in intervention, 69 in control group).	Interventions: Group Health Education = Medical information and instruction on glasses, optical aids, and lighting in areas of occupation included: self-care, meals, communication, orientation and mobility, food preparation, shopping, financial management, and cleaning. Control: Standard intervention for the target groups at the low vision clinics Outcome Measures: Perceived security in performing daily occupations	The values of perceived security in the Health Education Group varied from –0.09 to 0.47 with a median of 0.25. In the Individual Intervention Group, the range of perceived security varied from –0.32 to 0.15 with a median of –0.14. The Health Education Group changed toward an improved level of security in 20 daily activities compared to the Individual Intervention Group, who changed towards a deteriorated level of security.	High dropout rate
Foster, Taylor, Eldridge, Ramsay, & Griffiths (2007)	To assess the effectiveness of lay-led self-management programs for persons with chronic conditions	I—Meta-analysis Databases searched include Cochrane Central Register of Controlled Trials MEDLINE, EMBASE AMED, CINAHL, DARE, PsycInfo, and Science Citations Index through June 2006.	Interventions: Randomized controlled studies compared lay-led self-management programs against no intervention or clinician led. Outcome Measures: Knowledge, relaxation, pain, and self-care maintenance	Lay-led self-management education programs may lead to small, short-term improvements in participants' self-efficacy, self-rated health, cognitive symptom management, and frequency of aerobic exercise, but none for psychological health, symptoms or health-related quality of life, or health care use.	Wide range of included conditions and outcome measures

Source	Objective	Design/Sample	Intervention/Outcome Measures	Results	Limitations
Gitlin, Chernett, et al. (2008)	To evaluate the effectiveness of a Chronic Disease Self-Management Program (CDSMP) for delivery to older African-Americans at a senior center	III—Pretest–posttest design *N* = 519 African-American adults with a chronic condition > 60 yr recruited through a senior center	Intervention: Harvest Health (HH), a CDSMP tailored for African-American participants Outcome Measures: Physical activity, Cognitive Symptom Management, health status, illness intrusiveness, health care utilization, self-efficacy	There were small but significant improvements for HH participants for exercise, use of cognitive management strategies, energy/fatigue, self-efficacy, health distress, and illness intrusiveness in different life domains. There was no difference for health care use.	Lack of control group
Hibbard, Greene, & Tusler (2009)	To determine whether assessing patient capabilities for self-management and tailoring coaching support provides better outcomes for disease management	II—Nonrandomized controlled study *N* = 6,828 patients referred to 2 call centers for health coaching *n* = 4,254 Intervention *n* = 2,574 Control	Interventions: Health coaching for disease management based on Patient Activation Measure (PAM) Control: Telephone health coaching for disease management Outcome Measures: ▪ PAM ▪ Utilization rates of office visits ▪ Clinical indicators such as LDL cholesterol, blood pressure, medication	Activation scores increased, clinical indicator improved, and use rates declined significantly more in the intervention than control group.	Lack of full data for any variables Cost of intervention component was not included in the analysis
Holland et al. (2005)	To evaluate the outcomes of Health Matters program, a health promotion and fitness program from the California Public Employees Retirement System	I—Randomized controlled trial *N* = 504 participants with 1 or more chronic health conditions, > 65 yr in a managed care Medicare program *n* = 255 Intervention *n* = 249 Control	Interventions: Health Matters Program included a client-developed health action plan, health coaching, and patient education Control: Contacted by the Health Matters staff at 12-mo follow-up, and permitted to participate in Health Matters Outcome Measures: At baseline and 12 mo, self-report of chronic health conditions, health status, physical activities, social activity, ADL, IADL, health and social role, depression, medications, and communication with physician	At 12 mo, those participating in Health Matters took part in significantly more stretching and aerobic exercise than controls. Depressive symptoms decreased among those participants with moderate or higher symptom scores.	Results may not generalize to those in a nonmanaged care Medicare program Participants were aware of assignment status.

(continued)

Table F3. Health Management and Maintenance Interventions (continued)

Author/Year	Study Objectives	Level/Design/Participants	Intervention and Outcome Measures	Results	Study Limitations
Jerant, Moore-Hill, & Franks (2009)	To evaluate the effectiveness of Homing in on Health (HIOH), CDSMP over a 1-year follow-up period	I—Randomized controlled trial $N = 415$ outpatients with ≥ 1 chronic illnesses plus functional impairments $n = 138$ HIOH via home visit $n = 139$ HIOH via phone call $n = 138$ usual care control	Interventions: HIOH, a CDSMP delivered one-to-one either in participant's home or by telephone Control: Usual care plus initial visit by nurse Outcome Measures: • Self-efficacy • Short Form–36 (SF–36) • Functional ability • Quality of Life—EQ-5D, EQ-VAS	Compared with usual care, HIOH led to significantly higher illness management self-efficacy at 6 wks and 6 mo, but not at 1 yr. There was significant improvement on EQ-VAS through 1 yr. There were not differences for HIOH by telephone and for other outcome measures when delivered in-person.	Most participants were White, female, married, and well educated. Dropout rate was greater in intervention groups.
King et al. (2006)	To evaluate the effectiveness of a multifaceted physical activity intervention emphasizing participant choice for persons with type 2 diabetes	I—Randomized controlled trial $N = 335$ persons recruited from primary care physician $n = 174$ computer-assisted tailored self-management intervention $n = 161$ health risk appraisal with feedback control	Interventions: Tailored self-management focused on choice of physical activity Control: Participants filled out health risk appraisal and received feedback on assessment Outcome Measures: Community Health Activities Model Program for Seniors questionnaire, diet, demographics	At 2-mo follow-up, those in intervention group improved all physical activity and moderate physical activity compared to controls	Reliance on self-report Limited follow-up
Leveille et al. (1998)	To reduce risk factors for disability especially through increased physical activity, to promote social activities, and to enhance medical management and self-management of chronic illness	I—Randomized controlled trial. $N = 201$ patients ≥ 70 yr with 1 chronic condition (101 in intervention, 100 in control) Inclusion: Nonparticipation in the senior center, self-reported ability to perform all ADLs and walk independently	Interventions: Health Enhancement Project received treatment that focused on physical activity and chronic illness self-management. Participants met with a geriatric nurse practitioner from 1–8 times and were encouraged to participate in a variety of activities including self-management Control: Tour of the senior center Outcome Measures: • Health Assessment Questionnaire • PACE (Total leisure and work activity) • Short Form–36 (SF–36), self report (performance of ADLs) • Timed Up & Go • Chair Stand Time	Those in the intervention group reported a significant increase in physical activity, fewer days in the hospital, and reduced ADL difficulty. At 1 yr, there were no differences on SF–36 or on performance measures such as the Timed Up & Go test and the Chair Stand Time.	The study was limited to 1 year. Observed baseline differences between groups may have limited the ability to demonstrate a difference.

Citation	Purpose	Design/Sample	Intervention/Outcomes	Results	Comments
Lorig, Ritter, & Gonzalez (2003)	To evaluate the effectiveness of a 6-wk community-based program for Spanish speakers with heart disease, lung disease, or type 2 diabetes	I—Randomized controlled trial $N = 551$ Spanish speakers with chronic disease $n = 327$ peer-led program $n = 224$ wait-list controls	Interventions: Tomando Control de su Salud (Taking Care of Your Health), a standardized peer-led group that includes action planning Control: Wait list control Outcome Measures: ■ Physical activity scale ■ Self-rated health ■ Health distress and role function, pain, fatigue	At 4 mo, those in the peer-led group had improved health status, health behavior, and self-efficacy, as well as fewer emergency room visits compared with controls. Improvements were maintained at 1 year.	Study is of good quality.
Lorig, Ritter, Laurent, & Fries (2004)	To test the effectiveness of a mail-delivered, self-management intervention (SMART) for persons with arthritis	I—2 Randomized controlled trials Study 1 $N = 1090$ (mean age 62.2) $n = 522$ SMART $n = 568$ Usual Care Participants were recruited from a databank from several centers for patients with arthritis Study 2 $N = 341$ (mean age 65.2 yr) $n = 180$ SMART $n = 161$ Arthritis Self-Management Program (ASMP)	Interventions: SMART = Participant received a tailored action plan and letter based on diagnosis, pain disability, exercise levels, and other arthritis-related behaviors. Print materials also were provided. This was repeated every 4 mo for 1 year. ASMP = Small group intervention—standardized protocol for a period of 20 hours taught by peer leaders to teach skills to improve function, increase physical activity, and improve problem solving Control group: Usual care Outcome Measures: ■ Health-related quality of life ■ Health care utilization ■ Perceived self-efficacy	At 1 year, participants in SMART had decreased disability, improved role functioning, and improved self-efficacy. At 2 years, doctor visits and global severity were decreased and self-efficacy was improved. There were no significant differences between groups at Year 3. At 1 year, participants in SMART had greater decreases in disability and increases in self-efficacy than those in ASMP. There were no differences at Year 2, but at Year 3, those in ASMP had improvements in role function and doctor visits as compared to SMART.	There was some loss of data due to data collection being independent of intervention.
Lorig et al. (2001)	To assess the 1- and 2-year outcomes of the CDSMP	II—Longitudinal design as follow-up to a randomized controlled trial $N = 831 \geq 40$ yr (mean age = 65) At start of study, patients were randomized to CDSMP or 6-mo waiting period. After 6 mo, control group was offered CDSMP.	Interventions: CDSMP is based on the generic principles of the ASMP with 20 hours of peer training that includes information on exercises, medication management, problem solving, energy conservation, and modeling and social strategies to improve self-efficacy Outcome Measures: ■ Health status (self-rated health, disability, social/role activities limitations, energy/fatigue, and health distress) ■ Health care use ■ Perceived self-efficacy	82% completed at 1-year, and 76% completed at 2-year intervals. At the end of 2 years, emergency department/outpatient visits and health distress were reduced and self-efficacy was improved. There were no significant changes for other measures of health status, which can be indicative of the maintenance of health status.	Lack of control group

(continued)

Table F3. Health Management and Maintenance Interventions (continued)

Author/Year	Study Objectives	Level/Design/Participants	Intervention and Outcome Measures	Results	Study Limitations
Montgomery & Dennis (2003)	To determine the effectiveness of cognitive–behavioral interventions to improve the quality, duration, and efficiency of sleep for older adults	I—Systematic review $N = 6$ studies This Cochrane review searched Medline, EMBASE, CINAHL, PsycInfo, and Cochrane Library for randomized controlled trials for the systematic review	Interventions: Cognitive–behavioral treatments (CBT) for insomnia in older adults	The results of the meta-analysis indicated that there is a mild effect of CBT for sleep problems in older adults, particularly for insomnia related to sleep maintenance. Although there was initial improvement in total sleep duration, night waking, and sleep efficiency, the effects eroded over time.	Overlap between types of sleep hygiene interventions Did not use standard criteria for diagnosing sleep problems.
Murphy et al. (2010)	To examine the effects of tailored activity pacing on pain and fatigue in adults with knee or hip osteoarthritis	I—Randomized controlled trial $N = 32$ $n = 17$ tailored intervention $n = 15$ control participants	Interventions: Tailored activity pacing—education on activity pacing or alternating activity with rest plus tailored recommendations made by an occupational therapist based on personalized report. Outcome Measures: ■ Western Ontario & McMaster Universities (WOMAC) Osteoarthritis Index–Pain ■ Brief Fatigue Inventory ■ Fatigue Severity & Fatigue Interference Subscales	Participants in the tailored group had less fatigue interference than those in the control group at 10-wk follow-up with a large effect size for the group difference. Although there was no statistically significant difference between groups for fatigue severity, there was a moderate to large effect size for the group difference. There were no group differences for pain reduction.	Small sample size
Murphy et al. (2008)	To examine the effects of activity strategy training (AST) to teach adaptive strategies for symptom control and engagement in physical activity (PA)	I—Pilot randomized controlled trial $N = 54$ older adults with hip or knee osteoarthritis at senior centers/housing facilities $n = 28$ Exercise + AST $n = 26$ Exercise + Health Education	Interventions: Exercise + AST = Exercise plus group discussion, activity pacing plus occupational therapy session at home to individualize program Exercise + health education = Education program from Arthritis Foundation Outcome Measures: ■ WOMAC Osteoarthritis Index–Pain ■ Community Health Activities Model Program for Seniors–Physical Activity ■ Accelerometer–Physical Activity	Those in Exercise + AST had significantly higher levels of objective peak PA compared with those receiving Exercise + Health Education. There were no differences for other outcomes	Small sample size Study group was primarily White, well-educated women, which may limit generalizability.
Newbould, Taylor, & Bury (2006)	To evaluate the effectiveness of lay-led self-management in chronic illness	I—systematic review 12 databases were searched	Interventions: Lay-led chronic disease self-management programs, both disease-specific and generic. Seventeen articles and two conference papers met the criteria.	The evidence to date is indicative of short-term versus long-term benefits of lay-led self-management programs.	Study is of good quality.

Author (Year)	Study design / Sample	Interventions and Outcome Measures	Results	Comments
Ostasz- kiewicz, Chestney, & Roe (2004)	To assess the effectiveness of habit retraining for the management of urinary incontinence in adults	I—Systematic review This Cochrane review included all randomized or quasi-randomized trials of habit retraining for the management of urinary incontinence in adults.	Interventions: Habit retraining is a form of toileting assistance by caregivers for persons with incontinence. It is individualized based on the routines of each person. Outcome Measures: ■ Incidence or severity of incontinence ■ Cost, role strain, role burden ■ Incidence of skin rash, urinary tract infection, skin breakdown	There is limited evidence from the 4 trials included in the review that habit retraining is effective for the management of urinary incontinence in older adults. The results also indicate that habit retraining may be problematic for carers.	Varied features of programs The quality of the trials was modest, with poor reporting on levels of concealment to alloca- tion, interventions, and outcome assessment, as each trial had missing data, high attrition, and analyses did not use intention to treat.
Phelan et al. (2004)	To evaluate the efficacy of the Health Enhance- ment Program (HEP) to prevent and reduce disability ADLs in community-dwelling older adults	I—Randomized controlled trial $N = 201$ (101 interven- tion, 100 control) > 70 yr, independent in ADLs with 1 or more chronic conditions, and did not participate in senior center activities	Interventions: Group 1 = HEP—Participant developed a "health action plan" with a gerontologic nurse practitioner (GNP). Progress monitored toward health goals through follow-up visits and telephone calls. Group 2 = Tour of the senior center and a schedule of senior center activities Outcome Measures: Health Assessment Questionnaire Disability Index (HAQ)	Those in HEP demonstrated a greater improvement in ADL function over 12 mo among those with any ADL disability at baseline compared with those in the control group. There was no difference on the develop- ment of new ADL disability or on worsening of ADL function.	Authors reported a small sample size. No information provided on level of participation in HEP programs.
Reid et al. (2008)	To synthesize the scientific literature regarding self- management strategies for pain due to musculo- skeletal disorders, with a particular emphasis on studies that examine program outcomes among older adults with chronic pain and on programs and strategies appropriate for use in the community setting	I—Systematic review $N = 27$ articles Articles that were analyzed were selected 1980–2007 and published in English using the following key words: self- care, patient education, arthritis, osteoarthritis, pain, yoga, massage, Tai Chi, aged, chronic pain, self-management, and Arthritis Foundation	Interventions: Articles included evaluated self- management programs designed to reduce pain and improve function among older adults with chronic non-cancer pain or arthritis: Arthritis Foundation Self-Help Program, Arthritis Foundation Aquatic Program, yoga, massage therapy, Tai Chi Outcome Measures: Pain, disability, self-efficacy, depression, symptom bothersome, anxiety, sleep	The researchers found that in 96% (26 of 27) of studies examined, positive outcomes resulted. The outcome for pain ranged from an increase of 18% to a decrease of 85%, with a median 23% reduction. The changed in disability scores ranged from an increase of 2% to a 70% reduction, with a median 19% reduction.	Limited enrolment of ethnic minority elders. PsycInfo not included in search strategy.

(continued)

Table F3. Health Management and Maintenance Interventions (continued)

Author/Year	Study Objectives	Level/Design/Participants	Intervention and Outcome Measures	Results	Study Limitations
Rejeski et al. (2003)	To compare the effects of a traditional cardiac rehabilitation program (CRP) involving exercise training with a group-mediated cognitive–behavioral intervention (GMCB) on change in older adults' physical activity and fitness	I—Randomized controlled trial $N = 147$, CRP (37 men, 37 women) GMCB (40 men, 33 women) Mean age = 65 Targeting adults 50–80 yr who either were at high risk for CVD or had documented evidence of CVD Participants also had disability, defined as self-reported disability.	Interventions: Group 1 = CRP: Consisted of center-based training that included walking and upper body strength training. Group 2 = GMCB: Exercise therapy plus a 20–25 minute period of instruction and counseling with homework regarding self-regulatory tools to maintain long-term physical activity and functional independence. Outcome Measures: ■ MET level—symptom-limited maximal graded exercise test ■ Self-efficacy, self-reported physical activity —Physical Activity Recall	Although both men and women in each treatment arm made a positive change from baseline on all 3 outcome variables at both the 3- and 12-mo assessment, the results indicated that those in the GMCB group significantly better outcomes than those in the CRP group.	Study is of good quality.
Warsi, Wang, LaValley, Avorn, & Solomon (2004)	To evaluate the effectiveness of patient programs for chronic disease self-management	I—Systematic review MEDLINE and HealthSTAR search between 1964 and 1999 71 trials included	Interventions: Studies included in the review if there was a self-management education intervention, had a control group, and clinical outcomes were evaluated. Chronic conditions: arthritis, asthma, diabetes, hypertension, and miscellaneous	Small to moderate positive effects were found for diabetes and asthma. No difference was found for self-management programs for arthritis. The results of a metaregression indicated that face-to-face contact resulted in better outcomes.	Wide variation in trial methods and type of chronic illness

Note. PAM = Patient Activation Measure; LDL = low-density lipoprotein; ADL = activities of daily living; IADL = instrumental activities of daily living; CVD = cardiovascular disease.

Table F4. Occupation and Activity-Based Interventions

Author/Year	Study Objectives	Level/Design/Participants	Intervention and Outcome Measures	Results	Study Limitations
Aartsen et al. (2002)	To determine whether social, experiential, and developmental everyday activities have an effect on cognitive performance in the areas of immediate recall, learning, fluid intelligence, and information-processing speed	II—Cohort study Population-based sample N = 2,076 people 55–85 yr	Participants indicated engagement in social, experiential, and developmental (after an educational course or study during the past 6 months and doing outdoor sports) activities through 2 face-to-face interviews 6 yr apart. Outcome Measures: ■ Mini Mental Status Exam (MMSE) ■ The 15 Words Test ■ Raven's Coloured Progressive Matrices ■ Adaptation of the Coding Task	The everyday activities were not found to have causal effects on cognitive functioning after a duration of 6 yr when controlled for age, gender, level of education, and health. Information-processing speed appeared to affect developmental activity; those with good cognitive functioning participate in intellectually challenging activities.	A period of 6 yr may have been too short to evaluate the effects of everyday activities on cognitive functioning. Findings may be largely affected by socioeconomic status rather than by engagement in activities alone. Attrition in the study led to relatively younger sample of respondents after a 6-yr time period.
Avlund et al. (1998)	To identify aspects of social relations predictive of mortality in older adults	II—Cohort study N = 743 men and women (70-yr-old) from Copenhagen	Data taken in 1984 regarding social networks, education, income, and functional skills Outcome Measures: 1995 information about deaths from The Central National Register	An independent association was found between social relations and mortality. Men who had poor functional ability, did not help with repairs for others, and who lived alone had an increased risk of mortality. Women who had poor functional ability and had no social support for other tasks had an increased risk of mortality.	The measure of functional ability used was somewhat outdated. The wording of items may have caused information bias, because importance of help may have been considered or described.
Avlund et al. (2004)	To examine whether social relations are related to functional decline among nondisabled older adults	II—Cohort study N = 651 participants 75 yr old with no disabilities in Denmark and Finland from the Nordic Research on Ageing (NORA) study	Baseline data were collected 1989–1990 and follow-up data were collected 5 yr later. Outcome Measures: ■ Functional decline among survivors, as measured by the physical activities of daily living (PADL–H) Scale to assess necessary assistance to complete a variety of functional activities ■ Mortality ■ Structure and function of social relations	More women than men survived following functional decline. Less-than-weekly telephone contact and not being a member of a club were related to functional decline and mortality in men; less-than-weekly telephone contact, no membership in a retirement club, and not sewing for other people were related to functional decline and mortality for women.	Men and women with few social relations were less likely to participate in the study than others. No data on the quality of social relations or changes in social relations preceding baseline data of the study were available.

(continued)

Table F4. Occupation and Activity-Based Interventions (*continued*)

Author/Year	Study Objectives	Level/Design/Participants	Intervention and Outcome Measures	Results	Study Limitations
Ayalon (2008)	To determine the effect of different aspects of volunteering on mortality	II—Cohort study N = 5,055 Israeli adults ≥ 60 yr obtained from The Israeli Bureau of Statistics	During a face-to-face interview, participants were asked whether they volunteered and, if so, how many hours per week, for how many years, and whether the volunteering was within an organization or done independently. Outcome Measure: Time of death obtained from Israel's National Record	Participants volunteering for 10–14 yr had a significantly lower risk of death after adjusting for age, gender, education, baseline mental health and physical health, activity level, and social participation. This was seen for those volunteering independently compared with those volunteering with an organization. The number of hours per week spent volunteering was not a significant predictor of mortality.	Although the sample is representative of the Israeli population, it may not be representative of other cultures.
Ayis et al. (2006)	To investigate the associations between chronic health conditions, psychosocial and environmental factors, and catastrophic decline in mobility among older people	II—Longitudinal cohort study N = 427 adults obtained from a national cross-sectional survey of 999 people ≥ 65 yr, representative of British households	Initial interview questionnaire included chronic illnesses, social support, social engagement, perceived control Outcome Measure: Follow-up survey 12 mo later	The results of this study showed that psychosocial factors are strongly associated with catastrophic decline and deterioration in health status.	Low response rate may have biased the results. Those already experiencing catastrophic declines in mobility were not represented in the sample.
Barnes et al. (2004)	To examine the relationship between social resources and cognitive decline in older adults	II—Longitudinal cohort study N = 6,102 people ≥ 65 yr participating in the Chicago Health and Aging Project	Face-to-face interviews were conducted at baseline and twice at 3-yr intervals. Questions were about social and productive engagement and social networks, as well as sociodemographic variables and physical and cognitive performance. Outcome Measures: <ul><li>Immediate and delayed recall using the East Boston Story</li><li>Symbol Digit Modalities Test</li><li>MMSE</li></ul>	People with greater numbers of social networks and social and productive engagement experienced significantly less cognitive decline.	Measure of social engagement was limited by only 4 indicators, which may not have captured a broad spectrum of social and productive activities. The measure of social engagement used in the study may be less culturally relevant in the African-American population than in the White population.

| Bassuk et al. (1999) | To examine the relationship between social disengagement and cognitive impairment in community-dwelling older adults | II—Longitudinal cohort study

$N = 2,812$ people $\geq$ 65 yr

Participants were noninstitutionalized and lived in public housing, private housing, or community housing. | Participants were interviewed annually at home (4 times) or by telephone for 12 yr to gather information regarding their cognitive functioning, social engagement, and emotional support.

Outcome Measures:
- 10-Item Short Portable Mental Status Questionnaire (SPMSQ)
- Composite social disengagement index | As the number of social networks of participants increased, the likelihood of cognitive decline was reduced. Older people were less likely to report multiple social networks, as were people with less education, lower incomes, and decreased mental or physical health. Participants experiencing cognitive decline were twice as likely to be part of the most disengaged clients than the most engaged clients in the study. | A brief screening instrument of cognitive status (SPMSQ) was used and has a limited ability to detect mild cognitive deficits.

The nature of social interactions, which require varying levels of cognitive efforts, were not examined. |
| Bath & Morgan (1998) | To explore associations between customary physical activity (CPA) with all-cause mortality, disease-specific mortality, and change in general practitioner and personal social service use | II—Longitudinal cohort study

$N = 1,042 \geq 65$ yr from the Nottingham Longitudinal Study of Activity and Ageing (NLSAA)

The sample was obtained from a random sample from general practitioners' lists. | Baseline interviews were conducted in 1985. Follow-up surveys were conducts at 4-yr intervals between 1989 and 1993.

Outcome Measures:
- All-cause and disease-specific mortality
- Levels of CPA (customary physical activity)
- General health
- Grip strength
- Half-span measurement
- Weight | For all-cause mortality, survival rates were significantly related to activity levels. Compared with the high-activity level group, 12-yr mortality was significantly increased in the intermediate- and low-activity level groups for men and in the low- activity level group for women. Compared with the high-activity level group, the low-activity level groups had a significantly increased risk of dying from respiratory disease but a decreased risk of dying from cardiovascular disease versus dying from other primary causes of death for men.

Low activity levels also were associated with an increased likelihood of using health and personal services after 8 yr. | Results for disease-specific mortality should be interpreted with caution because only the primary cause of death was considered.

Because health status and smoking status were controlled for, it is unlikely that the activity gradings acted as proxies to physical health.

Health index scores may have been insensitive to some conditions. |
| Bennett et al. (2006) | To examine whether social network size is related to clinical expression of cognitive impairment in Alzheimer's disease | II—Cohort Study

$N = 89$ elderly people without known dementia in the Rush Memory and Aging Project | All participants underwent a clinical assessment that included a medical history, neurological examination, and neuropsychological performance testing.

Outcomes:
- MMSE
- Complex ideational material test
  Social network size
- Alzheimer's disease quantified by silver stain of brain | Cognitive functioning was inversely related to all measures of Alzheimer's disease pathology. Social network size had an effect on the association between pathology and cognitive functioning. Even when participants displayed more severe pathological symptoms, cognitive functioning remained higher for those with larger social networks. | Although a correlation between disease pathology, cognitive functioning, and social network size was established through the study, causation cannot be concluded with complete confidence.

The quality of participants' social networks and information regarding social networks in earlier life were not examined. |

(continued)

Table F4. Occupation and Activity-Based Interventions (continued)

Author/Year	Study Objectives	Level/Design/Participants	Intervention and Outcome Measures	Results	Study Limitations
Bookwala et al. (2004)	To examine caregiver-related factors related to concurrent and long-term use of community-based long-term care services in older adults caring for a disabled spouse	II—Longitudinal cohort study $N = 186$ older adults caring for a disabled spouse	Data from participants collected at 2 points (1 yr apart) of the Caregiver Health Effects Study (CHES) were used for the study. ■ Sociodemographic information ■ Functional limitations and memory and behavioral problems of care recipient ■ Information regarding caregiver-related variables, including caregiving demands, caregiver mental and physical health Outcome Measures: Service use was assessed by caregiver reports on the number of community and home care services used for their spouse or themselves.	Caregiver-related variables of caregiving assistance, restriction in engagement in personal and social activities because of caregiving, and mastery were significantly associated with formal service use. At the second point of data collection, more caregiver activity restriction and depressive symptoms predicted increased formal service use.	CHES participants tended to be younger, more educated, and healthier than the older adult population, limiting generalizability. Formal service use was measured as a range and not as an amount.
Bursztyn & Stessman (2005)	To examine whether the practice of the siesta is associated with increased cardiovascular mortality	II—Longitudinal cohort study $N = 455$ residents of Jerusalem, 70 yr old	Participants were asked if they napped every day and took part in a 2-part questionnaire. The first part was administered by a nurse or occupational therapist and was used to gather information regarding demography, personal history, life style, health services use, and function and cognitive status. The second part, administered by a physician, included a thorough medical history and examination. Outcome Measure: Survival 12 yr from baseline	A significant association was present between the history of the practice of the siesta at age 70 with increased 12-yr mortality. The increased mortality appeared to be independent of medical history as well as independence in ADLs and IADLs, physical activity, generalized fatigue, sleep satisfaction, and working status.	Information about the siesta was taken at only one point in time, so researchers do not know whether the siesta was voluntary or due to fatigue. Timing of the siesta is unknown, and no information is present regarding sleep-disordered breathing.
Bursztyn et al. (1999)	To examine the impact of engagement in a siesta on mortality in an elderly population	II—Cohort study $N = 455$ residents of Jerusalem, 70 yr old	Issue of safety of the siesta was studied using 6½ yr of mortality data in the cohort. At baseline, participants were asked about their afternoon sleeping habits. Information regarding background, lifestyle, and health status were previously gathered through interviews and examinations. Outcome Measure: ■ Mortality	Approximately 61% of participants practiced a siesta daily. More men engaged in a siesta compared with women; more survivors of myocardial infarctions engaged in the siesta as well. After 6.5 yr, 75 participants in the study died. For those who practiced the siesta, mortality was 20% versus the 11% that did not. Researchers concluded that the siesta appears to be associated with mortality, but association cannot be concluded as causal.	Cohort size was small. Taking a siesta was self-reported by participants. Information regarding the frequency of siesta was not obtained. Causality of the association between the siesta and mortality cannot be concluded.

Citation	Purpose	Study Design / Sample	Methods / Outcome Measures	Results	Limitations
Burton et al. (1999)	To determine whether the initiation and maintenance of a physically active lifestyle decreased the incidence of chronic disease in older adults	II—Longitudinal cohort study N = 2,507 community-dwelling adults $\geq$ 65 yr living in the Baltimore metropolitan area Participants were obtained from the Johns Hopkins Medicare Preventive Services Demonstration.	Three interviews were conducted over the course of 4 yr. Interview questions targeted aspects of health and physical activity. The interview also included questions about insurance status and communication about physical activity with the doctor. Outcome Measures: ■ Quality of Well-Being Scale ■ Goldberg's General Health Questionnaire ■ Self-mastery	Younger age, higher education level, lack of emotional distress, better physical health, and the level of importance that the participant placed on an active lifestyle were predictors of initiation physical activity.	All information about physical activity behaviors and physical and psychological health was obtained through self-report. Physical activity levels were not quantified.
Clark, Friedman, & Martin (1999)	To examine the extent to which religiosity in adulthood predicts mortality in the following 4 decades	II—Longitudinal cohort study N = 993 participants (n = 547 men, n = 446 women) Participants were a part of the Terman Life Cycle Study, which began in 1921, and were primarily White, middle class, and considered gifted.	Religiosity was measured with questions on a questionnaire given in 1950. Questionnaires also were used to obtain information about the following control variables: physical health, psychological well-being, adult income, educational level, marital status, organizational involvement, drinking, and smoking. Outcome Measure: Mortality	Women who were more religiously inclined had a 16% lower mortality rate than their peers who were less religious and were involved in more organizations, smoked and drank less than their less religious peers. There was no significant relationship between religiosity and mortality in males. Males who reported more religiosity were more likely to be in an intact marriage, were involved in more organizations, smoked and drank less than their less religious peers.	The sample used in this study was relatively homogenous in intelligence, ethnicity, and socioeconomic class. This makes the results less generalizable to the U.S. population as a whole. The measure used to determine religiosity could not determine between private religious participation and public religious participation.
Clay et al. (2008)	To study changes and racial differences in social support and psychosocial outcomes in dementia caregivers over 5 yr	II—Longitudinal cohort study N = 166 caregivers for people with dementia Average ages at baseline were 55.7 for African-Americans and 63.4 for Whites	Participants completed at least 2 of 4 caregiver assessments and self-reported information regarding demographic variables. Socioeconomic status was assessed using the Nam-Powers index of occupational status. Outcome Measures: ■ Center for Epidemiologic Studies–Depression (CES-D) ■ Life Satisfaction Index–Z ■ Social Support Questionnaire, Short Form–Revised	The total number of available social supports significantly declined with time in both racial groups. Older caregivers and African-American caregivers reported higher levels of satisfaction with social support. White caregivers reported consistently higher levels of depressive symptoms. African-American caregivers showed stability in life satisfaction over time, whereas White caregivers showed a decrease.	Cultural values and spiritual beliefs were not accounted for, which may explain group differences. Generalizability of results is questioned, because the entire sample lived within 50 mi of University of Alabama at Birmingham.

(continued)

Table F4. Occupation and Activity-Based Interventions (continued)

Author/Year	Study Objectives	Level/Design/Participants	Intervention and Outcome Measures	Results	Study Limitations
Crooks et al. (2008)	To examine whether social networks had a protective association with incidence of dementia among elderly women	II—Longitudinal cohort study N = 2,249 female members of Kaiser Permanente Southern California, ≥ 75 yr	Baseline scores were obtained for cognitive function in 1999 and social networks in 2001. Participants completed at least 1 follow-up interview between 2002 and 2005. Outcome Measures: ■ Telephone Interview for Cognitive Status–Modified ■ Telephone Dementia Questionnaire ■ Medical record review ■ Lubben Social Network Scale	Larger social networks were associated with decreased risk for dementia in the 4-yr follow-up. The findings of the study suggest that social networks may facilitate access to health care and increase engagement in healthy activities, therefore indirectly reducing conditions that may affect cognition.	Lack of minority participants in the study The results of the study may have had a different outcome if men were included. Selection and recall biases of the participants may have affected the data collected. Attrition resulted from death and dropping out.
Dahan-Oliel et al. (2008)	To systematically review the literature on social participation in the elderly, including the benefits and factors associated with it and the measures used to evaluate it	I—Systematic review of literature N = 46 articles that met the inclusion criteria: written in English, relevant to social participation, and includes healthy individuals > 60 yr	Review conducted in OVID Medline, CINAHL, and PsycINFO for articles between 1982 and 2008. Social participation is based on the *International Classification of Functioning, Disability, and Health (ICF)* definition of "actions and tasks required to engage in organized social life outside the family, in the community, and in social and civic areas of life." (p. 160) Outcome Measures: ■ Survival ■ Health related quality of life ■ Functional ability ■ Emotional well-being	Social participation has been found to be associated with functional, emotional, and cognitive skills; well-being; health-related quality of life; and survival. Both personal and environmental factors were found to affect social participation, either positively or negatively.	Many studies operationally define social participation differently. Majority of studies are cross-sectional, which does not establish direction in associations. Maintaining a consistent sample in the older adult population is challenging, so fewer longitudinal studies exist.
Dew et al. (2003)	To investigate specific electroencephalographic (EEG) sleep characteristics that may be predictive of survival of older adults	II—Longitudinal cohort study N = 185 older adults (60–85 yr) who were relatively healthy and without any noted psychiatric illness, sleep disturbances, or cognitive delay	At baseline, participants kept a sleep/wake journal. The sample also underwent an EEG examination as well as overnight sleep assessments. Outcome Measure: Survival	At baseline, participants who demonstrated longer sleep latencies, poor sleep efficiency, and reduced slow-wave sleep, were more likely to be deceased by the follow-up assessment. The relationship of these components of sleep to mortality was additive. Having more risk factors was associated with lower survival.	Small sample size The initial sample included only those older adults who were relatively healthy and therefore may reduce the generalizability of findings to other older adult populations.

Source	Purpose	Study Design / Sample	Methods / Outcome Measure	Results	Limitations
Dupre, Liu, & Gu (2008)	To investigate the characteristics of the oldest old in China and to examine whether factors associated with longevity vary with advanced age	II—Cohort study N = 13,297 oldest old in China, > 80 yr, collected 1998–2002 Chinese Longitudinal Health Longevity Survey data	Face-to-face interviews were completed at baseline. Information was obtained for demographic, social contact and support, religious activity, health behaviors and diet, health status, and psychological characteristics. Outcome Measure: ■ Age categorization of longevity	For urban men and women, education, economic independence, being married, and regularly eating vegetables were associated with advanced age. Participants who resided in large households were more likely to be the longest-living adults in urban areas, but not in rural areas.	Results from study population in China may not generalize to other populations.
Ertel et al. (2008)	To evaluate whether social integration protects against loss of memory and other cognitive disorders in older adulthood	II—Longitudinal cohort study N = 16,638 participants ≥ 50 yr	Telephone interviews gathered information about social integration, demographic characteristics, health conditions, and memory. Follow-up telephone interviews were conducted in 2000, 2002, and 2004 to assess memory. Memory was assessed with immediate and 5-minute delayed recall of 10 common nouns. Outcome Measure: Changes in memory score	Respondents with higher levels of social integration at baseline were significantly different for socio-demographic characteristics. They were more likely to be younger, White, male, better educated, and healthier. Respondents had similar baseline memory scores regardless of level of social integration; however, the ones with higher levels of social integration had slower rates of memory decline over time.	Measure of social integration did not include all possible types of social connections or the quality of contacts. The study relied on self-report for information on health conditions. Lack of data on physical and cognitive activity limited further control for outside variables.
Fratiglioni et al. (2000)	To examine whether components of social network and varying degrees of social relations affect dementia incidence	II—Longitudinal cohort study N = 1,368 participants ≥ 75 yr living at home with good cognition	Baseline information on social network for close social relationships (e.g., availability of resources, contact with resources, perceived sufficiency of support), demographic information, and cognitive and physical functioning was collected through personal interviews. Outcome Measure: Dementia incidence at 3-yr follow-up	A poor or restricted social network increased the probability of dementia by 60%. Being single and living alone was the strongest predictor of dementia. Having frequent but unsatisfying contact with children increased risk of dementia.	No specific measure was used to assess social network. Not all social activities were taken into account, nor was past social life.
Ghisletta et al. (2006)	To investigate the relationships between activity engagement and cognitive performance	II—Longitudinal cohort study N = 529 participants (n = 274 women; n = 255 men) 80–85 yr, consisting of 2 cohorts from the Swiss Interdisciplinary Longitudinal Study on the Oldest Old (SWILSO–O)	Frequency of engagement in 16 different activities, including media (listening to the radio, watching television, reading the newspaper), leisure (playing games, completing crossword puzzles), manual (gardening or craftwork), external-physical, social, religious Outcome Measures: Cognitive performance measured by Cross Out Test of the revised Woodcock–Johnson Psycho-Educational Battery and Category Fruit Test	Participants with the higher scores on the cross-out tended to have the largest declines in cognitive status. Cross-out performance did not significantly influence activity changes. Media and leisure activity scores may lessen decline in cognitive performance with respect to perceptual speed, but not for verbal fluency or performance.	Selection of potential activities was limited.

(continued)

Table F4. Occupation and Activity-Based Interventions (continued)

Author/Year	Study Objectives	Level/Design/Participants	Intervention and Outcome Measures	Results	Study Limitations
Giles et al. (2005)	To assess and examine the effects of social networks consisting of children, relatives, friends, and confidants on mortality of older Australian adults	II—Prospective longitudinal cohort study *N* = 1,477 participants ≥ 70 yr, living in the community and in residential care facilities in South Australia	Personal interviews were held, and topics included social networks, demographics, cognitive function, self-rated health. Social network information was gathered on children, relatives, friends, and confidants. Outcome Measures: Mortality rate after 10-yr period	The mean specific social network scores and total network scores were higher for the participants who were alive than for those who died. While social network scores for friends were predictive of mortality, those for children and relatives were not.	A wide range of covariates were used in the analysis, but some data were not available for certain factors. People who chose not to participate in the study may have been more socially isolated than participants.
Ginsburg et al. (1999)	To identify mortality risk factors; specifically, the relationship between IADLs and mortality	II—Longitudinal cohort study *N* = 605 participants age 70 yr, residents of Israel	Interviews of randomly selected participants included demographic information, IADLs and ADLs, confinement to bed, cognitive impairment, and health status. Outcome Measure: Mortality status at 6 yr	Those dependent in more than 1 IADL function were at a higher mortality risk. >90% of participants who had been sick in bed in the 2 weeks before the interview and had more than 1 IADL dysfunction died during the study period.	The study did not include a measure of the life events occurring in each participant's life.
Glass et al. (1999)	To examine any relationship between social, productive, and physical activity and survival in older adults	II—Longitudinal cohort study *N* = 2,761 participants ≥ 65 yr	Engagement in activity (social, productive, and fitness) and other measures were assessed by structured interviews at baseline in the participants' homes. Annual follow-up interviews were conducted in person or by phone. Outcome Measure: Mortality	After controlling for all other variables, all 3 types of activity were independently associated with survival.	Measurement of frequency or extent of participation was imprecise. The participants were asked only about their activity participation in the previous month.
Goldman et al. (2007)	To investigate the potential relationship between disruptive sleep patterns and poor daytime function among older women	II—Longitudinal cohort study *N* = 2,889 Participants were a part of an existing sample from the Study of Osteoporotic Fractures. Participants included community-dwelling women ≥ 65 yr.	Participants were assessed for night-time sleep patterns and daytime napping schedules over a 24-hr period. The following were also measured: medical history, weight, height, walking, depressive symptoms, mental status, and comorbidity index. Outcome Measures: ■ Gait speed, chair stand, intervals of sit to stand, and grip strength ■ Self-report—functional ability in IADL completion	Participants who either slept < 6 hr or > 7.5 hr reported more functional limitations than those women who averaged between 6.8–7.7 hr of sleep per night. In addition, women who slept more during the day reported increased functional limitations.	Sample consisted of a rather healthy population and thus results may not be generalized. Researchers use self-report measures of function. Portions of the results were cross-sectional in nature.

Study	Design	Methods	Results	Comments
Greenfield & Marks (2007)	To examine continuous participation in voluntary groups (recreational, religious, civic) as a protective psychological buffer against the negative psychological effects of developing functional limitation	II—Cohort design N = 4,646 participants 35–92 yr from the National Survey of Families and Households	In addition to demographic information, participation in voluntary groups was surveyed: recreational, religious, or civic. Outcome Measures: ■ 12-item version of the CES-D ■ Ryff's 3-item Personal Growth Index ■ Series of questions regarding physical or mental conditions that limit function	Continuous participation in religious groups but not recreational groups was found to be associated with smaller increases in depressive symptoms. Participation in civic groups was found to be associated with differences in depressive symptoms among men, but not women. Continuous participation in recreational groups and religious groups, but not civic groups, was associated with higher levels of personal growth.	The authors report that included groups did not cover all types of voluntary groups.
Gregg et al. (2003)	To examine if changes in physical activity level were associated with decreased mortality among community-dwelling older women	II—Cohort study N = 9,518 women ≥ 65 yr from the Study of Osteoporotic Fractures	A modified version of the Harvard Alumni Questionnaire assessed physical activity, including exercise and other leisure activities such as gardening, dancing, and swimming. A summary of estimated physical activity was calculated per week. Health measures included self-rated health status, hip fractures, hypertension, and body mass index. Outcome Measure: Mortality	Higher levels of physical activity and walking at baseline were associated with lower mortality rates for all-cause and cardiovascular disease. Women who were sedentary but became active had significantly decreased rate of mortality due to all causes and cancer compared with women who were sedentary at both collection points. Women who increased their activity levels had a 36% lower mortality rate than those who maintained the same physical activity levels.	Self-report The physical activity questionnaire may have been less sensitive to physical activities commonly performed by the oldest women and was also slightly modified between baseline and follow-up.
Hammerman-Rozenberg et al. (2005)	To determine the influence of employment in older adulthood on functional independence, health, and survival	II—Longitudinal cohort study N = 231 participants age 70 living in the community in Israel	Home-based interviews and physical examinations. Information gathered included social characteristics, medical status (illnesses and use of medical services), and full- or part-time work status. Follow-up after 7 yr Outcome Measures: ■ Survival ■ ADL independence	After 7 yr, those who were working at age 70 were in better health, had more ADL independence, and had increased survival rates.	The study does not include the nature of the participants' occupations. Authors reported that those electing to not participate in study may be more isolated and less likely to be employed, resulting in an overestimate of those continuing to work.

(continued)

Table F4. Occupation and Activity-Based Interventions (continued)

Author/Year	Study Objectives	Level/Design/Participants	Intervention and Outcome Measures	Results	Study Limitations
Hao (2008)	To determine the effect of paid work and formal volunteering on the rate of decline in mental health in later life	II—Longitudinal cohort study N = 7,830 participants 55–66 yr 4 waves of the Health and Retirement study Progressively smaller sample sizes in subsequent interviews	Information about experiencing depressive symptoms, paid work status, volunteering status, general health, functional disability, productive activities, engagement in 2 activities concurrently, and demographic characteristics was gathered during initial interview and subsequent reinterviews. Follow-up every 2 yr Outcome Measure: ■ Center for Epidemiological Studies Depression Scale (CES–D)	Both full-time employment and low-level volunteering separately protected against weakening in psychological well-being. Participants involved in both activities had a slower rate of decline than those involved in one.	The types of paid work and volunteering were not taken into account.
Harris & Thoresen (2005)	To examine the relationship of volunteering to survival when controlling for sociodemographics, medical and physical activity status, social integration, and support	II—Longitudinal cohort study N = 7,527 Participants were a part of Longitudinal Study of Aging (LSOA). Sample consisted of community-dwelling adults who were ≥ 70 yr. Follow-up was 96 months.	Data were collected about the following 4 areas: sociodemographics, health, physical activity, social functioning, and support. Participants also were asked whether they had volunteered and how frequently they had done so in the past year. Outcome Measure: Mortality	15.4% of the sample reported volunteering at baseline. More frequent volunteering was associated with delayed mortality even when socioeconomic status, medical and disability issues, self-rated physical health, and social support were controlled for.	No access to information about the type of volunteer work performed or the motivation behind performing it
Helm et al. (2000)	To examine the relationship between mortality and private religious activities and mortality for older adults	II—Prospective cohort study N = 3,851 community-dwelling adults ≥ 65 yr living in North Carolina. Data were obtained from the Duke University Established Populations for Epidemiologic Studies of the Elderly (Duke/EPESE).	Religious activities: Interview question regarding frequency of private religious activity (prayer, meditation, and Bible study). Other measurements were taken regarding church attendance, religious media use, demographics, physical health, and smoking status. Outcome Measures: Mortality after 6 yr	Although participants who reported rare participation in private religious activities were more likely to die within the follow-up time period, this association was not maintained after adjusting for covariates. Those with no ADL impairments who reported private religious activity had lower mortality rates.	The study lacked specificity and definition of private religious activity. Participants all reported being Protestants.

Author (year)	Study Objectives	Level of Evidence, Study Design/Participants	Intervention and Outcome Measures	Results	Study Limitations
Helzner et al. (2007)	To determine whether prediagnosis leisure activity affects the rate of cognitive decline in patients diagnosed with Alzheimer's disease (AD)	II—Longitudinal cohort study N = 283 Participants from an urban community with a mean age of 79 were followed for a mean of 5.3 yr.	Baseline information gathered included self-reported leisure activities, medical comorbidity, cognitive performance, and demographic characteristics. Diagnoses of AD were assessed on the basis of standardized physician-administered examinations. Outcome Measure: Change in a composite cognitive score from onset of diagnosis and during follow-up	Participants with higher leisure activity generally had higher baseline cognition, fewer medical comorbidities, and more years of education. Higher total leisure scores were linked to faster cognitive decline. The authors indicated that the higher cognitive reserve (those participating in more leisure activities) modulates the interaction between neurological disease and clinical manifestations.	Early dementia may have reduced leisure activity in some participants, thereby affecting results (leisure was only reported for 4 yr before the start of study). Frequency and intensity of activities were not considered.
Hebert et al. (2006)	To explore the association between dimensions of religion and mental health in active and bereaved dementia caregivers	II—Cohort study N = 1,229 participants ≥ 21 yr, with a mean age of 65. Participants were caregivers for people with dementia	Participants' religious activity was assessed on the basis of frequency of attendance in religious activities, frequency of prayer, and importance of faith. Demographic information including caregiver stressors, resources, and physical health were assessed as well. Outcome Measures: • At baseline, 6, 12, 18 mo • CES–D • Inventory of Complicated Grief	The 3 measures of religion were associated with less depressive symptoms in current caregivers, controlling for caregiver age, health, burden, and social integration. Frequent attendance was related to less depression and complicated grief in bereaved caregivers, which was associated also with increased social integration. Religious attendance increased after care recipients' deaths, whereas prayer and intensity of beliefs remained stable.	The study did not allow for inferring causal relationships. Subtleties in difference between different types of prayer were not reflected in the study. The sample was homogeneous with respect to high levels of religiosity.
Hinterlong et al. (2006/2007)	To examine the association between engagement in productive roles and the physical and mental health of adults ≥ 60 yr	II—Cohort study N = 1,644 adult participants ≥ 60 yr Data used from the Americans' Changing Lives Study: 1986, 1989, 1994	Participants reported on engagement in productive activity (paid worker, irregular paid worker, unpaid volunteer, caregiver, and provider of information social assistance) and hours of engagement in 5 roles during the 12 mo before the interview. Sociodemographic information collected at each phase Outcome Measure: Health status, including functional impairment, self-rated health, and depressive mood	Hours spent in productive activity dropped in each subsequent wave. Engagement status was significantly associated with better self-rated health and lesser functional impairment.	Findings are limited because of an inability to directly infer causation between productive engagement and health.

(continued)

Table F4. Occupation and Activity-Based Interventions (continued)

Author/Year	Study Objectives	Level/Design/Participants	Intervention and Outcome Measures	Results	Study Limitations
Hirvensalo, Rantanen, & Heikkinen (2000)	To study whether physical activity was able to predict dependence and mortality regardless of mobility status	II—Prospective cohort study N = 1,109 older adults 65–84 yr living in the community in Finland Participants and data were from the Evergreen Project. Follow-up was 8 yr.	Physical activity and mobility status were measured based on guidelines. Four groups were determined based on physical activity and mobility: Mobile–Active, Mobile–Sedentary, Impaired–Active, and Impaired–Sedentary Outcome Measures: ■ Mortality ■ Loss of independence based on specific criteria	After controlling for age, marital status, chronic conditions, smoking, and physical exercise earlier in life, the risk of death was 2 times higher in the Impaired–Active and 3 times higher in the Impaired-Sedentary groups for both men and women than in the Mobile–Active groups. There was a 3 times higher risk of becoming dependent in the Impaired–Active group, and approximately 5 times higher risk of dependency in the Impaired–Sedentary group than in the Mobile–Active group.	Physical activity and mobility were self-report.
Hsu (2007)	To determine the effect of social participation on mortality and cognition in older adults	II—Longitudinal cohort study N = 2,310, 60 yr old and were obtained from the Survey of Health and Living Status of the Elderly in Taiwan	Face-to-face interviews were conducted in 1989, 1993, 1996, and 1999. Social participation was measured through interview questions regarding paid and unpaid work and attendance of meetings of social groups/clubs but not leisure. Cognitive function was measured using the Short Portable Mental Status Questionnaire. Outcome Measure: Death	Engaging in paid or unpaid work can lower the risk for mortality 6 yr later. Among the women in the study, participating in a religious social group lowered the risk for mortality. Among men, participating in a political social group lowered the risk for cognitive impairment. Unpaid work was associated with higher rates of impaired cognitive functioning compared with nonworkers.	History of work and socialization before the study was not obtained. Social support was not examined. Volunteer and social group participation were combined into 1 variable because of low rates of volunteerism.
Hughes, Waite, LaPierre, & Luo (2007)	To examine how serving as a caregiver for grandchildren affects health behaviors as well as physical and mental well-being in older adults	II—Longitudinal cohort study This study included 12,872 grandparents 50–80 yr Participants were a part of the Health and Retirement Study (HRS). Data were taken from Waves 4, 5, and 6 of this study (between 1998 and 2002).	Grandchild care status was determined by asking how many hours participants spent caring for their grandchildren (if reported ≥ 100 hr/year). A variety of health indicators were measured through interviews. Outcome Measures: ■ Self-rated health ■ Chronic conditions ■ Depression ■ Functional limitations	There was no evidence to support that caring for grandchildren has a dramatic negative effect on the health and health behaviors of grandparents. There is some evidence showing that grandmothers caring for their grandchildren in skipped-generation homes (with no adult children) experience health declines. Those grandmothers providing 200–500 hr of care per year were more likely to exercise and reported fewer functional limitations and fewer depressive symptoms.	More than 25% of grandparents who live with their grandchildren are < 50 yr, but this study did not include participants who were < 50 yr.

Source	Design/Participants	Methods/Outcome Measures	Results	Limitations
Hughes et al. (2008)	To examine whether cognitive ability, speed/attention, and episodic memory for an older individual are influenced by having a social network of family and friends	II—Longitudinal study Participants were members of the Charlotte County Healthy Aging Study, a community-based, longitudinal study of aging. The final sample included 217 people. The mean age of the participants was 72.4 yr; 51.8% were women. Follow-up was 5 yr after baseline.	Participants were asked 26 questions regarding social resources and demographic information. NEO Five-Factor Inventory was used to assess personality. Outcome Measures: ■ Modified MMSE ■ Stroop Test (to test attention) ■ Trailmaking Test (to test perceptual speed) ■ Hopkins Verbal Learning Test	More negative social interactions (possibly indicative of more stimulation) and greater satisfaction with support were associated with better general cognitive ability. Better performance on speed and attention were associated with greater satisfaction with support. Less satisfaction with support was associated with decline in episodic memory performance.	Participants were all White, well educated, and in relatively good health, which may limit the generalizability of the results of this study. There was a high rate of attrition. People in the study had a fairly high stability in cognitive function over time, which may have decreased the ability to detect associations.
Inoue et al. (2006)	To examine whether the absence of outdoor activities is associated with increased mortality risk for older adults living at home	II—Cohort study N = 863 adults ≥ 65 yr, who lived at home in rural Japan and were capable of understanding and completing a baseline interview without assistance	A structured questionnaire was used to interview participants about demographics, functional impairments, ADLs, and outdoor activities (transporting self, initiative to leave home, and frequency of leaving home). Outcome measure: Mortality	Those who died during the study were more likely to be male, older, have more functional impairments, have more ADL impairments, and have fewer outdoor activities than did survivors. Participants not engaging in outdoor activities had a mortality rate almost twice as great as those who did.	Sample consisted of a homogeneous ethnic group. Medical information was not available for all participants.
Jacobs et al. (2008)	To examine the association between frequency of going outdoors and health/functional status among older people	II—Longitudinal cohort study N = 43 Jerusalem residents born between June 1920 and May 1921 Data collection took place at age 70 and then again at age 77. Mortality data were collected for 12 yr.	Participants were questioned about the frequency of going outside and they self-rated health and ADLs and IADLs. A physician completed a thorough evaluation of participants' health. Outcome Measures: ■ Mortality data ■ ADLs and IADLs ■ Self-rated health	Significant associations were found between going outdoors less at baseline and the new appearance of back/joint pain, poor sleep, loneliness, decreased independence in ADLs, decreased vision, poor self-rated health after 7 yr. There was no difference in mortality between participants who went outdoors daily and those who went outdoors less frequently.	There was a lack of information collected about why people went outdoors and where they went.

(continued)

Table F4. Occupation and Activity-Based Interventions (continued)

Author/Year	Study Objectives	Level/Design/Participants	Intervention and Outcome Measures	Results	Study Limitations
Jacobs et al. (2008)	To investigate the relationship of a solitary, non-strenuous activity (reading) and aging and mortality	II—Longitudinal cohort study N = 337 participants recruited from the Jerusalem Longitudinal Study, which was initiated in 1990 and followed an age homogenous cohort of Jerusalem residents who were born between June of 1920 and May of 1921	Demographic data, depression status, functional status and self-reported health were collected during the interview process. Reading activity was measured by asking participants "How often do you read a book?" Physical and other activities were also assessed. Outcome Measure: Mortality	There were significant differences in 8-yr survival among men but not women who read daily compared with those who read less than daily (83% vs. 61%).	The quality and content of the reading done by participants was unknown. The amount of time spent reading daily was unknown.
Janke, Nimrod, & Kleiber (2008)	To examine how leisure involvement changes with the transition to widowhood and to determine if change in leisure involvement during this time has an impact on widows' physical and mental health	II—Cohort study N = 154 widows ≥ 50 yr At the initial assessment, the mean age of the widows was 68.9, with almost 90% of the respondents being female. The average length of widowhood for participants was 2 yr.	Leisure participation was measured by 7 different leisure activities (talking, visiting, clubs, religion, walking, gardening, and sports) before and after widowhood and collected through self-report. Outcome Measures: ■ Health indicators ■ 10 common chronic conditions ■ Depressive symptoms ■ Life satisfaction ■ Coping and adaptation	The majority of widows in the sample experienced some change in leisure repertoire or frequency of leisure involvement following the death of their spouse. Sports and exercise were most likely added to leisure repertoire. Widowers reported having a more difficult time adjusting to the transition than widows because they reported less recovery from their loss.	Although the sample was derived from a large, national sample, the number of adults who experienced a transition to widowhood was relatively low, with very few widowers included in the sample. Gender differences were unable to be examined closely because the small number of male participants in the study.
Kaplan, Strawbridge, Cohen, & Hungerford (1996)	To study the association between leisure-time physical activity and risk of mortality from cardiovascular disease and all other causes	II—Cohort study N = 6,131 adult participants 16–94 yr from the Alameda County Study in Northern California	Participants were surveyed 4 times over 30 yr (in 1965, 1974, 1983, and 1994). Information regarding physical activity was gathered using a scale created from 3 questions. Outcome Measure: Mortality—all causes and from cardiovascular disease	Participants who were least active had the highest mortality rates. A protective effect of physical activity for all-cause and cardiovascular mortality was found.	Crude measurement was used to assess leisure-time physical activity.

Citation	Objective	Design & Sample	Methods / Outcome Measures	Results	Comments
Kaplan, Baltrus, & Raghunathan (2007)	To study the risk of and factors associated with self-reported health trajectories and mortality over 30 yr	II—Cohort study N = initial sample of 6,928 adult participants 16–94 yr from the Alameda County Study in Northern California (response rate ranged from 85% to 97%)	Participants were surveyed in 1965 at baseline, and they were asked to complete follow-up questionnaires in 1973, 1983, and 1994. Information regarding health status was gathered through self-reports. Outcome Measures: Mortality–Health trajectories were examined on the basis of self-reported health status and mortality data.	Physical activity was strongly related to health trajectories for men and women. Those with lower levels of physical activity were more likely to die and less likely to be "Alive in excellent health." Other associations were made between gender, smoking, alcohol consumption, and household income and health trajectories.	It is not possible to determine the effects of various diseases on the overall trajectory of health.
Keyes & Reitzes (2007)	To investigate whether religious identity explains unique variance of the self-esteem and depressive symptoms of older working and retired adults	II—Longitudinal cohort study N = 242 men and women 62–72 yr who participated in a larger 5-yr project begun in 1992 of older adult workers and retirees living in the Raleigh–Durham–Chapel Hill, North Carolina, metropolitan area	Outcome Measures: ■ Religious measures (religious attendance and religiosity) ■ Religious identity ■ Sociodemographic and health measures Outcome Measures ■ Self-esteem measured using the Rosenberg 10-item scale ■ CES–D	Self-esteem increased and depressive symptoms decreased as religious identify increased. Only religious identity, not religious attendance or religiosity, predicted mental health when all other variables were controlled.	Religious identity was added to the final wave of data collection in the longitudinal study, therefore leaving researchers unable to discern whether religious identity is a cause or a consequence of mental health.
Keysor (2003)	To systematically review the literature examining effects of late-life physical activity in older adults on outcomes of disablement	I—Systematic review of literature Articles published 1996–2002 addressing an older adult population, assessing disablement outcomes, and written in English were included.	Cochrane, Best Evidence, and Medline were searched for meta-analyses, systematic reviews, randomized controlled trials, and longitudinal observational studies examining the effects of late-life physical activity on functional limitations and physical disability. Outcome Measures: ■ Walking speed ■ Balance ■ Chair rise	Studies have shown that strength training and walking programs improve function, including walking and other functional activities. Although a protective effect of physical activity on functional limitations was found, there were inconsistent results for the effects of physical activity on disability.	Limitations within re-viewed articles, including (a) intensity or duration of physical activity were not examined, (b) physical inactivity measured at baseline in observational studies may be the result of poor health, (c) crude and potentially inaccurate measurements
Khokhar et al. (2001)	To explore the potential connection between mortality and participant-reported mobility deficit who also reported a lack of deficits in ADL function	II—Cohort study (prospective) N = 1,298 participants were functioning older adults who enrolled for Medicare services and resided in New York City They reported functional status at baseline and 2 yr later.	Self-reported mobility and ADL abilities or restrictions from the Comprehensive Assessment and Referral Evaluation Participant medical history was obtained from physicians. Outcome Measures: Mortality	At 2- and 4-yr follow-up of mortality, participants with reported mobility deficits without ADL limitations had a higher mortality risk measures. Female participants were more likely to report functional declines during follow-up.	The study relied on participant report. Results indicated a discrepancy be-tween physician- and participant-reported mobility deficit.

(continued)

Table F4. Occupation and Activity-Based Interventions (continued)

Author/Year	Study Objectives	Level/Design/Participants	Intervention and Outcome Measures	Results	Study Limitations
Kono et al. (2004)	To examine the relationship between the frequency of going outside and functional and psychosocial changes in ambulatory frail elders living at home	II—Prospective cohort study This was a 9-month prospective cohort study. Researchers collected data through questionnaires. N = 112 frail ambulatory elderly adults from Nagano Prefecture, a rural community in Japan	A questionnaire that included information about the frequency of going outdoors, and measures of ADLs, functional capacity, self-efficacy for daily activities, self-efficacy for health promotion, depression, and social support (measured at baseline and 9-months) was administered. Outcome Measures: Functional and psychosocial measures	There were significant differences in functional capacity and intellectual activities over time according to the frequency of going outdoors, even when controlling for baseline differences. There were similar relationships between frequency of going outdoors and changes in self-efficacy for both daily activities and for health promotion, with participants going outdoors most frequently improving significantly more.	Participants were selected by volunteers. "Frail adult" term was subjective.
Korten (1999)	To examine whether cognitive and psychosocial factors predict mortality in older adults	II—Prospective cohort study N = 897 community dwelling people ≥ 70 yr. who were drawn from the compulsory electoral roll in Australia participated in this study	An interview at baseline collected data on physical health, cognitive functioning, social support, psychiatric symptoms, personality, health behaviors, and socioeconomic status. Outcome Measure: Mortality	The most significant predictors of mortality were being male, having poor physical health, having poor cognitive functioning, and having low neuroticism. Social support did not add to the prediction of mortality following adjustment for cognitive and health factors.	Authors mentioned that other Australian studies have yielded no or limited relationship of social support to mortality, indicating that these results may not generalize to other populations.
Kunzmann (2008)	To examine performance-based and self-evaluative indicators of functioning in social and intellectual realms as predictors of individual differences and intra-individual changes in positive and negative affect	II—Cohort study N = 206 community-dwelling and institutionalized persons 70–103 yr from the Berlin Aging Study	Outcome Measures: At baseline and follow-up after approximately 4 yr ■ German translation of the Positive and Negative Affect Schedules ■ Social involvement assessed by number of social activities and number of social network partners ■ Quality of Life Test intelligence assessed by the Digit Letter and Identical Pictures, Spot-a-Word and Vocabulary, Animals and Letter S ■ Self-rated mental fitness	Indicators that were performance based and free of subjective evaluations (social involvement, test intelligence, and functional health) were associated with positive affect. Indicators that were self-evaluative and global (self-rated quality of life and mental fitness) were strongly associated with negative affect. The results revealed a negative correlation between age and those characteristics that are involved in the regulation of positive affect, supporting the finding that positive affect declines in later life, whereas negative affect remains the same.	Some constructs used to predict positive and negative affect were assessed by relatively few items.

Reference	Design / Sample	Measures	Results	Notes
la Cour et al. (2006)	II—Longitudinal cohort study $N = 734$ 70-yr-old former or present residents of Glostrup, Denmark 72% of the sample participated in a medical survey at the Copenhagen County Hospital in Glostrup. To analyze associations of religiosity and mortality in a secular region by examining the idea that religious affiliation, frequency of church attendance, and listening to religious services on radio and TV predict survival	At baseline, the survey measured: • Vital status and age • Religiosity (importance of religious affiliation and religious attendance) • Demography • Medical and mental health • Social connections • Health behavior (smoking, alcohol, and BMI) Outcome Measure: Vital status or age at death	Church attendance was found to significantly lower the risk of dying for the whole sample after controlling for covariates at the 20-yr follow-up period. Claiming religious affiliation was significantly related to mortality in women but not in men. Listening to religious media was not associated with mortality.	Although the current study includes 3 measures of religiosity, no measure was used to examine "religiousness." No standardized measure of depression or anxiety was used.
Lampinen, Heikkinen, Kauppinen, & Heikkinen (2006)	II—Longitudinal cohort study $N = 663$ participants 65–84 yr interviewed in 1988 and again in 1996 as part of a larger study entitled the Evergreen Project in Finland. To explore how participation in physical and leisure activities acts as a predictor of mental health and well-being of older adults	Outcome Measures (baseline and follow-up): • Physical activity • Leisure activities • Mobility status, number of chronic illnesses, and age • Revised version of Beck's 13-item depression scale • Anxiety, loneliness, mental vigor, and meaning in life	Physical activity was associated with a better mobility status and a higher level of participation in leisure activities. Mobility status and age predicted better mental well-being. Higher participation in physical and leisure activity along with a low number of chronic illnesses had an indirect effect on mental well-being at the follow-up assessment.	Self-report Mental well-being and independent variables were assessed using a 1-item scale.
Laukkanen et al. (1998)	II—Longitudinal cohort study Participants were born in 1914 ($n = 388$) and 1910 ($n = 291$) and were residents of the city of Jyvaskyla in central Finland. To examine baseline physical activity as a predictor of health and functional ability outcomes 5 yr later in older adults	Outcome Measures (baseline and follow-up): • Modified Finnish version of Grimby's 6-point physical activity questionnaire to assess physical activity, leisure, work, and domestic activities • Chronic diseases—physician report Follow-up: Mortality	More physically active participants had better health and functional ability compared to participants who were more sedentary. Degree of physical activity did not predict future disability, but had a predictive role at the level of disease severity.	Severity of chronic disease was not measured.
Lee & Markides (1990)	II—Longitudinal cohort study $N = 508$ Mexican Americans and Whites ≥ 60 yr residing in a 4-census tract area in San Antonio, Texas To examine the influence of the level of activity on mortality over an 8-yr period	Activity level was measured through a 10-item scale derived from factor analysis. Activity participation included movies, museums, sporting events, hunting, fishing, bingo, and traveling. Outcome Measure: Mortality	Activity was a significant predictor of mortality at the univariate level. However, when age, gender, education, marital status, ethnicity, and self-rated health were controlled for in the analysis, activity was no longer a significant predictor of mortality.	Measure of activity in the study may not have captured activities that promote health and longevity. Authors state that using a larger, more representative sample of older persons may have increased the association between activity and mortality.

(continued)

Table F4. Occupation and Activity-Based Interventions (continued)

Author/Year	Study Objectives	Level/Design/Participants	Intervention and Outcome Measures	Results	Study Limitations
Lennartsson & Silverstein (2001)	To determine whether engagement with life (involvement in social, leisure, and productive activities) had an effect on the survival of the oldest old people	II—Longitudinal cohort study N = 463 older adults Participants were part of the Swedish Panel Study of Living Conditions Among the Oldest Old (SWEOLD).	Baseline data about involvement in social, cultural, leisure, and productive activities was taken from interviews that were conducted for SWEOLD in 1992. Outcome Measure: Mortality	After adjustment, participants who were more involved in solitary-active activities (e.g., gardening, hobbies) had a significantly lower risk of mortality. This lowered risk of mortality was observed in men but not women.	No measures of affective ties or emotional support included. Activity categories included few examples of activities.
Lum & Lightfoot (2005)	To examine the association between volunteering and health among older adults	II—Longitudinal cohort study N = 7,322 people ≥ 70 yr who participated in the 1993 and 2000 panels of the Asset and Health Dynamics Among the Oldest Old Study (AHEAD) survey	At 1993 survey, participants were asked about formal volunteering for religious or charitable organizations (time spent volunteering); if > 100 hr, exact number described Demographic information Outcome Measure: Health and functional status mortality rate, and rate of residing in a nursing home	Formal volunteering by older adults is positively correlated with self-reported health, lower mortality, depression levels, and functioning levels as measured by ADLs and IADLs but not physician-diagnosed medical conditions or admission to a nursing home. The threshold for volunteering appears to be 100 hr/yr.	AHEAD's 100-hr minimum threshold for volunteering does not allow researchers to examine the idea that more limited participation affects self-reported health or mortality.
Luoh & Herzog (2002)	To examine how volunteer and paid work affects health and survival outcomes for older adults	II—Longitudinal cohort study N = 4,860 participants who were born in 1923 Participants were taken from the AHEAD Study, 1993–2000	Outcome Measures (baseline and follow-up): ■ Survey that asked questions about volunteer work, paid work, health, demographic and socioeconomic status ■ Telephone Interview of Cognitive Status ■ Mortality	Participants who reported volunteering or working for pay for ≥ 100 hr were less likely to have died at follow-up than those who did not volunteer ≥ 100 hr (5.6% vs. 16.8%). They were also less likely to report poor health and activity limitations.	Difficulty of accurately measuring volunteer and work participation in survey format
Marottoli et al. (1997)	To determine the relationship between driving cessation and depressive symptoms in older adults using longitudinal data	II—Longitudinal cohort study N = 1,316 participants taken from the New Haven site of the Established Populations for Epidemiologic Studies of the Elderly (EPESE) program	Surveys were conducted every 3 yr (1982–1988). The 1989 interview included older adults' driving history and current driving practices. Survey included questions on ADLs, health, demographic, social, and cognitive status. Outcome Measures: CES–D	Substantially higher depressive symptoms were found with older adults who no longer drive after controlling for sociodemographic and health-related factors. Driving cessation is among the highest predictors of depressive symptoms in older adults.	There was a lack of information on the precise time that the older adult ceased driving and changes in depressive symptoms.

McCamish-Svensson et al. (1999)	To examine the relationship between family and friend social support, health, and life satisfaction	II—Cohort study $N = 212$ participants age 80 living in Lund, Sweden followed annually for 4 yr	Data were collected related to housing conditions, social networks, feelings of loneliness, family and childhood conditions, and other demographic variables. Outcome Measures (baseline and follow-up): ■ Social Support Network ■ Health, including doctor-rated and self-rated health using Likert scales ■ Life satisfaction using Life Satisfaction Index A (LSIA) ■ Mortality	A greater percentage of people who died reported help from children and had the poorest health. Those alive at follow-up indicated the greatest satisfaction with friends, had the least need of assistance, had the highest doctor and self-rated health, and had the highest level of life-satisfaction. Satisfaction with sibling contact was significantly associated with doctor and self-rated health at age 80 yr and with life satisfaction at both 80 and 83 yr.	Generalizability of results is limited because of cultural factors implied by homogenous group of Swedish participants.
McCullough et al. (2000)	To examine the association between religious involvement and mortality in older adults	I—Meta-analysis $N = 29$ studies of nearly 126,000 participants	Studies included in the meta-analysis if a measure of religious involvement was a predictor of all-cause mortality. Some results were based on multiple, but varied studies of the same dataset (e.g., different length of follow-up).	42 effect sizes were computed. Religious involvement was associated with lower rates of mortality in older adults with an odds ratio of 1.29 and a small effect size.	Many studies included in the review used a single measure of religious participation and religiousness that may have limited reliability.
McCullough & Laurenceau (2005)	To look at the relationship between religiousness and self-rated health over the life span of an adult	II—Longitudinal cohort study Data from the Terman Life Cycle Study of Children with High Ability were used. Data from 1,119 of the original participants were used.	Data were collected through questionnaires at baseline and follow-up on the following topics: self-rated health, religiousness, conscientiousness, extraversion, agreeableness, neuroticism, body mass, alcohol use, adjustment difficulties, and social support/activities. Outcome Measures Self-rated health model developed from questionnaire items	Women, but not men, who were very religious in 1940 had higher mean self-rated health across their life spans and slower rates of linear decline after controlling for health behaviors, social support, and social activities.	Sample consisted of a homogenous and highly selective group of gifted people, limiting the generalizability of the results. Religiousness, personality traits, health behaviors, and social support/social activity were measured only once in mid adulthood.
Mendes de Leon, Glass, & Berkman (2003)	To determine whether there is an association between social engagement and reduced risk of disability in community-dwelling older adults 65 yr and older	II—Longitudinal cohort study $N = 2,812$ participants ≥ 65 yr obtained from the New Haven site of the Established Populations for Epidemiologic Studies of the Elderly (EPESE) program.	A series of 9 annual interviews addressed 11 types of social activities. Information was gathered regarding the adult's frequency of social interactions in groups and during paid employment. Outcome Measures: ■ Katz ADL scale–self-care ■ Rosow-Breslau Functional Health Scale	A strong cross-sectional association between social engagement and disability was found. More socially active older adults reported lower levels of disability. Although this was maintained during follow-up, the effect decreased slightly during follow-up.	Social engagement was measured by putting together aspects of interview information rather than a specific measure of social engagement.

(continued)

Table F4. Occupation and Activity-Based Interventions (continued)

Author/Year	Study Objectives	Level/Design/Participants	Intervention and Outcome Measures	Results	Study Limitations
Mendes de Leon et al. (1999)	To determine whether social network ties are associated with lower levels of disability in community-dwelling older adults	II—Longitudinal cohort study *N* = 2,812 participants taken from the New Haven site of the Established Populations for Epidemiologic Studies of the Elderly (EPESE) program	Yearly interviews were conducted to determine the participants' demographics, disability status, and social network ties. Physical health Medical conditions—self-report SPMSQ Outcome Measures: ■ Katz ADL scale (used to determine disability status) ■ Rosow-Breslau Index (adults' ability to do heavy work around the house, use stairs, and walk a ½ mi)	The results of this study showed that social network ties had a positive effect on survival in older adults. The presence of a strong social network decreased the likelihood of developing an ADL disability as well as increased recovery from an ADL disability. Emotional and instrumental support accounted for part of the positive effects of recovery from ADL disability but not on the development of ADL disability.	Although social network size tends to remain stable over time, changes in social network variables were not accounted for during follow-up. Information was gathered through participant self-report.
Menec (2003)	To longitudinally examine the relationship between engagement in everyday activities and successful aging, specifically well-being, function, and mortality	II—Longitudinal cohort study *N* = 2,291 participants obtained from the Aging in Manitoba study	Overall functioning—ADL and IADL performance as well as results from a cognitive assessment (The Mental Status Questionnaire) Outcome Measures: ■ LSIA ■ Questions based on a Likert scale were used to determine happiness ■ Mortality	Higher levels of activity were associated with increased well-being, function, perception of overall happiness, and lower mortality rates. Participation in sport activities was associated with higher life satisfaction. Social, solitary, and productive activities were related to happiness.	Participants in this study were generally active and healthy. The LSIA may not be the best measure of well-being. Time spent and frequency of activity engagement was not assessed.
Miller et al. (2000)	To identify how physical activity may delay the onset of disability in older adults, therefore prolonging independent living	II—Longitudinal cohort study *N* = 5,151 participants from the Longitudinal Study of Aging (LSOA) a supplement of the National Health Interview Survey	Four interviews were conducted between 1984 and 1990. Interviews included information on age, gender, comorbid conditions, level of functional limitations, ADLs, and IADLs. Disability and functional limitations were based on interview items and were ordinally categorized. Physical activity Outcome measures: ■ Lower body limitation ■ ADL/IDL performance	Older adults with at least a minimal level of physical activity showed a slowed progression of physical limitations. Low levels of physical activity slow the progression of ADL/IADL disability.	Information was gathered through participant self-report.

Author	Study Design	Methods	Results	Comments
Mullee et al. (2008)	II—Longitudinal cohort study $N = 328$ participants > 65 yr in England To analyze the predictive value of reported activity and attitude to participant's activity level on longevity	Information was gathered regarding reported activities, health status, cognitive functioning, and self-evaluation. ■ Cognitive functioning ■ Wakefield Depression Scale ■ Southampton Self-Esteem and Sources of Self-Esteem Scale ■ Chicago Life Satisfaction Scale Outcome Measure: Mortality	Decreased risk of mortality was associated with increased activity scores, activity self-evaluation, and health self-evaluation. Whereas positive health self-perception was significantly associated with decreased mortality in participants 65–74 yr at baseline, it did not hold true for those ≥ 75 yr.	Number of participants studied was not large.
Musick, Herzog, & House (1999)	II—Longitudinal cohort study $N = 2,348$ respondents ≥ 65 yr were obtained from the Americans Changing Lives study To establish the association between volunteering and mortality among older adults ≥ 65 yr	Participants were interviewed about their participation in volunteer activities (e.g., religious, educational, political, senior citizen group). Frequency of participation was noted. In addition, the following were surveyed: social interaction, physical activity, health. Outcome Measure: Mortality	A moderate amount of volunteering lowers the risk of mortality in older adults. The protective effect does not hold for those who volunteer for more extended periods of time.	Information was gathered through participant self-report. The type of work done by the participants while volunteering was not addressed; 69% of the volunteers did so with religious organizations, raising the question of whether or not it was religious involvement that affects mortality.
Musick & Wilson (2003)	II—Longitudinal cohort study $N = 3,617$ respondents obtained from the Americans Changing Lives study To determine the effect of volunteering on the mood, specifically depression and anxiety, on adults ≥ 65 yr	Face-to-face, in-home, and telephone interviews were conducted in 1986, 1989, and 1994. Participants were asked about health, psychological resources, social resources, and amount and type of volunteering Outcome Measures: ■ CES–D ■ A 3-item index of self-esteem	For adults > 65 yr, volunteering resulted in lower depression. The longer an individual participated in volunteering, the better the impact on mood was.	Information was gathered through participant self-report.

(continued)

Table F4. Occupation and Activity-Based Interventions (continued)

Author/Year	Study Objectives	Level/Design/Participants	Intervention and Outcome Measures	Results	Study Limitations
Oman & Reed (1998)	To determine whether religious service attendance is associated with lower mortality among older adults	II—Longitudinal cohort study $N = 2,023$ community-dwelling adults ≥ 55 yr	Religious attendance was measured through a single question, "How often do you usually attend religious services" Demographics, health status, physical functioning, health habits, social functioning, and support were all evaluated through self-report questionnaires. ■ CES-D ■ East Boston ■ Memory Test Outcome Measure: Mortality	After adjustment for covariates, individuals who attend religious services have lower rates of mortality.	Limited questions related to religiosity A large number of participants were highly affluent and White, which limits the generalizability of the findings. The researchers state that "inaccurate measurement of covariables" and "unidentified confounders" could explain the results of this study.
Oman et al. (1999)	To determine whether volunteerism predicted lower mortality, independent of potentially confounding factors, such as health practices and social support	II—Longitudinal cohort study $N = 2,025$ community-dwelling residents of Marin County, California, first examined in 1990–1991 Respondents were ≥ 55 yr at baseline	Participants were asked about number of hours volunteering and number of organizations volunteering for. Covariates were measured in questionnaire administered at baseline (physical health and health habits, sociodemographics, social functioning and support, psychological functioning) Outcome Measure: Mortality	Volunteering in $= 2$ organizations ("high" volunteering) offered a more persistent protective effect against mortality in an elderly population compared with nonvolunteers. High volunteering had a 44% reduction in mortality, compared with physical mobility (39%), exercise four times weekly (30%), and weekly attendance at religious activities (29%), and was only slightly smaller than the reduction associated with not smoking (49%).	Mortality and morbidity were not examined by the specific types of volunteer activities in which participants engaged.
Park et al. (2008)	To examine the effect of religious involvement on the trajectories of functional status of community-dwelling older adults	II—Prospective cohort study $N = 784$ adults, ≥ 65 yr, from the University of Alabama at Birmingham Study of Aging Participants completed interviews every 6 months between December 1999 and February 2004.	Religiousness was measured by a modified version of the Duke University Religion Index Sociodemographic information—age, ethnicity, gender, residence, marital. Resources to individuals in maintaining functional capacity marital status, income, social support Outcome Measures: Functional difficulties—ADLs and 6 IADLs.	Religious service attendance was predictive of slower increases for frequent churchgoers and steeper increases for less frequent churchgoers for IADL problems. Protective effects from religious service attendance were identified only for IADL problems and not ADL problems.	All participants were from 1 Southern state. The religiousness of participants may have been different or more diverse if the study had taken place in another state or in multiple states throughout the country. IADL and ADL problems were measured by presence or absence of problems, instead of degree of difficulty.

Study	Purpose	Design/Sample	Methods/Outcome Measures	Results	Limitations
Scarmeas et al. (2001)	To investigate the potential role of leisure occupations in reducing the development of incident dementia	II—Longitudinal cohort design N = 1,772 older adults (≥65 yr) from the Manhattan area in New York City	Cognitive and neurological assessments Participation in leisure activities (e.g., hobbies, walking or exercise, volunteering, attending religious services, reading, playing cards, going to movies) Outcome Measures: The number of people who developed dementia over the 7-yr period	Participants with reported high levels of leisure activity, social activity, mild-moderate physical activity, and cognitive activity were associated with a reduced risk for incident dementia, after controlling for ethnicity, education, baseline cognitive function, health limitations, cerebrovascular disease and depression. The lowest rate of incident dementia was associated with cognitive stimulating occupations.	The study included only those who lived in an urban setting, which can limit the ability to generalize the results to people living in more isolated or rural areas of the country.
Schulz et al. (2001)	To examine pre-death versus post-death changes in self-reported and objective health outcomes among older adults providing varying levels of care before their spouse's death	II—Prospective cohort study N = 129 participants 66–96 yr, whose spouses died during an average 4-yr follow-up	Participants were classified into 1 of 3 groups: noncaregivers, non-strained caregivers, and strained caregivers. Participants completed 3 annual structured interviews conducted in person. Socio-demographic variables, baseline prevalent cardiovascular disease, caregiving status, CES–D scale, antidepressant use, health risk behaviors, and weight were assessed during the interviews. Outcome Measures: ■ Changes in depression symptoms as measured by the 10 item CES–D ■ Antidepressant medication use ■ 6 health risk behaviors ■ Weight	CES–D scores remained high but did not change, health risk behaviors improved, and weight did not change significantly for strained caregivers. CES–D scores increased and health risk behaviors showed no significant change among non-strained caregivers and noncaregivers. Nontricyclic antidepressant use was most widely used by the noncaregiver group after the death of their spouses.	Small sample size
Seeman (1995)	To investigate the relationship of behavioral factors, social network characteristics, and psychological characteristics with physical function in an elderly cohort	II—Longitudinal cohort study N = 1,189 Participants were from the MacArthur Research Network on Successful Aging Community Study.	The following areas were measured at baseline: ■ Behavioral factors ■ Social network characteristics ■ Psychological characteristics Covariates included gender, race, education, income, baseline biomedical, health status, and cognitive measures. Outcome Measure: At baseline and follow-up Summary measure of physical performance based on five tests of physical ability (balance, gait, chair stands, foot taps, and manual ability)	Physical exercise and emotional support from one's social network were found to predict better physical performance over a 2.5-yr follow-up period.	Cohort used represents only high-functioning adults 70–79 yr.

(continued)

Table F4. Occupation and Activity-Based Interventions (*continued*)

Author/Year	Study Objectives	Level/Design/Participants	Intervention and Outcome Measures	Results	Study Limitations
Seeman & Chen (2002)	To investigate lifestyle and psychosocial elements that may impact continued physical functioning in old age	II—Longitudinal cohort study *N* = 1,189 The sample was selected from the MacArthur Study of Successful Aging. All participants resided in three communities along the east coast of the United States. The MacArthur Study included those older adults, 70–79 yr, who were generally high functioning.	At baseline and 2.5-yr follow-up, participants were asked to report on chronic conditions, demographics, physical activity, psychological health and social networks. Outcome Measures: Measures of physical function (e.g., balance, sit to stand, ambulation)	Participants who engaged in habitual physical activity demonstrated better functioning over time. Positive social support systems and self-efficacy were associated with better function in participants living with chronic conditions (i.e., heart disease, diabetes, orthopedic injuries).	The results may not generalize to the total population of older adults. Severity of chronic conditions was not reported.
Seeman et al. (2001)	To examine to potential correlation between socialization and support mechanisms to patterns of cognitive maturing	II—Longitudinal cohort study *N* = 1,189 Participants were sampled from the MacArthur Studies of Successful Aging.	At baseline and follow-up, cognitive function and social ties and support were measured. Demographic measures included age, education, ethnicity, and income. Health measures included physical health, depression, self-efficacy, and physical activity. Outcome Measures: Cognitive function	Nearly half of the participants demonstrated a small to moderate decline in cognitive function. Over time, positive emotional support was the only baseline social mechanism that correlated with better cognitive maturing.	As a result of the sampling procedures, the results may not have the ability to be generalized. The authors reported that the longitudinal data may demonstrate regressions to the mean instead of actual change over time.
Shmotkin et al. (2003)	To investigate the effects of coexisting volunteer work and lifestyle activities	II—Cohort study *N* = 1,343 The random sample was taken from the Cross-Sectional and Longitudinal Aging Study in Israel. A total of 148 participants were designated as volunteers, whereas 1,195 participants were included as nonvolunteers. The age ranged from 75–94 yr.	Participants reported volunteer activity, physical activity, everyday leisure activities, function, cognitive health, depressive symptoms, relationships, and subjective life satisfaction. Outcome Measure: Mortality	Volunteer and physical activity was found to be predictive of a lowered risk for mortality in older adults. Reduced mortality was seen for those volunteering on a weekly or monthly, but not less frequent basis.	The results may not be generalizable to other populations or groups, because the results may be indicative of cultural norms. The self-report measures did not include questions relating informal volunteering and religious organizations.

Silverstein & Parker (2002)	To determine whether changes in leisure participation affected the perception of quality of life among older adults	II—Longitudinal cohort study N = 324 community-dwelling older adults obtained from the SWEOLD	Social participation was evaluated in both the 1981 and the 1992 surveys and addressed leisure participation in domains: culture-entertainment, productive-personal growth, outdoor-physical, recreation-expressive, friendship, and formal-group. Demographics, health, income, social support Outcome Measure: Quality of life	Increasing opportunities for social participation were associated with improvement in quality of life. This association was the strongest among older adults who were widowed, developed functional impairments, or had low contact with family.	Measurement of quality of life was obtained through a single, self-report item. Findings may represent the experiences of the culture of older adults in Sweden and therefore may not be generalizable to all older adults.
Stessman et al. (2000)	To study the association between physical activity and mortality in older adults	II—Longitudinal cohort study N = 456 participants ≥ 70 yr, representative of the residents living in Israel, and born between 1920 and 1921	Initial interviews included information about demographics, religious practices, ADLs, IADLs, support networks, and physical aids. Also included medical history, physical examination, assessment of physical activity, depression, a cognitive test, a self-administered psychological profile, physical activity. Outcome Measure: Mortality	After a 6-yr period, mortality rates consistently decreased with increased physical activity from 23.4% among participants walking less than 4 hr per week to 3.85% among participants walking at least 1 hr daily. Participants found to be depressed were less likely to participate in physical activity.	This study demonstrated a lack of data on the amount of time in which participants had maintained their reported level of exercise.
Stessman et al. (2002)	To determine the effect that engagement in physical activity has on autonomy and execution of ADLs and IADLs	II—Longitudinal cohort study N = 287 adults born between June 1920 to May 1921 in Israel	At baseline and at follow-up 7 yr later, the participants completed interviews on self-reported physical exercise and ease of performance in ADLs and IADLs. Information on demographics, social survey, and functional independence were included in baseline and follow-up	Those participants who reported physical exercise 4 times per week at age 70 where more likely to report continued independence and ease in performing ADLs and IADLs after 7 yr. Men and women reporting consistent physical exercise tended to maintain autonomy and ease in ADLs, but in IADLs only for men.	Use of self-report measures
Stessman et al. (2005)	To explore the health and social factors that may affect the livelihood and function of older adults; to identify potential inherited characteristics that may relate to the identified differences	II—Longitudinal cohort study N = 463 adults 70 yr old completed the study. All participants were located in Jerusalem.	At 70 and 77 yr, interviewing consisted of 2 interview sessions. The first session highlighted the participants' ability to complete ADLs and IADLs through observation and participant self-report. The second session involved more formalized medical testing, including a physical examination of cognition. Outcome Measure: Survival at 12 yr	Those who continued to be independent in ADLs and IADLs had a reduced risk for mortality. Continued engagement in physical exercise and work—paid or unpaid—tended to affect both continued ADL function and increased survival rates.	The study failed to examine potential environmental factors that may affect mortality rates.

(continued)

Table F4. Occupation and Activity-Based Interventions (continued)

Author/Year	Study Objectives	Level/Design/Participants	Intervention and Outcome Measures	Results	Study Limitations
Strawbridge, Cohen, & Shema (2000)	To analyze the effects on long-term survival of frequent religious attendance compared with 4 widely accepted beneficial health behaviors, including cigarette smoking, physical activity, alcohol consumption, and nonreligious involvement	II—Longitudinal cohort study N = 5,894 participants 21–75 yr at baseline from the Alameda County Study (a longitudinal study conducted in 1965 with follow-up assessments in 1974, 1983, and 1994)	Religious attendance scored as weekly, monthly, or yearly/never. Health behaviors included cigarette smoking, physical activity, alcohol consumption, and social involvement. Outcome Measure: Mortality rate after 29-yr period	Weekly religious attendance, never smoking, often being physically active, moderate alcohol consumption, and social involvement with both individuals and groups were all protective for survival. The protective effect of engagement in weekly religious activities is strong for women, but moderately protective for men.	Quality of religious involvement not noted.
Strawbridge et al. (1997)	To explore the effect of religious practices on older adult mortality	II—Longitudinal cohort study N = 5,286 At baseline, participants were 16–94 yr of age. The Alameda County sample was followed for 28 yr.	Survey examined frequency of religious attendance, health practices (i.e., physical exercise, smoking, alcohol use), health conditions, and the extent of socialization. Outcome Measure: Survival	Those who regularly participated in religious activities demonstrated reduced mortality rate and better social relations; however, when comparing women to men with the same participation rate, men had a higher rate of mortality. Women who regularly engaged in religious practice were more likely than men to maintain positive health behaviors.	The quality of the religious practices was not assessed.
Strawbridge, Shema, Cohen, & Kaplan (2001)	To investigate the effect of religious service attendance on mental health, use of preventive medicine, and social connectedness among older adults	II—Longitudinal cohort study N = 2,676 Participants 17–65 yr from 1 county in California were interviewed at baseline in 1965 and then participated through the follow-up in 1994.	Comparisons were made between participants who weekly attended religious activities and those who did not, with a focus on alcohol consumption, use of preventive medical care, mental health, social relations, and marriage.	Weekly religious attendance was related to improve health behaviors, mental health, and social connectedness. Greater frequency of religious activities was connected to quitting smoking, increased physical activity, reduced onset of depression, and a greater amount of personal relationships.	There were limited number of participants engaged in some health behaviors (e.g., stopping heavy drinking).

Tucker et al. (1995)	To determine the association between playing with pets and health, and analyze whether frequency of playing with pets predicts mortality risk over a 13-yr period	II—Longitudinal cohort study $N = 643$ of 1,528 people who participated in the Terman Life Cycle Study, which was conducted from 1921 through 1991 living at the time of the 1977 follow-up.	Participants were asked about playing with pets in the 1977 follow-up. At different points in time, participants were asked about self-rated health and health-related behaviors, which included assessing alcohol consumption and smoking, social ties, childhood psychosocial characteristics, and education. Outcome Measure: Survival in 1991	In survival analyses of documented longevity, playing with pets in 1977 was not associated with less mortality risk or health behaviors through 1991 for the total sample, nor for those who were unmarried or less satisfied with their human relationships.	First, the researchers stated they cannot be certain the degree to which "playing with a pet" measures an individual's attachment to the pet. Second, the sample in the study was homogeneous in nature and included gifted, White, middle-class individuals.
Unger, Johnson, & Marks (1997)	To examine the effect of socialization and physical activity on the deterioration of functional independence	II—Longitudinal cohort study $N = 7,527$ adults ≥ 70 yr The sample was obtained from the Longitudinal Study of Aging of the National Health Interview Survey.	The authors analyzed the amount of social-ization with friends and family, the amount of physical activity (i.e., walking, exercise routines, level of activity). Covariates included age, gender, education, income, minority status, and past history of chronic disease. Outcome Measures: Physical functioning—the ability to complete ADLs and IADLs	Older adults who continued to participate in social and physical activity demonstrated fewer physical limitations and tended to sustain independence in ADLs and IADLs. Continued physical activity had a stronger effect on health compared with socialization.	The data were collected on the basis of partici-pants' self-report of physical and social activity.
Unger et al. (1999)	To examine the influ-ence of social support systems on the func-tion of the older adult	II—Longitudinal cohort study $N = 850$ Participants were taken from the MacArthur Studies. Participants were mostly high-functioning adults 70–79 yr.	Participants were asked about emotional and instrumental social support of spouse, children, friends, and relatives. Covariates included age, gender, ethnicity, education, income, health behaviors, and baseline physical and psychological health. Outcome Measures: Changes in physical function over 7 yr (Nagy Physical Functioning Scale)	Older adults with positive social relationships tended to have better continued functioning over the 7 yr. The effects of social relations were strongest for men and those partici-pants who demonstrated reduced baseline physical function.	The study did not account for the other confounding variables, including personality traits and certain health behaviors.

(continued)

Table F4. Occupation and Activity-Based Interventions (continued)

Author/Year	Study Objectives	Level/Design/Participants	Intervention and Outcome Measures	Results	Study Limitations
Van Willigen (2000)	To explore the potential effect of volunteer activity on the emotional and physical health of older adults To evaluate the difference in benefits between older and younger volunteers	II—Longitudinal cohort study N = 2,867 adults ≥ 25 yr Those ≥ 60 yr were sampled more frequently than younger participants. Sample was taken from the Americans' Changing Lives Survey.	Self-reported: Type of volunteer activity and frequency of volunteer activity Also examined were participant social roles, socioeconomic status, functional impairment, social relations, social support, and life control. Outcome Measures: Physical well-being—perceived health, life satisfaction	Those participants who volunteered less (but not > 100 hr) were also less likely to report good health and greater satisfaction with life. Those who volunteered tended to report higher levels of life satisfaction. Although physical impairment was a predictor of volunteer activity, physical and psychosocial well-being were not.	Detailed information on how participants volunteered their time was not available.
Verghese et al. (2003)	To identify how intellectual and physical leisure occupation can influence the occurrence of dementia in a sample of older adults	II—Longitudinal, prospective cohort study N = 469 Older adults ≥ 75 were included who resided in Bronx, NY, and were community dwelling. Those selected did not demonstrate dementia symptoms and did not have visual or auditory deficits.	Assessments were conducted in relation to neurological function and participation in leisure activity at baseline and follow-up. Cognitive and physical activity scales were derived. Outcome Measures: Diagnosis of dementia–Blessed test followed by computed tomographic scanning, blood test, and case conference	A high level of leisure engagement was associated with decreased risk for the development of dementia, independent of education and intellectual level. Participants who engaged in cognitive stimulating leisure activity (i.e. crosswords, reading, board games) demonstrated decreased risk for developing dementia. A relationship between continued physical activity and dementia was not found.	Because the study was observational in nature, it is possible that other potential confounders contributed to the association. The leisure occupations included in the study were identified by the participants and may not represent a consensus for the general population.
Walter-Ginzburg et al. (2002)	To determine elements of social networks that are most significantly linked to mortality among the old-old in Israel	II—Longitudinal cohort study N = 1,340 participants 75–94 yr	Social network characteristics and social engagement, including solitary and group activities, sociodemographic variables, health, cognitive status, depression, and function, were assessed during personal interviews that took place between 1989 and 1992. Follow-up was for up to 8 yr, for an average of 5.3 yr. Outcome Measure: Mortality	Those who engaged in activities that clearly involved others and those who frequently engaged in group or solitary leisure activities were at a lower risk of mortality. Those living in the community without a spouse and with a child and living in an institution were at a higher risk of mortality. Those with no contact or the most contact with their children had the highest mortality, those with lower levels of contact had lower mortality	Self-reports of functional status may not be valid, particularly for the old-old population. Potential for bias from the sample having used only nonproxy respondents; those represented by proxies were demographically different. The measures of social support did not separate potentially supportive relationships from support that was actually received.

Wang et al. (2002a)	To explore and examine the relationship between social and leisure activities and the development of dementia	II—Longitudinal cohort design *N* = 776 participants living in the community of the Kungsholmen district of Stockholm, Sweden, ≥ 75 yr in October of 1987, and were nondemented at first follow-up in 1991. Second follow-up was in 1994.	Personal interviews regarding information on social and leisure activities Confounders in the analysis included age, sex education, cognitive function, comorbidity, depressive symptoms, and physical function. Outcome Measures: Dementia was diagnosed according to the *DSM–III–R*.	Participants who participated in activities had a lower incidence of dementia than participants who did not participate in mental, physical, social, productive, or recreational activities. The incidence of dementia decreased with increased frequency of participation in the 3 types of activities studied.	An open question was used to acquire information about social and leisure activities, which may not provide enough details about the activities.
Wang et al. (2002b)	To determine risk factors that may relate to changes in older adults' functional status	II—Longitudinal, prospective cohort study *N* = 2,578 adults ≥ 65 yr who resided in the Seattle area	Potential predictor variables (i.e., hypertension, cancer, physical exercise) were evaluated to determine the potential causes for change in functional status. Outcome Measures: Changes in ADLs, IADLs, and physical functioning	Those who exercised consistently and ingested minimal amounts of alcohol had better performance over time on ADLs, IADLs, and demonstrated superior physical function. Although poorer performance was observed for those with coronary heart disease, it was better for participants exercising regularly.	Certain participants with specific diagnosis (lower baseline cognitive function and diabetes mellitus) tended to drop out of the study more frequently than others. The authors reported that this might lead to an underestimate of study results.
Welin et al. (1992)	To examine the relationship between social network and activities and causes of death	II—Prospective cohort study *N* = 989 male participants living in Gothenburg, Sweden, and 50 or 60 yr	Information regarding cholesterol, blood pressure, smoking habits, alcohol use, prior stroke or myocardial infarction, marital status, people living in their household, activity engagement (home activities, outside home activities, and social activities), and self-rated health status Outcome Measures: Mortality	Men who died from any cause lived in households with fewer people than men who survived. After controlling for covariates, no social network and activity variables were predictive of death due to cancer, whereas social activities were weakly but significantly predictive of death due to cardiovascular disease. A low home activity score was predictive of mortality for all other causes of death.	The sample consisted of men only. Social factors, such as marital status and level of income, may have affected one's choice to participate in the study. Quality of home activities, outside activities, and social activities were not measured.

(continued)

Table F4. Occupation and Activity-Based Interventions (continued)

Author/Year	Study Objectives	Level/Design/Participants	Intervention and Outcome Measures	Results	Study Limitations
Wilson et al. (2002)	To examine the association between cognitively stimulating activities and incidence of Alzheimer's disease	II—Cohort study N = 801 Catholic nuns, priests, and brothers without dementia at baseline and ≥ 65 yr	Assessment of cognitive activity Composite score: Participants were asked about time spent in common activities and physical activities. Uniform evaluations included medical history, neurological examination, assessment of cognitive function, and a review of a brain scan when possible. 10-item form of the CES-D Outcome Measures: Clinical diagnosis of Alzheimer's disease by a board-certified neurologist	The relative risk of developing Alzheimer's disease was decreased by 33% for every 1 point increase in cognitive activity measures. Using random-effects models, a 1-point increase in cognitive activity was associated with a 47% reduced decline in global cognition, a 60% reduced decline in working memory, and a 30% less decline in perceptual speed.	The cohort was selected and differs from many other older persons living in the U.S. population. Results are applicable only to the measures of cognitive activity used in this study.
Wu, McCrone, & Lai (2008)	To examine the transitions of disability over 5 yr among older adults and the influences of health behaviors on these transitions	II—Longitudinal cohort study N = 3,067 community-dwelling adults participating in the National Long-Term Care Survey in 1994 and followed up in 1999	Participants were asked about lifestyle habits (e.g., alcohol, vitamins, working on a hobby) as well as ■ Social connection ■ Demographics (race, living location, marital status, and income) ■ Height and weight ■ Functional limitation ■ IADL limitation ■ Comorbidity Outcome Measures: ■ Physical disability assessed by the ADL scale ■ Mortality	Physical activity was strongly associated with the onset of disability. Among those who reported being disabled, the risk of status decline was higher for those underweight or physically inactive; those taking vitamin or mineral supplements regularly or working in a hobby were less likely to further decline in disability status. Having more contacts with friends, having regular social activities, and having a BMI ≥ 25 were beneficial to survival.	Self-reported height and weight were used to calculate BMI.
Xue et al. (2008)	To assess the association between life-space constriction and incidence of frailty	II—Cohort study N = 599 community-dwelling women ≥ 65 yr who were not frail at baseline that were part of a Baltimore community-based study.	Standardized questionnaires and physical examinations over a period of 1 yr; physical function disabilities and MMSE scores. Life-space assessment—an abbreviated Life Space Questionnaire—examined whether participant left the house or neighborhood, chronic diseases and physical and cognitive function, 30-item Geriatric Depression Scale Outcome measure: Frailty phenotype—weakness, slowness, low physical activity, weight loss, exhaustion	The amount of life space constriction at baseline increased with increasing age and decreasing education level, income, and MMSE score. The risk of frailty and the risk of frailty-free mortality increased with decreased life space. Participants in the slightly constricted group (leaving the neighborhood less frequently) were 1.7 times more likely to become frail than the participants with no constriction.	The sample was restricted to a cohort of disabled women living in the community. The study used only a limited number of questions from the larger life-space assessment.

		Participants were asked about physical activity—city blocks walked and stairs climbed, modified Paffenbarger Scale, and total physical activity expended in kilocalories per week. Additional information collected included age, history of comorbid health conditions, weight, height, body mass index, current medications, gait speed, overall self-rating of health status, amount of difficulty with specific daily activities, modified version of the Stanford Health Assessment Questionnaire, and the Geriatric Depression Scale.	The odds of developing cognitive decline (after controlling for covariates) were 37% lower in the highest quartile of blocks walked as compared with the lowest quartile, and 35% lower in the highest quartile of total kilocalories expended as compared with the lowest quartile.	Physical activity was based on a subject's self-report.
Yaffe et al. (2001)	To examine the association between physical activity and cognitive decline in older community-dwelling women	II—Nonrandomized cohort design			Participants did not partake in a clinical assessment for dementia.
		N = 5,925 predominately White community-dwelling women ≥ 65 yr participating in the Study of Osteoporotic Fractures			There was some attrition among participants.
				Overall, there is an association between physical activity and cognitive decline in older women.	A possible association between subclinical cognitive impairment and physical activity level may have influenced results.
			Outcome Measure: Modified MMSE at baseline and follow-up 6–8 yr later.		All participants were women, and the majority of participants were White.
Zhang (2008)	To determine whether participation in religious activity impacts the mortality of older adults	II—Longitudinal cohort study	Participants were asked about frequency of religious activity, self-reported health, psychological resources, and engagement in leisure and physical activity.	After controlling for covariates, increased frequency of religious activity correlated with reduced levels of mortality among oldest old women and individuals in poor health.	The quality of the religious practice and level of involvement or commitment of the participant were not measured.
		N = 6,747 Chinese adults 80–105. Participants were selected from the Chinese Longitudinal Healthy Longevity Survey (CLHLS) conducted in 1998 and 2000.	Outcome Measure: Mortality	Engagement in physical and leisure activities was also significant and partially accounted for the reduced mortality risk.	Limited period of follow-up

Note. ADLs = activities of daily living; *DSM–III–R* = *Diagnostic and Statistical Manual of Mental Disorders, 3rd Edition;* IADLs = instrumental activities of daily living; BMI = body mass index.

References

AARP, & American Council of Life Insurers. (2007). *What now? How retirees manage money to make it last through retirement. Report of findings.* Washington, DC: Authors. Available online at: http://assets. aarp. org/rgcenter/econ/guaranteed_income.pdf

Aartsen, M. J., Smits, C. H. M., van Tilburg, T., Knipscheer, K. C. P. M., & Deeg, D. J. H. (2002). Activity in older adults: Cause or consequence of cognitive functioning? A longitudinal study on everyday activities and cognitive performance in older adults. *Journal of Gerontology: Psychological Sciences, 57B,* P153–P162.

Academy for Certification of Vision Rehabilitation, & Education Professionals. (n.d.). *Certified low vision therapist scope of practice.* Retrieved May 1, 2011, from http://www.acvrep.org/Certified-Low-Vision-Therapist-Scope-of-Practice.php

Accreditation Council for Occupational Therapy Education. (2011). *Standards and interpretive guidelines.* Bethesda, MD: Authors. Available online at http://www.aota.org/Educate/Accredit/StandardsReview/guide/42369.aspx?FT=.pdf

Accreditation Council for Occupational Therapy Education. (2012a). Accreditation standards for a doctoral-degree-level educational program for the occupational therapist. *American Journal of Occupational Therapy, 66.*

Accreditation Council for Occupational Therapy Education. (2012b). Accreditation standards for a master's-degree-level educational program for the occupational therapist. *American Journal of Occupational Therapy, 66.*

Accreditation Council for Occupational Therapy Education. (2012c). Accreditation standards for an educational program for the occupational therapist assistant. *American Journal of Occupational Therapy, 66.*

Administration on Aging. (2010). *A profile of older Americans.* Rockville, MD: U.S. Department of Health and Human Services. Retrieved February 10, 2011, from http://www. aoa.gov/aoaroot/aging_statistics/Profile/2010/docs/2010profile.pdf

Agency for Healthcare Research and Quality. (2008). *2007 national healthcare disparities report.* Rockville, MD: U.S. Department of Health and Human Services.

Alp, A., Kanat, E., & Yurtkuran, M. (2007). Efficacy of a self-management program for osteoporotic subjects. *American Journal of Physical Medicine and Rehabilitation, 86,* 633–640.

American Geriatrics Society, & British Geriatrics Society. (2010). *Clinical practice guideline: Prevention of falls in older persons.* Retrieved March 14, 2012, from http://www.americangeriatrics.org/files/documents/health_care_pros/Falls.Summary.Guide.pdf

American Geriatrics Society. (n.d.). *Trends in the elderly population.* Retrieved February 21, 2011, from http://www.healthinaging.org/agingintheknow/chapters_print_ch_trial.asp?ch=2#Trends%20in%20Health%20and%20Functioning

American Medical Association. (2012). *CPT 2011.* Chicago: Author.

American Occupational Therapy Association. (1979). *Occupational therapy product outpower reporting system and uniform terminology for reporting occupational therapy services.* (Available from the American Occupational Therapy Association, 4720 Montgomery Lane, P.O. Box 31220, Bethesda, MD 20824–1220)

American Occupational Therapy Association. (1984). *Uniform terminology for occupational therapy*. (Available from the American Occupational Therapy Association, 4720 Montgomery Lane, P.O. Box 31220, Bethesda, MD 20824-1220)

American Occupational Therapy Association. (1989). *Uniform terminology for occupational therapy* (2nd ed.). (Available from the American Occupational Therapy Association, 4720 Montgomery Lane, P.O. Box 31220, Bethesda, MD 20824–1220)

American Occupational Therapy Association. (1994). Uniform terminology for occupational therapy (3rd ed.). *American Journal of Occupational Therapy, 48,* 1047–1054.

American Occupational Therapy Association. (2002). Occupational therapy practice framework: Domain and process. *American Journal of Occupational Therapy, 56,* 609–639.

American Occupational Therapy Association. (2006a). *Occupational therapy's role in senior centers.* Retrieved March 23, 2011, from http://www.aota.org/Practitioners/PracticeAreas/Aging/Tools/38509.aspx

American Occupational Therapy Association. (2006b). Policy 1.44: Categories of occupational therapy personnel. In *Policy manual* (2011 ed., pp. 33–34). Bethesda, MD: Author.

American Occupational Therapy Association. (2008a). Guidelines for documentation of occupational therapy. *American Journal of Occupational Therapy, 62,* 684–690.

American Occupational Therapy Association. (2008b). Occupational therapy practice framework: Domain and process (2nd ed.). *American Journal of Occupational Therapy, 62,* 625–683.

American Occupational Therapy Association. (2008c). Occupational therapy services in the promotion of health and the prevention of disease and disability. *American Journal of Occupational Therapy, 62*(6), 694–703.

American Occupational Therapy Association. (2008d). *Occupational therapy—Referral requirements.* Retrieved March 23, 2011, from http://www.aota.org/practitioners/licensure/stateregs/referral/36361.aspx?ft=.pdf

American Occupational Therapy Association. (2009a). Guidelines for supervision, roles, and responsibilities during the delivery of occupational therapy services. *American Journal of Occupational Therapy, 63,* 779–803.

American Occupational Therapy Association. (2009b). Occupational therapy's perspective on the use of environments and contexts to support health and participation in occupations. *American Journal of Occupational Therapy, 63,* S57–S69.

American Occupational Therapy Association. (2010a, April 1). *Nearly recession-proof profession celebrates national awareness month* [Press Release]. Retrieved February 12, 2012, from http://aota.org/News/Media/PR/2010-Press-Releases/2010OTMonth.aspx?FT=.pdf

American Occupational Therapy Association. (2010b). Occupational therapy code of ethics and ethics standards (2010). *American Journal of Occupational Therapy, 64,* S17–S26

American Occupational Therapy Association. (2010c). Scope of practice. *American Journal of Occupational Therapy, 64,* S70–S77.

American Occupational Therapy Association. (2010d). Standards of practice for occupational therapy. *American Journal of Occupational Therapy, 64,* S106–S111.

American Occupational Therapy Association. (2011a). *Critically appraised topic, occupation and activity based interventions, focused question: What is the evidence for the effect of occupation and activity-based interventions on the performance of selected instrumental activities of daily living (IADL) for community-dwelling older adults?* Retrieved February 20, 2011, from http://www.aota.org/CCL/Occupation/IADL.aspx

American Occupational Therapy Association. (2011b). *Critically appraised topic, occupation and activity based interventions, focused question: What is the evidence that participation in occupations and activities supports the health of community-dwelling older adults?* Retrieved February 20, 2011, from http://www.aota.org/CCL/Occupation/Occupation-and-Health.aspx

American Occupational Therapy Association. (2011c). *Home modifications and occupational therapy* (Fact Sheet). Retrieved February 20, 2011, from http://www.aota.org/Consumers/Professionals/WhatIsOT/PA/Facts/39470.aspx?FT=.pdf

American Occupational Therapy Association. (n.d.). *The road to the Centennial Vision.* Retrieved July 27, 2009, from http://www.aota.org/News/Centennial.aspx

Americans With Disabilities Act of 1990, P.L. 101-336. Retrieved May 10, 2011 from http://www.ada.gov/pubs/ada.htm

Anderson, R. N., Miniño, A. M., Fingerhut, L. A., Warner, M., & Heinen, M. A. (2004). Deaths: injuries, 2001. *National Vital Statistics Report, 52*(21). Retrieved June 15, 2005, from http://www.cdc.gov/nchs/data/nvsr/nvsr52/nvsr52_21acc.pdf

Anzik, M. A., & Weaver, D. A. (2001). *Reducing poverty among elderly women* (Social Security Administration Office of Policy Office of Research, Evaluation, and Statistics No. 87). Retrieved February 20, 2011, from http://www.ssa.gov/policy/docs/workingpapers/wp87.pdf

Arbesman, M., & Lieberman, D. (2012). Methodology for the systematic reviews on occupation- and activity-based intervention related to productive aging. *American Journal of Occupational Therapy, 66,* 271–276.

Arbesman, M., & Mosley, L. (2012). Systematic review of occupation- and activity-based health management and maintenance interventions for community-dwelling older adults. *American Journal of Occupational Therapy, 66,* 277–283.

Arbesman, M., & Pellerito, J. M., Jr. (2008). Evidence-based perspective on the effect of automobile-related modifications on the driving ability, performance, and safety of older adults. *American Journal of Occupational Therapy, 62,* 173–186.

Arthritis Foundation, Association of State and Territorial Health Officials, & Centers for Disease Control and Prevention. (1999). *National arthritis action plan: A public health strategy.* Atlanta: Arthritis Foundation. Retrieved February 12, 2011, from http://www.arthritis.org/media/Delia/NAAP_full_plan.pdf http://www.healthypeople.gov/2020/exitDisclaimer.as

Arthritis Foundation. (2011a). *Help others take control of arthritis.* Retrieved April 12, 2011, from http://www.arthritis.org/media/offering-programs/Leader%20Brochure.pdf

Arthritis Foundation. (2011b). *Instructor position description.* Retrieved April 12, 2011, from http://www.arthritis.org/media/offering-programs/Offering%20Programs/positiondescriptionExercise_Leader_Instructor.doc

Atwal, A., & Caldwell, K. (2003). Ethics, occupational therapy and discharge planning: Four broken principles. *Australian Occupational Therapy Journal, 50*(4), 244–251.

Avlund, K., Damsgaard, M. T., & Holstein, B. E. (1998). Social relations and mortality: An eleven-year follow up study of 70 year-old men and women in Denmark. *Social Science Medicine, 47,* 635–643.

Avlund, K., Lund, R., Holstein, B. E., Due, P., Sakari-Rantala, R., & Heikkinen, R. (2004). The impact of structural and functional characteristics of social relations as determinants of functional decline. *Journal of Gerontology: Social Sciences, 59B,* S44–S51.

Ayalon, L. (2008). Volunteering as a predictor of all-cause mortality: What aspects of volunteering really matter? *International Psychogeriatrics, 20,* 1000–1013.

Ayis, S., Gooberman-Hill, R., Bowling, A., & Ebrahim, S. (2006). Predicting catastrophic decline in mobility among older people. *Age and Ageing, 35,* 382–387.

Backman, K., & Hentinen, M. (1999). Model for the self-care of home-dwelling elderly. *Journal of Advanced Nursing, 30,* 564–572.

Baker, M. W. (2005). Creation of a model of independence for community-dwelling elders in the United States. *Nursing Research, 54,* 288–295.

Barnes, L. L., Mendes de Leon, C. F., Wilson, R. S., Bienias, J. L., & Evans, D. A. (2004). Social resources and cognitive decline in a population of older African Americans and Whites. *Neurology, 63,* 2322–2326.

Barras, S. (2005). A systematic and critical review of the literature: The effectiveness of Occupational Therapy Home Assessment on a range of outcome measures. *Australian Occupational Therapy Journal, 52*(4), 326–336.

Bartels, S. J., Forester, B., Mueser, K. T., Miles, K. M., Dums, A. R., Pratt, S. I., . . . Perkins, L. (2004). Enhanced skills training and health care management for older persons with severe mental illness. *Community Mental Health Journal, 40,* 75–90.

Bass, S. A., & Caro, F. G. (2001). Productive aging: A conceptual framework. In N. Morrow-Howell, J. Hinterlong, & M. Sherraden (Eds.). *Productive aging: Concepts, cautions, and challenges* (pp. 37–78). Baltimore: Johns Hopkins University Press.

Bassuk, S. S., Glass, T. A., & Berkman, L. F. (1999). Social disengagement and incident cognitive decline in community-dwelling elderly persons. *Annals of Internal Medicine, 131,* 165–173.

Bath, P. A., & Morgan, K. (1998). Customary physical activity and physical health outcomes in later life. *Age and Ageing, 27*(S3), 29–34.

Baum, C. M., Connor, L. T., Morrison, T., Hahn, M., Dromerick, A. W., & Edwards, D. F. (2008). Reliability, validity, and clinical utility of the Executive Function Performance Test: A measure of executive function in a sample of people with stroke. *American Journal of Occupational Therapy, 62*(4), 446–455.

Baum, C. M., & Edwards, D. (2008). *Activity card sort (ACS).* Bethesda, MD: AOTA Press.

Benartzi, S. (2010). *Behavioral finance and the post-retirement crisis: A response to the Department of Treasury/ Department of Labor request for information regarding lifetime income options for participation and beneficiaries in retirement plans.* New York: Allianz of America. Retrieved February 18, 2011, from http://www.allianzinvestors. com/MarketingPrograms/External%20Documents/ Allianz_DOL_RFI_Response.pdf

Bennett, D. A., Schneider, J. A., Tang, Y., Arnold, S. E., & Wilson, R. S. (2006). The effect of social networks on the relation between Alzheimer's disease pathology and level of cognitive function in old people: A longitudinal cohort study. *Lancet Neurology, 5,* 406–412.

Beswick, A. D., Rees, K., Dieppe, P., Ayis, S., Gooberman-Hill, R., Horwood, J., & Ebrhamim, S. (2008). Complex interventions to improve physical function and maintain independent living in elderly people: A systematic review and meta-analysis. *Lancet, 371,* 725–735.

Betancourt, J. R., & King, R. K. (2003). Unequal treatment: The Institute of Medicine report and its public health implications. *Public Health Reporter, 118*(4), 287–292.

Betancourt, J. R., Maina, A. W., & Soni, S. M. (2005). The IOM report on unequal treatment: Lessons for clinical practice. *Delaware Medical Journal, 77*(9), 339–348.

Bookwala, J., Zdaniuk, B., Burton, L., Lind, B., Jackson, S., & Schulz, R. (2004). Concurrent and long-term predictors of older adults' use of community-based long-term care services: The

Caregiver Health Effects Study. *Journal of Aging and Health, 16,* 88–115.

Brachtesende, A. (2005a). New markets emerge from society's needs. *OT Practice.* Retrieved March 1, 2011, from http://www.aota.org/Educate/EdRes/StuRecruit/Working/38380.aspx?FT=.pdf

Brachtesende, A. (2005b). The turnaround is here! *OT Practice, 23*(1), 13–19.

Brault, M. W., Hootman, J., Helmick, C. G., & Theis, K. A. (2009). Prevalence and most common causes of disability among adults, United States, 2005. *MMWR, 58*(16), 421–426.

Brawley, L., Rejeski, W. J., & Lutes, L. (2000). A group-mediated cognitive–behavioral intervention for increasing adherence to physical activity in older adults. *Journal of Applied Biobehavioral Research, 5*(1), 47–65.

Breyer, F., Costa-Font, J., Felder, S. (2010). Ageing, health, and health care. *Oxford Review of Economic Policy, 25*(4), 674–690.

Buchner, D. M., Cress, M. E., de Lateur, B. J., Esselman, P. C., Margherita, A. J., Price, R., & Wagner, E. H. (1997). The effect of strength and endurance training on gait, balance, fall risk and health services use in community-living older adults. *Journal of Gerontology: Medical Sciences, 52A*(4), M218–M224.

Bursztyn, M., Ginsberg, G., Hammerman-Rozenberg, R., & Stessman, J. (1999). The siesta in the elderly: Risk factor for mortality? *Archives of Internal Medicine, 159,* 1582–1586.

Bursztyn, M., & Stessman, J. (2005). The siesta and mortality: Twelve years of prospective observations in 70-year-olds. *Sleep, 28,* 345–347.

Burton, L. C., Shapiro, S., & German, P. S. (1999). Determinants of physical activity initiation and maintenance among community-dwelling older persons. *Preventive Medicine, 29,* 422–430.

Busse, E. W. (1969). Theories of aging. In E. W. Busse & E. Pfeiffer (Eds.), *Behavior and adaptation in later life.* Boston: Little Brown.

Butler, R. N. (2002). The study of productive aging. *Journals of Gerontology, 57*(6), S323.

Butler, R. N., & Gleason, H. P. (1985). *Productive aging: Enhancing vitality in later life.* New York: Springer.

Butrica, B. (2008). *Older Americans' reliance on assets.* Washington, DC: Urban Institute. Retrieved March 3, 2011, from http://www.urban.org/UploadedPDF/411632_relianceonassets.pdf

Butrica, B. A., Murphy, D., & Zedlewski. S. R. (2008). *How many struggle to get by in retirement?* Washington, DC: Urban Institute.

California State University, Fullerton, Center for Successful Aging. (2008). *Fullerton Advanced Balance (FAB) Scale.* Retrieved March 23, 2011, from http://hhd.fullerton.edu/csa/CenterProducts/centerproducts_assessment.htm

California State University, Fullerton, Center for Successful Aging. (n.d.). *Modified clinical test of sensory interaction in balance.* Retrieved March 13, 2012, from http://www.patientsafety.gov/SafetyTopics/fallstoolkit/resources/educational/Balance_Assessment_Handbook.pdf

Campbell, A. J., Robertson, M. C., Gardner, M. M., Norton, R. N., Tilyard, M. W., & Buchner, D. M. (1997). Randomised controlled trial of a general practice programme of home-based exercise to prevent falls in elderly women. *British Medical Journal, 315,* 1065–1069.

Campbell, A. J., Robertson, M. C., La Grow, S. J., Kerse, N. M., Sanderson, G. F., . . . Hale, L. A. (2005). Randomised controlled trial of prevention of falls in people aged >75 with severe visual impairment: The VIP trial. *British Medical Journal, 331*(7520), 817.

Campion, E. J. (1994). The oldest old. *New England Journal of Medicine, 330,* 1819–1820.

Caro, F. G., Bass, S. A., & Chen, P-C. (1993). Introduction. In S. A. Bass, F. G. Caro, & Y.-C. Chen, (eds.) *Achieving a productive aging society* (pp. 3–25). Westport, CT: Auburn House.

Center for Medicare Advocacy. (2004). *Summary of the Medicare Act of 2003.* Retrieved February 23, 2011, from http://www.nls.org/conf2004/summary-medicare-act-2003.htm

Center for Medicare and Medicaid Services, Office of Legislation. (2004). *CMS legislative summary: Medicare Prescription Drug, Improvement, and Modernization Act of 2003, Public Law 108-173.* Retrieved March 5, 2011, from https://www.cms.gov/MMAUpdate/downloads/PL108-173summary.pdf

Center for Participatory Change. (n.d.). *The components of a grant proposal.* Retrieved March 2, 2011, from http://www.cpcwnc.org/resources/toolbox/the-components-of-a-grant-proposal

Centers for Disease Control and Prevention. (2006). Self-reported falls and fall-related injuries among persons aged >65 years. *MMWR.* Retrieved February 23, 2011, from http://www.cdc.gov/mmwr/preview/mmwrhtml/mm5709a1.htm.

Centers for Disease Control and Prevention. (2011). *Older drivers and prevention.* Retrieved March 9, 2011, from http://www.cdc.gov/Features/OlderDrivers/

Centers for Medicare and Medicaid Services. (2011). *Program of All Inclusive Care for the Elderly (PACE).* Retrieved February 23, 2011, from www.cms.gov/pace/

Chandler, J., Duncan, P., Weiner, D., & Studentski, S. (2001). The Home Assessment Profile—A reliable and valid assessment tool. *Topics in Geriatric Rehabilitation, 16,* 77–88.

Chang, J. T., Morton, S. C., Rubenstein, L. Z., Mojica, W. A., Maglione, M. Suttorp, M.J., Shekelle, P. G. (2004). Interventions for the prevention of falls in older adults: Systematic review and meta-analysis of randomised clinical trials. *British Medical Journal, 328*(7441), 680.

Chappell, N. L., & Dujela, C. (2008). Caregiving: Predicting at-risk status. *Canadian Journal of Aging, 27,* 169–179.

Chase, C. A., Mann, K., Wasek, S. & Arbesman, M. (2012). Systematic review of the effect of home modification and fall prevention programs on the performance of community-dwelling older adults. *American Journal of Occupational Therapy, 66,* 284–291.

Chen, Y. M., & Thompson, E. A. (2010). Understanding factors that influence success of home- and community-based services in keeping older adults in community settings. *Journal of Aging and Health, 22,* 267–291.

Cheng, P. T., Liaw, M. Y., Wong, M. K., Tang, F. T., Lee, M. Y., & Lin, P. S. (1998). The sit-to-stand movement in stroke patients and its correlation with falling. *Archives of Physical Medicine and Rehabilitation, 79,* 1043–1046.

Cheng, S., Fung, H. H., & Chan, A. C. M. (2008). Living status and psychological wellbeing: Social comparison as a moderator in later life. *Aging and Mental Health, 12,* 654–661.

Chodosh, J., Morton, S. C., Mojica, W., Maglione, M., Suttorp, M. J., Hilton, L. Shekelle, P.G., et al. (2005). Meta-analysis chronic disease self-management programs for older adults. *Annals of Internal Medicine, 143,* 427–438.

Christensen, K., Doblhammer, G., Rau, R., & Vaupel, J. W. (2009). Ageing populations: The challenges ahead. *Lancet, 374,* 1196–1208.

Clark, F., Azen, S. P., Zemke, R., Jackson, J., Carlson, M., Mandel, D., & Lipson, L. (1997). Occupational therapy for independent-living older adults: A randomized controlled trial. *JAMA, 278,* 1321–1326.

Clark, F., Azen, S. P., Carlson, M., Mandel, D., LaBree, L., Hay, J., & Lipson, L. (2001). Embedding health-promoting changes into the daily lives of independent-living older adults: Long-term follow-up of occupational therapy intervention. *Journals of Gerontology Series B-Psychological Sciences and Social Sciences, 56,* 60–63.

Clark, F., Jackson, J., Carlson, M., Chou, C., Cherry, B. J., Jordan-Marsh, M., & Azen, S. P. (2011). Effectiveness of a lifestyle intervention in promoting the well-being of independently living older people: Results of the Well Elderly2 Randomised Controlled Trial. *Journal of Epidemiology and Community Health.* Retrieved April 2, 2011, from http://jech.bmj.com/content/early/2011/06/01/jech.2009.099754.abstract

Clark, K. M., Friedman, H. S., & Martin, L. R. (1999). A longitudinal study of religiosity and mortality risk. *Journal of Health Psychology, 4,* 381–392.

Clay, O. J., Roth, D. L., Wadley, V. G., & Haley, W. E. (2008). Changes in social support and their impact on psychosocial outcome over a 5-year period for African American and White dementia caregivers. *International Journal of Geriatric Psychiatry, 23,* 857–862.

Clemson, L. (1997). *Home fall hazards. A guide to identifying fall hazards in the homes of elderly people and an accompaniment to the assessment tool, the Westmead Home Safety Assessment (WeHSA).* West Brunswick, Victoria, Australia: Coordinates Publications.

Clemson, L., Cumming, R. G., Hendig, H., Swann, M., Heard, R., & Taylor, K. (2004). The effectiveness of a community-based program for reducing the incidence of falls in the elderly: A randomized trial. *Journal of the American Geriatrics Society, 52,* 1487–1494.

Close, J., Ellis, M., Hooper, R., Glucksman, E., Jackson, S., & Swift, C. (1999). Prevention of falls in the elderly trial (PROFET): A randomized controlled trial. *The Lancet, 353,* 93–97.

Collier, T. (1991). The screening process. In W. Dunn (Ed.), *Pediatric occupational therapy: Facilitating effective service provision* (pp. 11–33). Thorofare, NJ: Slack.

Cooper, B., Letts, L., Rigby, P., Stewart, D., & Strong, S. (2005). Measuring environmental factors. In M. Law, C. Baum, & W. Dunn (Eds.), *Measuring occupational performance: Supporting best practice in occupational therapy* (2nd ed., pp. 326–327). Thorofare, NJ: Slack.

Cornwell, E. Y., & Waite, L. J. (2009). Social disconnectedness, perceived isolation, and health among older adults. *Journal of Health and Social Behavior, 50*(1), 31–48.

Crooks, V. C., Lubben, J., Petitti, D. B., Little, D., & Chiu, V. (2008). Social network, cognitive function, and dementia incidence among elderly women. *American Journal of Public Health, 98,* 1221–1227.

Cumming, R. G., Thomas, M., Szonyi, G., Frampton, G., Salkeld, G., & Clemson, L. (2001). Adherence to occupational therapist recommendations for home modifications for fall prevention. *American Journal of Occupational Therapy, 55*(6), 644–648.

Cumming, R. G., Thomas, M., Szonyi, G., Salkeld, G., O'Neill, E., Westbury, C., & Frampton, G. (1999). Home visits by an occupational therapist for assessment and modification of environmental hazards: A randomized trial of falls prevention. *Journal of the American Geriatrics Society, 47*(12), 1397–1402.

Dahan-Oliel, N., Gélinas, I., & Mazer, B. (2008). Social participation in the elderly: What does the literature tell us? *Critical Reviews in Physical and Rehabilitation Medicine, 20,* 159–176.

Dahlin Ivanoff, S., Sonn, U., & Svensson, E. (2002). A health education program for elderly persons with visual impairments and perceived security in the performance of daily occupations: A randomized study. *American Journal of Occupational Therapy, 56,* 322–330.

Darzins, P. (2010). Can this patient go home? Assessment of decision-making capacity. *Australian Occupational Therapy Journal, 57,* 65–67.

Davison, J., Bond, J., Dawson, P., Steen, I. N., & Kenny, R. A. (2005). Patients with recurrent falls attending accident and emergency benefit from multi-factorial intervention—A randomized controlled trial. *Age and Aging, 34*(2), 162–168.

Day, L., Fildes, B., Gordon, I., Fitzharris, M., Flamer, H., & Lord, S. (2002). Randomised facto-rial trial of falls prevention among older people living in their own homes. *British Medical Journal, 325,* 128–133.

de Vreede, P. L., Samson, M. M., van Meeteren, N. L. U., Duursma, S. A., & Verhaar, H. J. J. (2005). Functional-task exercise versus resistance strength exercise to improve daily function in older women: A randomized, controlled trial. *Journal of the American Geriatrics Society, 53,* 2–10.

de Vreede, P. L., Samson, M. M., van Meeteren, N. L., van der Bom, J. G., Duursma, S. A., & Verhaar, H. J. (2004). Functional tasks exercise versus resistance exercise to improve daily function in older women: A feasibility study. *Archives of Physical Medicine and Rehabilitation, 85,* 1952–1961.

DeForge, R. T., Cormack, C., Byrne, K., Hillier, L. M., Mackenzie, R., & Gutmanis, I. A. (2008). Barriers and facilitators to recommendation adherence follow-ing discharge from geriatric rehabilitation. *Topics in Geriatric Rehabilitation, 24*(4), 345–353.

Dew, M. A., Hoch, C. C., Buysse, D. J., Monk, T. H., Begley, A. E., Houck, P. R., . . . Reynolds, C. F. (2003). Healthy older adults' sleep predicts all-cause mortality at 4 to 19 years of follow-up. *Psychosomatic Medicine, 65,* 63–73.

Dickerson, A. E., Molnar, L. J., Eby, D. W., Adler, G., Bédard, M., Berg-Weger, M., & Trujillo, L. (2007).

Transportation and aging: A research agenda for advancing safe mobility. *Gerontologist, 47*(5), 578–590.

Dilworth, J., & Kingsbury, N. (2005). Home-to-job spillover for Generation X, Boomers, and Matures: A comparison. *Journal of Family and Economic Issues, 26*(2), 267–281.

Dobek, J. C., White, K. N., & Gunter, K. B. (2006). The effect of a novel ADL-based training program on performance of activities of daily living and physical fitness. *Journal of Aging and Physical Activity, 15,* 13–25.

Doble, S. E., Fisk, J. D., Lewis, N., & Rockwood, K. (1999). Test–retest reliability of the Assessment of Motor and Process Skills (AMPS) in elderly adults. *Occupational Therapy Journal of Research, 19,* 203–215.

Duncan, P. W., Weiner, D. K., Chandler, J., & Studen-ski, S. (1990). Functional reach: A new clinical measure of balance. *Journal of Gerontology, 45*(6), M192–M197.

Dunn, W., McClain, L. H., Brown, C., & Youngstrom, M. J. (1998). The ecology of human performance. In M. E. Neistadt & E. B. Crepeau (Eds.), *Willard and Spackman's occupational therapy* (9th ed., pp. 525–535). Philadelphia: Lippincott Williams & Wilkins.

Dupre, M. E., Liu, G., & Gu, D. (2008). Predictors of longevity: Evidence from the oldest old in China. *American Journal of Public Health, 98,* 1203–1208.

Durocher, E., & Gibson, B. E. (2010). Navigating ethical discharge planning: A case study in older adult rehabilita-tion. *Australian Occupational Therapy Journal, 57,* 2–7.

Easton, L., & Herge, E. A. (2011). Adult day care: Providing meaningful and purposeful leisure. *OT Practice, 16*(1), 20–23.

Eklund, K., Sonn, U., & Dahlin-Ivanoff, S. (2004). Long-term evaluation of a health education programme for elderly persons with visual impairment. A randomized study. *Disability and Rehabilitation, 26,* 401–409.

Elbert, K. B., & Neufeld, P. S. (2010). Indicators of a successful naturally occurring retirement community: A case study. *Journal of Housing for the Elderly, 24*(3), 322–334.

Enright, P. L., McBurnie, M. A., Bittner, V., Tracy, R. P., McNamara, R., Arnold, A., & Newman, A. B. (2003). The 6-minute walk test: A quick measure of functional status in elderly adults. *Chest, 123*(2), 387–398.

Ertel, K. A., Glymour, M. M., & Berkman, L. F. (2008). Effects of social integration on preserving memory function in a nationally representative U.S. elderly population. *American Journal of Public Health, 98,* 1215–1220.

Evans, D. M., Conte, K., Gilroy, M., Marvin, T., Theysohn, H., & Fisher, G. (2008). Occupational therapy—Meeting the needs of older adult workers? *Work, 31,* 73–82.

Faber, M. J., Bosscher, R. J., China Paw, M. J., & van Wieringen, P. C. (2006). Effects of exercise programs on falls and mobility in frail and pre-frail older adults: A multicenter randomized controlled trial. *Archives of Physical Medicine Rehabilitation, 87,* 885–896.

Fange, A., & Iwarsson, S. (2005). Changes in ADL dependence and aspects of usability following housing adaptation: A longitudinal perspective. *American Journal of Occupational Therapy, 59,* 296–304.

Farrell, D. J., & Murphy, S. L. (2010, May 24). Promoting physical activity in older adults. *OT Practice,* pp. 8–11.

Federal Interagency Forum on Aging-Related Statistics. (2010). *Older Americans 2010: Key indicators of wellbeing.* Retrieved February 20, 2011, from http://www.aoa.gov/agingstatsdotnet/Main_site/Data/Data_2010.aspx

Fields, J., & Casper, L. M. (2001). *American's families and living arrangements.* Washington, DC: U.S. Printing Office.

Fillenbaum, G. G. (2005). *Multidimensional functional assessment of older adults: The Duke Older American Resources and Services Procedures.* Hillsdale, NJ: Lawrence Erlbaum.

Fisher, A. G., Atler, K., & Potts, A. (2007). Effectiveness of occupational therapy with frail community living older adults. *Scandinavian Journal of Occupational Therapy, 14,* 240–249

Fisher, G., Civitella, H., & Perez, V. (2006). *The Cougar Home Safety Assessment—Version 4.0.* Dallas, PA: College Misericordia.

Fisher, K. J., & Li, F. (2004). A community-based walking trial to improve neighborhood quality of life in older adults: A multilevel analysis. *Annals of Behavioral Medicine, 28,* 186–194.

Fischer, L. R., & Schaffer, K. B. (1993). *Older volunteers: A guide to research and practice.* Newbury Park, CA: Sage.

Foster, G., Taylor, S. J. C., Eldridge, S., Ramsay, J., & Griffiths, C. J. (2007). Self-management education programmes by lay leaders for people with chronic conditions. *Cochrane Database of Systematic Reviews, 4,* CD005108.

Fratiglioni, L., Wang, H., Ericsson, K., Maytan, M., & Winblad, B. (2000). Influence of social network on occurrence of dementia: A community-based longitudinal study. *Lancet, 355,* 1315–1319.

Gardner, M. (1997). *Home-based exercises to prevent falls in elderly women.* Unpublished doctoral dissertation, University of Otago, Dunedin, New Zealand.

Gerber, L., & Furst, G. (1992). Validation of the NIH activity record: A quantitative measure of life activities. *Arthritis Care Research, 5,* 81–86.

Ghisletta, P., Bickel, J., & Lövdén, M. (2006). Does activity engagement protect against cognitive decline in old age? Methodological and analytical considerations. *Journal of Gerontology: Psychological Sciences, 61B,* P253–P261.

Giles, L. C., Glonek, G. F., Luszcz, M. A., & Andrews, G. R. (2005). Effect of social networks on 10-year survival in very old Australians: The Australian longitudinal study of aging. *Journal of Epidemiology and Community Health, 59*, 574–579.

Gill, T. M., & Kurland, B. F. (2003). Prognostic effect of prior disability episodes among nondisabled community-living older persons. *American Journal of Epidemiology, 158*, 1090–1096.

Gill T. M., Williams, C. S., Robison, J. T., & Tinetti, M. E. (1999). A population-based study of environmental hazards in the homes of older persons. *American Journal of Public Health, 89*(4), 553–556.

Gillespie, L. D., Gillespie, W. J., Robertson, M. C., Lamb, S. E., Cumming R. G., & Rowe, B. H. (2003). Interventions for preventing falls in elderly people. *Cochrane Database of Systematic Reviews, 4*, CD000340.

Gillespie, L. D., Robertson, M. C., Gillespie, W. J., Lamb, S. E., Cumming, R. G., & Rowe, B. H. (2009). Interventions for preventing falls in older people living in the community. *Cochrane Database of Systematic Reviews, 2*, CD007146.

Ginis, K. A. M., Latimer, A., Brawley, L. R., Jung, M. E., & Hicks, A. L. (2006). Weight training to activities of daily living: Helping older adults make a connection. *Medicine and Science in Sports and Exercise: Official Journal of the American College of Sports Medicine, 38*, 116–121.

Ginsberg, G. M., Hammerman-Rozenberg, R., Cohen, A., & Stessman, J. (1999). Independence in instrumental activities of daily living and its effect on mortality. *Aging Clinical and Experimental Research, 11*, 161–168.

Gitlin L. N. (2003). Conducting research on home environments: Lessons learned and new directions. *The Gerontologist, 43*(5), 628–637.

Gitlin, L. N., Chernett, N. L., Harris, L. F., Palmer, D., Hopkins, P., & Dennis, M. P. (2008). Harvest health: Translation of the chronic disease self-management program for older African-Americans in a senior setting. *The Gerontologist, 48*, 698–705.

Gitlin, L. N., Schinfeld, S.,Winter, L., Corcoran, M., Boyce, A. A., & Hauck, W. (2002). Evaluating home environments of persons with dementia: Interrater reliability and validity of the Home Environmental Assessment Protocol (HEAP). *Disability and Rehabilitation, 24*, 59–71.

Gitlin, L. N., Winter, L., Dennis, M. P., Corcoran, M., Schinfeld, S., & Hauck, W. W. (2006). A randomized trial of a multicomponent home intervention to reduce functional difficulties in older adults. *Journal of the American Geriatrics Society, 54*, 809–816.

Gitlin, L. N., Winter, L., Dennis, M. P., & Hauck, W. W. (2008). Variation in response to a home intervention to support daily function by age, race, sex, and education. *Journal of Gerontology: Medical Sciences, 63A*, 745–750.

Glass, T. A., Mendes de Leon, C. F., Marottoli, R. A., & Berkman, L. F. (1999). Population based study of social and productive activities as predictors of survival among elderly Americans. *British Medical Journal, 319*, 478–483.

Goldman, S. E., Stone, K. L., Ancoli-Israel, S., Blackwell, T., Ewing, S. K., Boudreau, R., . . . Newman, A. B. (2007). Poor sleep is associated with poorer physical performance and greater functional limitations in older women. *Sleep, 30*, 1317–1324.

Gourley, M. (2007). *A visionary center.* Retrieved March 2, 2011, from http://www.aota.org/Practitioners/PracticeAreas/Emerging/PA/LowVision/36248.aspx

Grantwritersonline. (2006). *Components of a grant proposal.* Retrieved March 12, 2011,from http://www.grantwritersonline.com/components-of-a-grant-proposal-2.html

Gray, J. M. (1998). Putting occupation into practice: occupation as ends, occupation as means. *American Journal of Occupational Therapy, 52*, 354–364.

Green, A. (2008). Sleep, occupation and the passage of time. *British Journal of Occupational Therapy, 71*(8), 339–347.

Greenfield, E. A., & Marks, N. F. (2007). Continuous participation in voluntary groups as a protective factor for the psychological well-being of adults who develop functional limitations: Evidence from the National Survey of Families and Households. *Journals of Gerontology: Social Sciences, 62B,* S60–S68.

Gregg, E. W., Cauley, J. A., Stone, K., Thompson, T. J., Bauer, D. C., Cummings, S. R., & Ensrud K. E. (2003). Relationship of changes in physical activity and mortality among older women. *JAMA, 289,* 2379–2386

Grimm, R., Jr., Spring, K., & Dietz, N. (2007). *The health benefits of volunteering: A review of recent research.* Washington, DC: Office of Research and Policy Development.

Grisbrooke, J., & Scott, S. (2009). Moving into housing: Experiences of developing specialist occupational therapy posts in local authority housing departments. *British Journal of Occupational Therapy, 72*(1), 29–36.

Gu, M. O., & Conn, V. S. (2008). Meta-analysis of the effects of exercise interventions on functional status in older adults. *Research in Nursing and Health, 31,* 594–603.

Gupta, J., & Sabata, D. (2010, April). Maximizing occupational performance of older workers. *OT Practice, 15*(7), CE1–CE8.

Gurland, B., Golden, R. R., Teresi, J. A., & Challop, J. (1984). The SHORT-CARE: An efficient instrument for the assessment of depression, dementia, and disability. *Journal of Gerontology, 39,* 166–169.

Hagsten, B., Svensson, O., & Gardulf, A. (2006). Health-related quality of life and self-reported ability concerning ADL and IADL after hip fracture: A randomized trial. *Acta Orthopaedica, 77,* 114–119.

Hammerman-Rozenberg, R., Maaravi, Y., Cohen, A., & Stessman, J. (2005). Working late: The impact of work after 70 on longevity, health and function. *Aging Clinical and Experimental Research, 17,* 508–513.

Hao, Y. (2008). Productive activities and psychological well-being among older adults. *Journal of Gerontology: Social Sciences, 63B,* S64–S72.

Harris, A. H. S., & Thoresen, C. E. (2005). Volunteering is associated with delayed mortality in older people: Analysis of the Longitudinal Study of Aging. *Journal of Health Psychology, 10,* 739–752.

Hauer, K., Rost, B., Rütschle, K., Opitz, H., Specht, N., Bärtsch, P., & Schlierf, G. (2001). Exercise training for rehabilitation and secondary prevention of falls in geriatric patients with a history of injurious falls. *Journal of the American Geriatrics Society, 49,* 10–20.

Hay, J., LaBree, L., Luo, R., Clark, F., Carlson, M., Mandel, D., & Azen, S. P. (2002). Cost-effectiveness of preventive occupational therapy for independent-living older adults. *Journal of the American Geriatrics Society, 50,* 1381–1388.

Haynes, S. A., Johnson, A. W., & Heyes, A. D. (2001). Preliminary investigation of the responsiveness of the Melbourne Low Vision ADL Index to low-vision rehabilitation. *Optometry and Vision Science, 78*(6), 373–380.

Hays, R. D., Sherbourne, C. D., & Mazel, R. M. (1993). The RAND 36-Item Health Survey 1.0. *Health Economics, 2,* 217–227.

He, W., Sengupta, M., Velkoff, V. A., & Debarros, K. A. (2005). *65+ in the United States: U.S. Census Bureau Current population reports* (pp. 23–209). Washington, DC: U.S. Government Printing Office.

Hebert, R. S., Dang, Q., & Schulz, R. (2006). Preparedness for the death of a loved one and mental health in bereaved caregivers of patients with dementia: Findings from the REACH study. *Journal of Palliative Medicine, 9,* 683–693.

Helm, H. M., Hays, J. C., Flint, E. P., Koenig, H. G., & Blazer, D. G. (2000). Does private religious activity prolong survival? A six-year follow-up study of 3,851 older adults. *Journal of Gerontology: Medical Sciences, 55A,* M400–M405.

Helzner, E. P., Scarmeas, N., Cosentino, S., Portet, F., & Stern, Y. (2007). Leisure activity and cognitive decline in incident Alzheimer disease. *Archives of Neurology, 64,* 1749–1754.

Herd, P. (2009). Women, public pensions, and poverty: What can the United States learn from other countries? *Journal of Women, Politics and Policy, 30*(2), 301–334.

Herzog, A. R., Kahn, R. L., Morgan, J. N., Jackson, J. S., & Antonucci, T. C. (1989). Age differences in productive activities. *Journals of Gerontology, 44*(4), S129–S138.

Hewitt, A., Howie, L., & Feldman, S. (2010). Retirement: What will you do? A narrative inquiry of occupation-based planning for retirement: Implications for practice. *Australian Occupational Therapy Journal, 57,* 8–16.

Hibbard, J. H., Greene, J., & Tusler, M. (2009). Improving the outcomes of disease management by tailoring care to the patient's level of activation. *American Journal of Managed Care, 15,* 353–360.

Hinojosa, J., Kramer, P., & Crist, P. (Eds.). (2010). *Evaluation: Obtaining and interpreting data* (3rd ed.). Bethesda, MD: AOTA Press.

Hinterlong, J. E. (2008). Productive engagement among older Americans: Prevalence, patterns, and implications for public policy. *Journal of Aging and Social Policy, 20*(2), 141–164.

Hinterlong, J. E., & Williamson, A. (2006/2007). The effects of civic engagement of current and future cohorts of older adults. *Generations, 30*(4), 10–17.

Hirvensalo, M., Rantanen, T., & Heikkinen, E. (2000). Mobility difficulties and physical activity as predictors of mortality and loss of independence in the community-living older population. *Journal of the American Geriatrics Society, 48,* 493–498.

Hoffman, T., & McKenna, K. (2004). A survey of assistive equipment use by older people following hospital discharge. *British Journal of Occupational Therapy, 67*(2), 75–82.

Hogan, D. B., MacDonald, F. A., Betts, J., Bricker, S., Ebly, E. M., Delarue, B., & Metcalf, B. (2001). A randomized controlled trial of community-based consultation service to prevent falls. *Canadian Medical Association Journal, 165*(5), 587–588.

Holland, S. K., Greenberg, J., Tidwell, L., Malone, J., Mullan, J., & Newcomer, R. (2005). Community-based health coaching, exercise, and health service use. *Journal of Aging and Health, 17,* 697–716.

Hootman, J. M., & Helmick, C. G. (2006). Projections of US prevalence of arthritis and associated activity limitations. *Arthritis and Rheumatism, 54*(1), 226–229.

Horgas, A., & Abowd, G. (2004). The impact of technology on living environments for older adults. In R. W. Pew & S. B. Van Hemel (Eds.), *Technology for adaptive aging: Steering Committee for the Workshop on Technology for Adaptive Aging* (pp. 244–252). Washington, DC: National Academies Press. Retrieved from December 5, 2008, from http://www.geron.uga.edu/pdfs/BooksOnAging/AdaptiveAging.pdf#page=244

Hornbrook, M. C., Stevens, V. J., Wingfield, D. J., Hollis, J. F., Greenlick, M. R., & Ory, M. G. (1994). Preventing falls among community-dwelling older persons: Results from a randomized trial. *The Gerontologist, 34*(1), 16–23.

Horowitz, B. P., & Chang, P. J. (2004). Promoting well-being and engagement in life through occupational therapy life redesign: A pilot study within adult day programs. *Topics in Geriatric Rehabilitation, 20,* 46–58.

Hsu, H. C. (2007). Does social participation by the elderly reduce mortality and cognitive impairment? *Aging and Mental Health, 11,* 699–707.

Hughes, T. F., Andel, R., Small, B. J., Borenstein, A. R., & Mortimer, J. A. (2008). The association between social resources and cognitive change in older adults: Evidence from the Charlotte County Healthy Aging Study. *Journal of Gerontology: Psychological Sciences, 63B,* P241–P244.

Hughes, M. E., Waite, L. J., LaPierre, T. A., & Luo, Y. (2007). All in the family: The impact of caring for grandchildren on grandparents' health. *Journals of Gerontology: Psychological Sciences and Social Sciences, 62,* S108–A119.

Hunt, L. A., & Arbesman, M. (2008). Evidence-based and occupational perspective of effective interventions for older clients that remediate or support improved driving performance. *American Journal of Occupational Therapy, 62,* 136–148.

Idyll Arbor Leisure Battery. (2010). Retrieved March 9, 2011, from http://www.idyllarbor.com/agora.cgi?p_id=A145&xm=on

Inoue, K., Shono, T., & Matsumoto, M. (2006). Absence of outdoor activity and mortality risk in older adults living at home. *Journal of Aging and Physical Activity, 14,* 203–211.

Institute for the Future. (2003). *Health and health care 2010: The forecast, the challenge.* Princeton, NJ: Jossey-Bass.

Institute for Work and Health. (2006). *The DASH outcome measure: Disabilities of the arm, shoulder, and hand.* Retrieved March 9, 2011, from http://www.dash.iwh.on.ca/conditions.htm

Institute of Medicine. (2008). *Retooling for an aging America: Building the health care workforce.* Washington, DC: National Academies Press.

Isernhagen, S. J. (n.d.). *A brief history of the Isernhagen-DSI Work Solutions Functional Capacity Assessment.*

Retrieved March 9, 2011, from http://dsiworksolutions.com/history.htm

Jacobs, J. M., Hammerman-Rozenberg, R., Cohen, A., & Stessman, J. (2008). Reading daily predicts reduced mortality among men from a cohort of community-dwelling 70-year-olds. *Journal of Gerontology: Social Sciences, 63B,* S73–S80.

Janke, M. C., Nimrod, G., & Kleiber, D. A. (2008). Leisure patterns and health among recently widowed adults. *Activities, Adaptation, and Aging, 32,* 19–39.

Jenkinson, N., Ownsworth, T., & Shum, D. (2007). Utility of the Canadian Occupational Performance Measure in community-based brain injury rehabilitation. *Brain Injury, 21,* 1283–1294.

Jerant, A., Moore-Hill, M., & Franks, P. (2009). Home-based, peer-led chronic illness self-management training: Findings from a 1-year randomized controlled trial. *Annals of Family Medicine, 7,* 319–327.

Johns Hopkins Medicine. (2009). *Depression and anxiety special report: Report on substance abuse and aging.* Retrieved May 12, 2011, from http://www.johnshopkinshealthalerts.com/reports/depression_anxiety/2943–1.html

Johnson, R. W., & Schaner, S. G. (2005). *Older caregiving.* Retrieved May 12, 2011, from http://www.wiserwomen.org/index.php?id=585&page=Older_Caregivers

Johnson, R. W., Soto, M., & Zedlewski, S. R. (2008). *How is the economic turmoil affecting older Americans?* Washington, DC: Urban Institute. Retrieved May 1, 2011, from http://www.globalaging.org/elderrights/us/2008/turmoil.pdf

Kaiser Family Foundation. (2011). *Focus on health reform: Summary of the health reform law.* Retrieved March 9, 2012, from http://www.kff.org/healthreform/upload/8061.pdf Patient Protection and Accountable Care Act of 2010.

Kaldenberg, J., & Smallfield, S. (in press). *Occupational therapy practice guidelines for older adults with low vision.* Bethesda, MD: AOTA Press.

Kaminsky, T. (2010, April 5). The role of occupational therapy in successful aging. *OT Practice,* 11–14.

Kaplan, G. A., Baltrus, P. T., & Raghunathan, T. E. (2007). The shape of health to come: Prospective study of the determinants of 30-year health trajectories in the Alameda County Study. *International Journal of Epidemiology, 36,* 542–548.

Kaplan, G. A., Strawbridge, W. J., Cohen, R. D., & Hungerford, L. R. (1996). Natural history of leisure-time physical activity and its correlates: Associations with mortality from all causes and cardiovascular disease over 28 years. *American Journal of Epidemiology, 144,* 793–797.

Katzman, R., Brown, T., Fukd, P., Peck, A., Schechter, R., & Shimmel, H. (1983). Validation of a short orientation–memory–concentration test of cognitive impairment. *American Journal Psychiatry, 140*(6), 734–739.

Keyes, C. L., & Reitzes, D. C. (2007). The role of religious identity in the mental health of older working and retired adults. *Aging and Mental Health, 11,* 434–443.

Keysor, J. J. (2003). Does late-life physical activity or exercise prevent or minimize disablement?: A critical review of the scientific evidence. *American Journal of Preventative Medicine, 25,* 129–136.

Kharicha, K., Iliffe, S., Harari, D., Swift, C., Gillmann, G., & Stuck, A. E. (2007). Healthrisk appraisal in older people 1: Are older people living alone an "at-risk" group? *British Journal of General Practice, 57,* 271–276.

Khokhar, S. R., Stern, Y., Bell, K., Anderson, K., Noe, E., Mayeux, R., & Albert, S. M. (2001). Persistent mobility deficit in the absence of deficits in activities of daily living: A risk factor for mortality. *Journal of the American Geriatrics Society, 49,* 1539–1543.

Kielhofner, G., Fogg, L., Braveman, B., Forsyth, K., Kramer, J., & Duncan, E. (2009). A factor analytic study of the Model of Human Occupation Screening Tool of Hypothesized Variables. *Occupational Therapy in Mental Health, 25*(2), 127–137.

King, D. K., Estabrooks, P. A., Strycker, L. A., Toobert, D. J., Bull, S. S., & Glasgow, R. E. (2006). Outcomes of a multifaceted physical activity regimen as part of adiabetes self-management intervention. *Annals of Behavioral Medicine, 31*(2),128–137.

Kominski, G. F., Simon, P. A., Ho, A., Luck, J., Lim, Y. W., & Fielding, J. E. (2002). Assessing the burden of disease and injury in Los Angeles County using disability-adjusted life years. *Public Health Report, 117*(2), 185–191.

Kondo, T., Mann, W. C., Tomita, M., & Ottenbacher, K. J. (1997). The use of microwave ovens by elderly persons with disabilities. *American Journal of Occupational Therapy, 51,* 739–747.

Kono, A., Kai, I., Sakato, C., & Rubenstein, L. Z. (2004). Frequency of going outdoors: A predictor of functional and psychosocial change among ambulatory frail elders living at home. *Journal of Gerontology: Medical Sciences, 59A,* 275–280.

Korten, A. E., Jorm, A. F., Jiao, Z., Letenneur, L., Jacomb, P. A., Henderson, A. S., . . . Rogers, B. (1999). Health, cognitive, and psychosocial factors as predictors of mortality in an elderly community sample. *Journal of Epidemiology and Community Health, 53,* 83–88.

Kua, A., Korner-Bitensky, N., Desrosiers, J., Man-Son-Hing, M., & Marshall, S. (2007). Older driver retraining: A systematic review of evidence of effectiveness. *Journal of Safety Research, 38,* 81–90.

Kunzmann, U. (2008). Differential age trajectories of positive and negative affect: Further evidence from the Berlin Aging Study. *Journal of Gerontology: Psychological Sciences, 63B,* P261–P270.

la Cour, P., Avlund, K., & Schultz-Larsen, K. (2006). Religion and survival in a secular region. A twenty-year follow-up of 734 Danish adults born in 1914. *Social Science and Medicine, 62,* 157–164.

Lajoie, Y., & Gallagher, S. P. (2004). Predicting falls within the elderly community: Comparison of postural sway, reaction time, the Berg balance scale and ABC scale for comparing fallers and non-fallers. *Archives of Gerontology and Geriatrics, 4*(38), 11–26.

Lampinen, P., Heikkinen, R.-L., Kauppinen, M., & Heikkinen, E. (2006). Activity as a predictor of mental well-being among older adults. *Aging and Mental Health, 10,* 454–466.

Laukkanen, P., Kauppinen, M., & Heikkinen, E. (1998). Physical activity as a predictor of health and disability in 75- and 80-year-old men and women: A five-year longitudinal study. *Journal of Aging and Physical Activity, 6,* 141–156.

Law, M., Baptiste, S., Carswell, A., McColl, M., Polatajko, H., & Pollock, N. (2005). *Canadian Occupational Performance Measure* (4th ed.). Ottawa, Ontario, Canada: CAOT Publications ACE.

Law, M., Baptiste, S., McColl, M. A., Carswell, A., Polatajko, H., & Pollock, N. (1998). *Canadian Occupational Performance Measure* (3rd ed.). Toronto, Ontario: Canadian Association of Occupational Therapists.

Law, M., & Baum, C. (1998). Evidence-based occupational therapy. *Canadian Journal of Occupational Therapy, 65,* 131–135.

Lee, D. J., & Markides, K. S. (1990). Activity and mortality among aged persons over an eightyear period. *Journal of Gerontology: Social Sciences, 45,* S39–S42.

Lee, R. E., & King, A. C. (2003). Discretionary time among older adults: How do physical activity promotion interventions affect sedentary and active behaviors? *Annals of Behavioral Medicine, 25,* 112–119.

Lennartsson, C., & Silverstein, M. (2001). Does engagement with life enhance survival of elderly people in Sweden? The role of social and leisure activities. *Journal of Gerontology: Social Sciences, 56B,* S335–S342.

Letts, L., Minezes, J., Edwards, M., Berenyi, J., Moros, K., O'Neill, C., & Toole, C. E. (2011). Effectiveness of interventions designed to modify and maintain perceptual abilities in people with Alzheimer's disease and related dementias. *American Journal of Occupational Therapy, 65,* 505–513.

Leveille, S. G., Wagner, E. H., Davis, C., Grothaus, L., Wallace, J., LoGerfo, M., & Kent, D. (1998). Preventing disability and managing chronic illness in frail older adults: A randomized trial of a community-based partnership with primary care. *Journal of American Geriatrics Society, 46,* 1191–1198.

Lin, M. R., Wolf, S. L., Hwang, H. F., Gong, S. Y., & Chen, C. Y. (2007). A randomized, controlled trial of fall prevention programs and quality of life in older fallers. *Journal of the American Geriatrics Society, 55,* 499–506.

Liu, C.-J., & Latham, N. K. (2007). Progressive resistance strength training for improving physical function in older adults. *Cochrane Database of Systematic Reviews, 4,* CD002759.

Liu, S. Y., & Lapane, K. L. (2009). Residential modifications and decline in physical function among community-dwelling older adults. *The Gerontologist, 49*(3), 344–354.

Logan, P. A., Coupland, C. A. C., Gladman, J. R. F., Sahota, O., Stoner-Hobbs, V. Robertson, K., . . . Avery, A. J. (2010). Community falls prevention for people who call an emergency ambulance after a fall: Randomized controlled trial. *British Medical Journal, 340,* c2102.

Lord, S. R., Tiedemann, A., Chapman, K., Munro, B., Murray, S. M., & Sherrington, C. (2005). The effect of an individualized fall prevention program on fall risk and falls in older people: A randomized, controlled trial. *Journal of the American Geriatrics Society, 53,* 1296–1304.

Lord, S. R., Ward, J. A., Williams, P., & Strudwick, M. (1995). The effect of a 12-month exercise trial on balance, strength, and falls in older women: A randomized controlled trial. *Journal of the American Geriatrics Society, 43,* 1198–1206.

Lorig, K. R., Ritter, P. L., & Gonzalez, V. M. (2003). Hispanic chronic disease self-management: A randomized community-based outcome trial. *Nursing Research, 52,* 361–369.

Lorig, K. R., Ritter, P. L., Laurent, D. D., & Fries, J. F. (2004). Long-term randomized controlled trials of tailored-print and small-group arthritis self-management interventions. *Medical Care, 42,* 346–354.

Lorig, K. R., Ritter, P., Stewart, A. L., Sobel, D. S., Brown, B. W., Jr., Bandura, A., . . . Holman, H.R. (2001). Chronic disease self-management program: 2-year health status and healthcare use outcomes. *Medical Care, 39*(11), 1217–1223.

Lum, T. Y., & Lightfoot, E. (2005). The effects of volunteering on the physical and mental health of older people. *Research on Aging, 27,* 31–55.

Luoh, M., & Herzog, A. R. (2002). Individual consequences of volunteer and paid work in old age: Health and mortality. *Journal of Health and Social Behavior, 43,* 490–509.

Luukinen, H., Lehtola, S., Jokelainen, J., Väänänen-Sainio, R., Lotvonen, S., & Koistinen, P. (2007). Pragmatic exercise-oriented prevention of falls among the elderly: A population-based randomized, controlled trial, *Preventive Medicine, 44,* 265–271.

Mackenzie, L., Byles, J., & Higginbotham, N. (2002). Reliability of the Home Falls and Accidents Screening Tool (HOME FAST) for measuring falls risk for older people. *Disability and Rehabilitation, 24,* 266–274.

Manini, T., Marko, M., VanArnam, T., Cook, S., Fernhall, B., Burke, J., & Ploutz-Snyder, L. (2007). Efficacy of resistance and task-specific exercise in older adults who modify tasks of everyday life. *Journal of Gerontology: Medical Sciences, 62A,* 616–623.

Mann, W. C., Ottenbacher, K. J., Fraas, L., Tomita, M., & Granger, C. V. (1999). Effectiveness of assistive technology and environmental interventions in maintaining independence and reducing home care costs for the frail elderly. *Archives of Family Medicine, 8,* 210–217.

Marottoli, R. A., Allore, H., Araujo, K. L., Iannone, L. P., Acampora, D., Gottschalk, M., . . . Peduzzi, P. (2007a). A randomized trial of a physical conditioning program to enhance the driving performance of older persons. *Journal of General Internal Medicine, 22,* 590–597.

Marottoli, R. A., Van Ness, P. H., Araujo, K. L. B., Iannone, L. P., Acampora, D., Charpentier, P., & Peduzzi, P. (2007b). A randomized trial of an education program to enhance older driver performance. *Journal of Gerontology: Medical Sciences, 62A,* 1113–1119.

Marottoli, R. A., Mendes de Leon, C. F., Glass, T. A., Williams, C. S., Cooney, L. M. C., Jr., Berkman, L. F., et al. (1997). Driving cessation and increased depressive symptoms: Prospective evidence from the New Haven EPESE. *Journal of the American Geriatrics Society, 45,* 202–206.

Masoro, E. J., & Austad, S. N. (Eds). (2006). *Handbook of the biology of aging.* Amsterdam: Elsevier.

Mathew Greenwald & Associates. (2003). *These four walls: American 45+ talk about home and community.* Washington, DC: AARP. Available online at: http://assets.aarp.org/rgcenter/il/four_walls. pdf

Matteliano, M., Mann, W. C., & Tomita, M. (2002). Comparison of home-based older patients who received occupational therapy with patients not receiving occupational therapy. *Physical and Occupational Therapy in Geriatrics, 21,* 21–33.

Mausner, J. S., & Bahn, A. K. (1974) *Epidemiology: An introductory text.* Philadelphia: W. B. Saunders.

McCabe, P., Nason, F., Demers Turco, P., Friedman, D., & Seddon, J. M. (2000). Evaluating the effectiveness of a vision rehabilitation intervention using an objective and subjective measure of functional performance. *Ophthalmic Epidemiology, 7,* 259–270.

McCaffery, M., & Beebe, A. (1993). *Pain: Clinical manual for nursing practice.* London: Mosby.

McCamish-Svensson, C., Samuelsson, G., Hagberg, B., Svensson, T., & Dehlin, O. (1999). Social relationships and health as predictors of life satisfaction in advanced old age: Results from a Swedish longitudinal study. *International Journal of Aging and Human Development, 48,* 301–324.

McCullough, M. E., Hoyt, W. T., Larson, D. B., Koenig, H. G., & Thoresen, C. (2000). Religious involvement and mortality: A meta-analytic review. *Health Psychology, 19,* 211–222.

McCullough, M. E., & Laurenceau, J. P. (2005). Religiousness and the trajectory of self-rated health across adulthood. *Personality and Social Psychology Bulletin, 31,* 1–14.

McNamarra, T., Dobbs, J., Healey, P., & Kane, K. (2007). *Social security and older workers* (Center of Aging and Work, Workplace Flexibility at Boston College, Fact Sheet 04). Retrieved February 23, 2011, from http://agingandwork.bc.edu/documents/FS04_SocialSec_OlderWrkr.pdf

Means, K. M., Rodell, D. E., & O'Sullivan, P. S. (2005). Balance, mobility and falls among community-dwelling elderly persons: Effects of a rehabilitation exercise program. *American Journal of Physical Medicine and Rehabilitation, 84*(4), 238–250.

Medicare Prescription Drug, Improvement, and Modernization Act of 2003, P. L. 108–173, 117 Stat. 2066.

Mendes de Leon, C. F., Glass, T. A., Beckett, L. A., Seeman, T. E., Evans, D. A., & Berkman, L. F. (1999). Social networks and disability transitions across eight intervals of yearly data in the New Haven EPESE. *Journal of Gerontology: Social Sciences, 54B,* S162–S172.

Mendes de Leon, C. F., Glass, T. A., & Berkman, L. F. (2003). Social engagement and disability in a community population of older adults: The New Haven EPESE. *American Journal of Epidemiology, 157,* 633–642.

Menec, V. H. (2003). The relation between everyday activities and successful aging: A 6-year longitudinal study. *Journal of Gerontology: Social Sciences, 58B,* S74–S82.

Merryman, M. B. (2002). Networking as an entrée to paid community practice. *OT Practice,* Retrieved March 12, 2011, from http://www.aota.org/Pubs/OTP/1997-2007/Features/2002/f-051302.aspx

Meyer, A. (1922). The philosophy of occupational therapy. *Archives of Occupational Therapy, 1,* 1–10.

Miller, M. E., Rejeski, W. J., Reboussin, B. A., Ten Have, T. R., & Ettinger, W. H. (2000). Physical activity, functional limitations, and disability in older adults. *Journal of the American Geriatrics Society, 48,* 1264–1272.

Montgomery, P., & Dennis, J. (2003). Cognitive behavioural interventions for sleep problems in adults aged 60+. *Cochrane Database of Systematic Reviews, 1,* CD003161.

Morgan, R. O., Virnig, B. A., Duque, M., Abdel-Moty, E., & DeVito, C. A. (2004). Low-intensity exercise and reduction of the risk for falls among at-risk elders. *Journals of Gerontology, 59A*(10), 1062–1067.

Moyers, P., & Dale, L. (2007). *The guide to occupational therapy practice* (2nd ed.). Bethesda, MD: AOTA Press.

Mullee, M. A., Coleman, P. G., Briggs, R. S. J., Stevenson, J. E., & Turnbull, J. C. (2008). Self-rated activity levels and longevity: Evidence from a 20-year longitudinal study. *International Journal of Aging and Human Development, 67,* 171–186.

Murphy, L. B., Hootman, J., Langmaid, G. A., Brady, T. J., Helmick, C. G., Cheng, Y. J., & Bolen J. (2006). Prevalence of doctor-diagnosed arthritis and arthritis-attributable activity limitation—United States, 2003–2005. *MMWR, 55*(40), 1089–1092.

Murphy, S. L., Gretebeck, K. A., & Alexander, N. B. (2007). The bath environment, the bathing task, and the older adult: A review and future directions for bathing disability research. *Disability and Rehabilitation, 29*(14), 1067–1075.

Murphy, S. L., Lyden, A. K., Smith, D. M., Dong, Q., & Koliba, J. F. (2010). Research Scholars Initiative—Effects of a tailored activity pacing intervention on pain and fatigue for adults with osteoarthritis. *American Journal of Occupational Therapy, 64,* 869–876.

Murphy, S. L., Nyquist, L. V., Strasburg, D. M., & Alexander, N. B. (2006). Bath transfers in older adult congregate housing residents: Assessing the person–environment interaction. *Journal of the American Geriatrics Society, 54*(8), 1265–1270

Murphy, S. L., Strasburg, D. M., Lyden, A. K., Smith, D. M., Koliba, J. F., Dadabhoy, D. P., & Wallis SM. (2008). Effects of activity strategy training on pain and physical activity in older adults with knee or hip osteoarthritis: A pilot study. *Arthritis and Rheumatism, 59,* 1480–1487.

Musick, M. A., Herzog, A. R., & House, J. S. (1999). Volunteering and mortality among older adults: Findings from a national sample. *Journal of Gerontology: Social Sciences, 54B,* S173–S180.

Musick, M. A., & Wilson, J. (2003). Volunteering and depression: The role of psychology and social resources in different age groups. *Social Science and Medicine, 56,* 259–269.

Myers, A. M., Fletcher, P. C., Myers, A. N., & Sherk, W. (1998). Discriminative and evaluative properties of the ABC Scale. *Journal of Gerontology A: Biological Sciences, Medical Sciences, 53,* M287–M294.

Narro, P., & Clarke, E. (2007). The sensitivity and specificity of the Blankenship FCE system's indicators of sincere effort. *Journal of Orthopaedic and Sports Physical Therapy, 37*(4), 161–168.

Nasreddine, Z. (2011). *Montreal Cognitive Assessment (MoCA).* Retrieved February 29, 2011, from http://www.mocatest.org/

National Academy on an Aging Society. (2000). *Challenges for the 21st century: Chronic and disabling conditions, 7.* Retrieved February 20, 2011, from http://ihcrp.georgetown.edu/agingsociety/pdfs/ Caregiving.pdf

National Association of Professional Geriatric Care Managers. (n. d.). *What is a geriatric care manger?* Retrieved March 1, 2011, from http://www.caremanager.org/displaycommon.cfm?an=1&subarticlenbr=76

National Center for Health Statistics. (2011). *Health, United States, 2010: With special feature on death and dying.* Hyattsville, MD: Author.

National Institute of Mental Health. (2007). *Older adults: Depression and suicide factsheet.* Retrieved March 15, 2011, from http://www.nimh.nih.gov/health/publications/older-adults-depression-and-suicide-facts-fact-sheet/index.shtml

Neal, M. B., Wagner, D. L., Bonn, J. B., & Niles-Yokum, K. (2008). Caring from a distance: Contemporary care issues. In A. Martin-Mathews & J.E. Phillips (Eds.), *Aging and caring at the intersection of work and home life* (pp. 107–128). New York: Psychology Press.

Neugarten, B. L. (1974). Age groups in American society and the rise of the young old. *Annals of the American Academy of Political and Social Science, 415,* 187–198.

Newbould, J., Taylor, D., & Bury, M. (2006). Lay-led self-management in chronic illness: A review of the evidence. *Chronic Illness, 2,* 249–261.

Newcomer, K. L., Krug, H. E., & Mahowald, M. L. (1993). Validity and reliability of the timed-stands test for patients with rheumatoid arthritis and other chronic diseases. *Journal of Rheumatology, 20,* 21–27.

Nickens, H. (1986). Report of the Secretary's Task Force on Black and Minority Health: A summary and a presentation of health data with regard to blacks. *Journal of the National Medical Association, 78*(6), 577–580.

Nikolaus, T., & Bach, M. (2003). Preventing falls in community-dwelling frail older people using a home intervention team (HIT): Results from the randomized falls HIT trial. *Journal of the American Geriatric Society, 52,* 300–305.

Nishimura, T. C., & Myers, M. (2007). Community based practice: The secrets of successful fund-raising. *OT Practice, 12*(9), 23–25.

Nitz, J. C., & Choy, N. L. (2004). The efficacy of a specific balance-strategy training programme for preventing falls among older people: A pilot randomized controlled trial. *Age and Aging, 32,* 52–58.

Non-Profit Guides. (n. d.). *Grant writing tools for non-profit organizations.* Retrieved February 23, 2011, from http://www.npguides.org/

O'Hayer, B. (2009). Expanding your practice to meet the needs of aging Baby Boomers. *OT Practice, 14*(14), 7–8.

Oida, Y., Kitabatake, Y., Nishijima, Y., Nagamatsu, T., Kohno, H., Egawa, K., & Arao, T. (2003). Effects of a 5-year exercise-centered health-promoting programme on mortality and ADL impairment in the elderly. *Age and Ageing, 32,* 585–592.

Oliver, R., Blath Wayt, J., Brackley, C., & Tamaki, T. (1993). Development of the Safety Assessment of Function and the Environment for Rehabilitation (SAFER) tool. *Canadian Journal of Occupational Therapy, 60,* 78–82.

Oman, D., & Reed, D. (1998). Religion and mortality among the community-dwelling elderly. *American Journal of Public Health, 88,* 1469–1475.

Oman, D., Thoresen, C. E., & McMahon, K. (1999). Volunteerism and mortality among the community-dwelling elderly. *Journal of Health Psychology, 4,* 1359–1053.

Orellano, E., Colón, W. I., & Arbesman, M. (2012). Effect of occupation- and activity-based interventions on the performance of instrumental activities of daily living among community-dwelling older adults: A systematic review. *American Journal of Occupational Therapy, 66,* 292–300.

Ostaszkiewicz, J., Chestney, T., & Roe, B. (2004). Habit retraining for the management of urinary incontinence in adults. *Cochrane Database of Systematic Reviews, 2,* CD002801.

Owsley, C., Stalvey, B., Wells, J., & Sloane, M. E. (1999). Older drivers and cataracts: Driving habits and crash risk. *Journal of Gerontology A, 54*(4), M203–M211.

Pahor, M., Blair, S. N., Espeland, M., Fielding, R., Gill, T. M., Guralnick, J. M., . . . Studenski, S. (2006). Effects of a physical activity intervention on measures of physical performance: Results of the Lifestyle Interventions and Independence for Elders pilot (LIFE–P) study. *Journal of Gerontology Series A: Biological and Medical Sciences, 61,* 1157–1165.

Park, N. S., Klemmack, D. L., Roff, L. L., Parker, M. W., Koenig, H. G., Sawyer, P. & Allman, R. A. (2008). Religiousness and longitudinal trajectories in elders' functional status. *Research on Aging, 30,* 279–298.

Parry, C., & Coleman, E. A. (2010). Active roles for older adults in navigating care transitions: Lessons learned from the care transitions intervention. *Open Longevity Science, 4,* 43–50.

ParyPatient Protection and Affordable Care Act, P. L. 111–148 § 3502, 124 Stat. 119, 124 (2010).

Patrick, D. L., Richardson, M., Starks, H. E., Rose, M. A., & Kinne, S. (1997). Rethinking prevention for people with disabilities part II: A framework for designing interventions. *American Journal of Health Promotion, 11*, 261–263.

Peloquin, S. M. (1991a). Looking Back—Occupational therapy service: Individual and collective understandings of the founders, Part 1. *American Journal of Occupational Therapy, 45*, 352–360.

Peloquin, S. M. (1991b). Looking Back—Occupational therapy service: Individual and collective understandings of the founders, Part 2. *American Journal of Occupational Therapy, 45*, 733–744.

Perlmutter, M. S., Bhorade, A., Gordon, M., Hollingsworth, H. H., & Baum, M. C. (2010). Cognitive, visual, auditory, and emotional factors that affect participation in older adults. *American Journal of Occupational Therapy, 64*(4), 570–579.

Peterson, E. W., & Clemson, L. (2008). Understanding the role of occupational therapy in fall prevention for community-dwelling older adults. *OT Practice, 18*(3), CE1–CE8.

Peterson, E. W., & Murphy, S. (2002). Fear of falling. Part II: Assessment and intervention. *Home and Community Special Interest Section Newsletter, 9*(1), 1–4.

Petersson, I., Kottorp, A., Bergström, J., & Lilja, M. (2009). Longitudinal changes in everyday life after home modifications for people aging with disabilities. *Scandinavian Journal of Occupational Therapy, 16*, 78–87.

Pettersson, A., & Malmberg, G. (2009). Adult children and elderly parents as mobility attractions in Sweden. *Population, Space, and Place, 15*(4), 299–304.

Phelan, E. A., Williams, B., Penninx, B. W., LoGerfo, J. P., & Leveille, S. G. (2004). Activities of daily living function and disability in older adults in a randomized trial of the health enhancement program. *Journals of Gerontology. Series A, Biological Sciences and Medical Sciences, 59*(8), 838–843.

Phipps, S., & Richardson, P. (2007). Occupational therapy outcomes for clients with traumatic brain injury and stroke using the Canadian Occupational Performance Measure. *American Journal of Occupational Therapy, 61*, 328–334.

Pighills, A. C., Torgerson, D. J., Sheldon, T. A., Drummond, A. E., & Bland, J. M. (2011). Environmental assessment and modification to prevent falls in older people. *Journal of the American Geriatric Society, 59*, 26–33.

Podsiadlo, D., & Richardson, S. (1991). The Timed Up and Go: A test of basic functional mobility for frail elderly persons. *Journal of the American Geriatrics Society, 39*(2), 142–148.

Powell, L. E., & Myers, A. M. (1998). The Activities-Specific Balance Confidence (ABC) Scale. *Journal of Gerontology, Medical Sciences, 50*(1), M28–M34.

Ratnoff, C., Becker-Omvig, M., Elliott, S. J., O'Sullivan, A., & V. Talley. (2002). Occupational therapy and Area Agencies on Aging—A partnership. *Home and Community Health Special Interest Section Quarterly, 9*(3), 1–3.

Reid, M. C., Papaleontiou, M., Ong, A., Breckman, R., Wethington, E., & Pillemer, K. (2008). Self-management strategies to reduce pain and improve function among older adults in community settings: A review of the evidence. *Pain Medicine, 9*, 409–424.

Rejeski, W. J., Brawley, L. R., Ambrosius, W. T., Brubaker, P. H., Focht, B. C., Foy, C. G., & Fox, L. D. (2003). Older adults with chronic disease: Benefits of group-mediated counseling in the promotion of physically active lifestyles. *Health Psychology, 22*, 414–423.

Rejeski, W. J., King, A. C., Katula, J. A., Kritchevsky, S., Miller, M. E., Walkup, M. P., Glynn, N. W., & Pahor, M. (2008). Physical activity in prefrail older adults: Confidence and satisfaction related to physical function. *Journals of Gerontology: Series B: Psychological Sciences and Social Sciences, 63B,* P19–P26.

Rejeski, W. J., Marsh, A. P., Chmelo, E., Prescott, A. J., Dobrosielski, M., Walkup, M. P., & Kritchevsky, S. (2009). The Lifestyle Interventions and Independence for Elders Pilot (LIFE–P): 2-year follow-up. *Journals of Gerontology and Biological Sciences and Medical Sciences, 64A,* 462–467.

Richardson, J., Law, M., Wishart, L., & Guyatt, G. (2000). The use of a simulated environment (Easy Street) to retrain independent living skills in elderly persons: A randomized controlled trial. *Journals of Gerontology: Medical Sciences, 55,* M578–M584.

Rikli, R. E., & Jones, C. J. (2001). *Senior fitness test manual.* Champaign, IL: Human Kinetics.

Riley, L. D., & Bowen, C. (2005). The Sandwich Generation: Challenges and coping strategies of multigenerational families. *Family Journal, 13*(1), 52–59.

Rizza, F. T. (2010). The gerontologist: Counselor and coach. *Educational Gerontology, 36,* 46–51.

Robertson, M. C., Devlin, N., Gardner, M. M., & Campbell, A. J. (2001). Effectiveness and economic evaluation of a nurse-delivered home exercise programme to prevent falls. 1: Randomised controlled trial. *British Medical Journal, 322,* 697–701.

Robinson, B. C. (1983). Validation of a Caregiver Strain Index. *Journal of Gerontology, 38,* 344–348.

Robinson-Brown, R., & Robinson, M. (2010). Meeting the needs of the client who is not homebound. *Home and Community Health Special Interest Section Quarterly, 17*(1), 1–3.

Rogers, J. C., & Holm, M. B. (1989). *Performance Assessment of Self-Care skills (PASS–Home).* Unpublished tests. Pittsburgh: University of Pittsburgh.

Routasalo, P. E., Savikko, N., Tilvis, R. S., Strandberg, T. E., & Pitkälä, K. H. (2006). Social contacts and their relationship to lonliness among aged people: A population-based study. *Gerontology, 52*(3), 181–187.

Rowe, J. W. (2007, September). *Opportunities and challenges of an aging society.* Speech presented at the MacArthur Foundation Research Network on an Aging Society, University of Michigan. Retrieved February 27, 2011, from http://www.agingsocietynetwork.org/speech

Rowe, J. W., & Kahn, R. L. (1998). *Successful aging.* New York: Pantheon.

Russell, M. A., Hill, K. D., Blackberry, I., Day, L. M., & Dharmage, S. C. (2008). The reliability and predictive accuracy of the Falls Risk for Older People in the Community assessment (FROP–Com) tool. *Age and Ageing, 37,* 634–639.

Sackett, D. L., Rosenberg, W. M., Muir Gray, J. A., Haynes, R. B., & Richardson, W. S. (1996). Evidence-based medicine: What it is and what it isn't. *British Medical Journal, 312,* 71–72.

Scarmeas, N., Levy, G., Tang, M.-X., Manly, J., & Stern, Y. (2001). Influence of leisure activity on the incidence of Alzheimer's disease. *Neurology, 57,* 2236–2242.

Schaber, P. (2010). *Occupational therapy practice guidelines for adults with Alzheimer's disease and related disorders.* Bethesda, MD: AOTA Press.

Schulz, R., Beach, S. R., Lind, B., Martire, L. M., Zdaniuk, B., Hirsch, C., et al. (2001). Involvement in caregiving and adjustment to death of a spouse: Findings from the Caregiver Health Effects Study. *JAMA, 285,* 3123–3129.

Seeman, T. E., Berkman, L. F., Charpentier, P. A., Blazer, D. G., Albert, M. S., & Tinetti, M. E. (1995).

Behavioral and psychosocial predictors of physical performance: MacArthur Studies of Successful Aging. *Journals of Gerontology: Biological Sciences and Medical Sciences, 50,* M177–M183.

Seeman, T. E., & Chen, X. (2002). Risk and protective factors for physical functioning in older adults with and without chronic conditions: MacArthur Studies of Successful Aging. *Journal of Gerontology: Social Sciences, 57B,* S135–S144.

Seeman, T., Lusingnolo, T. M., Albert, M., & Berkman, L. (2001). Social relationships, social support, and patterns of cognitive aging in healthy, high-functioning older adults: MacArthur Studies of Successful Aging. *Health Psychology, 20,* 243–255.

Shmotkin, D., Blumstein, T., & Modan, B. (2003). Beyond keeping active: Concomitants of being a volunteer in old-old age. *Psychology and Aging, 18,* 602–607.

Shrestha, L. B. (2006). *Life expectancy in the United States* (Congressional Research Services Report for Congress, Report #RL32792). Retrieved February 22, 2011, from http://aging.senate.gov/crs/aging1.pdf

Shumway-Cook, A., Silver, I. F., LeMier, M., York, S., Cummings, P., & Koepsell, T. D. (2007). Effectiveness of a community-based multifactorial intervention on falls and fall risk factors in community-living older adults: A randomized controlled trial. *Journals of Gerontology, 62A*(12), 1420–1427.

Shumway-Cook, A., & Woollacott, M. (1995). *Motor control theory and applications.* Baltimore: Lippincot Williams & Wilkins.

Siebert, C. (2005). *Occupational therapy practice guidelines for home modifications.* Bethesda, MD: AOTA Press.

Silverstein, M., & Parker, M. G. (2002). Leisure activities and quality of life among the oldest old in Sweden. *Research on Aging, 24,* 528–548.

Sivrioglu, E. Y., Sivrioglu, K., Ertan, T., Ertan, F. S., Cankurtaran, E., Aki, O., . . . Kirli, S. (2009). Reliability and validity of the Geriatric Depression Scale in detection of poststroke minor depression. *Journal of Clinical and Experimental Neuropsychology, 31*(8), 999–1006.

Skelton, D., Dinan, S., Campbell, M., & Rutherford, O. (2005). Tailored group exercise (Falls Management Exercise—FaME) reduces falls in community-dwelling older frequent fallers (an RCT). *Age and Ageing, 34*(6), 636–639.

Smith, N. R., Kielhofner, G., & Watts, J. H. (1986). The relationships between volition, activity pattern, and life satisfaction in the elderly. *American Journal of Occupational Therapy, 40*(4), 278–283.

Social Security Administration. (1984). *In depth research: Legislative history of Public Law 98–21, (H.R. 1900) Social Security amendments of 1983.* Retrieved February 22, 2011, from http://www.ssa.gov/history/1983amend.html

Social Security Administration. (2011). *Retirement benefits by year of birth.* Retrieved February 22, 2011, from http://www.socialsecurity.gov/retire2/agereduction.htm

Soer, R., Van der Schans, C. P., Geertzen, J. H., Groothoff, J. W., Brouwer, S., Dijkstra, P. U., & Reneman, M. F. (2009). Normative values for a functional capacity evaluation. *Archives of Physical Medicine and Rehabilitation, 90*(10), 1785–1794.

St. John, P. D., Blandford, A. A., & Strain, L. A. (2006). Depressive symptoms among older adults in urban and rural areas. *International Journal of Geriatric Psychiatry, 21,* 1175–1180.

Stanford School of Medicine. (2011). *Chronic disease self-management program.* Retrieved from http://patienteducation.stanford.edu/programs/cdsmp.html

Stav, W. B. (2008). Review of the evidence related to older adult community mobility and driver licensure policies. *American Journal of Occupational Therapy, 62,* 149–158.

Stav, W. B., Arbesman, M., & Lieberman, D. (2008). Background and methodology of the older driver: Evidence-based systematic literature review. *American Journal of Occupational Therapy, 62*(2), 130–135.

Stav, W. B., Hallenen, T., Lane, J., & Arbesman, M. (2012). Systematic review of occupational engagement and health outcomes among community-dwelling older adults, *American Journal of Occupational Therapy, 66,* 301–310.

Stav, W. B., Hunt, L. A., & Arbesman, M. (2006). *Occupational therapy practice guidelines for driving and community mobility for older adults.* Bethesda, MD: AOTA Press.

Stel, V. S., Smit, J. H., Plujim, S. M. F., & Lips, P. (2004). Consequences of falling in older men and women and risk factors for health service use and functional decline. *Age and Ageing, 33,* 58–65.

Stephens, M. A. P., & Franks, M. M. (2009). All in the family: Providing care to chronically ill and disabled older adults. In S. H. Quals & S. H. Zarit (Eds.), *Aging families and caregiving* (pp. 61–84). Hoboken, NJ: Wiley.

Stessman, J., Hammerman-Rozenberg, R., Maaravi, Y., Azoulay, D., & Cohen, A. (2005). Strategies to enhance longevity and independent function: The Jerusalem Longitudinal Study. *Mechanisms of Ageing and Development, 126,* 327–331.

Stessman, J., Hammerman-Rozenberg, R., Maaravi, Y., & Cohen, A. (2002). Effect of exercise on ease of performing activities of daily living and instrumental activities of daily living from age 70 to 77: The Jerusalem Longitudinal Study. *Journal of the American Geriatric Society, 50,* 1934–1938.

Stessman, J., Maaravi, Y., Hammerman-Rozenberg, R., & Cohen, A. (2000). The effects of physical activity on mortality in the Jerusalem 70-Year-Olds Longitudinal Study. *Journal of the American Geriatrics Society, 48,* 499–504.

Steuljens, E. M. J., Dekker, J., Bouter, L. M., Jellema, S., Bakker, E. B., & van den Ende, C. H. M. (2004). Occupational therapy for community-dwelling elderly people: A systematic review. *Age and Aging, 33,* 453–460.

Stevens, J., Corso, P., Finkelstein, E., & Miller, T. (2006). The costs of fatal and nonfatal falls among older adults. *Injury Prevention, 12,* 290–295.

Stevens, M., Holman, C. D. J., Bennett, N., & de Klerk, N. (2001). Preventing falls in older people: Outcome evaluation of a randomized controlled trial. *Journal of the American Geriatric Society, 49,* 1448–1455.

Strawbridge, W. J., Cohen, R. D., & Shema, S. J. (2000). Comparative strength of association between religious attendance and survival. *International Journal of Psychiatry in Medicine, 30,* 299–308.

Strawbridge, W. J., Cohen, R. D., Shema, S. J., & Kaplan, G. A. (1997). Frequent attendance at religious services and mortality over 28 years. *American Journal of Public Health, 87,* 957–961.

Strawbridge, W. J., Shema, S. J., Cohen, R. D., & Kaplan, G. A. (2001). Religious attendance increases survival by improving and maintaining good health behaviors, mental health, and social relationships. *Annals of Behavioral Medicine, 23,* 68–74.

Strong, J. G., Jutai, J. W., Russell-Minda, E., & Evans, M. (2008). Driving and low vision: An evidence-based review of rehabilitation. *Journal of Visual Impairment and Blindness, 102,* 410–419.

Substance Abuse and Mental Health Services Administration, Office of Applied Studies. (December 29, 2009). *The NSDUH Report: Illicit drug use among older adults.* Rockville, MD: Author.

Suchy, Y., Williams, P., Kraybill, M., Franchow, E., & Butner, J. (2010). Instrumental activities of daily living among community-dwelling eldery: Personality associations with self-report, performance, and awareness of functional difficulties. *Journal of Gereontology: Series B, Psychological Sciences, 65B*(5): 542–550.

Tennstedt, S., Howland, J., Lachman, M., Peterson, E., Kasten, L., & Jette A. (1998). A randomized, controlled trial of a group intervention to reduce fear of falling and associated activity restriction in older adults. *Journal of Gerontology, 53,* 384–392.

Theeke, L. A. (2009). Predictors of loneliness in U.S. adults over age sixty-five. *Archives of Psychiatric Nursing,* 23(5), 387–396.

Thoits, P. L., & Hewitt, L. N. (2001). Volunteer work and well-being. *Journal of Health and Social Behavior, 42,* 115–131.

Timonen, L., Rantanen, T., Makinen, E., Timonen, T., Tormakangas, T., & Sulkava, R. (2006). Effects of a group-based exercise program on functional abilities in frail older woman after hospital discharge. *Aging Clinical and Experimental Research, 18,* 50–56.

Tinetti, M., Inouye, S., Gill, T., & Doucette, J. (1995). Shared risk factors for falls, incontinence and functional dependence. *JAMA, 273,* 1348–1353.

Tinetti, M., Richman, D., & Powell, L. (1990). Falls efficacy as a measure of fear of falling. *Journal of Gerontology, 45,* 239.

Tinetti, M. E., & Williams, C. S. (1997). Falls, injuries due to falls, and the risk of admission to a nursing home. *New England Journal of Medicine, 337*(18), 1279–1284

Tomita, M. R., Mann, W. C., Stanton, K., Tomita, A. D., & Sundar, V. (2007). Use of currently available smart home technology by frail elders: Process and outcomes. *Topics in Geriatric Rehabilitation, 23*(1), 24–34.

Townsend, E. A., & Wilcock, A. A. (2004). Occupational justice. In C. H. Christiansen & E. A. Townsend (Eds.), *Introduction to occupation: The art and science of living* (pp. 243–273). Upper Saddle River, NJ: Prentice Hall.

Trombly, C. A. (1993). The Issue Is—Anticipating the future: Assessment of occupational function. *American Journal of Occupational Therapy, 47,* 253–257.

Trombly, C. A. (1995). Occupation: Purposefulness and meaningfulness as therapeutic mechanisms. *American Journal of Occupational Therapy, 49,* 960–972.

Trombly, C. A., Radomski, M. V., & Davis, E. S. (1998). Achievement of self-identified goals by adults with traumatic brain injury: Phase I. *American Journal of Occupational Therapy, 52,* 810–818.

Tucker, J. S., Friedman, H. S., Tsai, C. M., & Martin, L. R. (1995). Playing with pets and longevity among older people. *Psychology and Aging, 10,* 3–7.

U.S. Bureau of Labor Statistics. (2011). *Volunteering in the United States, 2010.* Retrieved March 13, 2011, from http://www.bls.gov/news.release/volun.toc.htm

U.S. Bureau of the Census. (2004). *We the people: Aging in the U.S.* Retrieved February 23, 2011, from http://www.census. gov/prod/2004pubs/censr-19.pdf

U.S. Bureau of the Census. (2008). *The American community survey.* Retrieved February 23, 2011, from http://www.census.gov/acs/www/guidance_for_data_users/guidance_main/

U.S. Bureau of the Census. (2009). *U. S. population projections.* Retrieved February 23, 2011, from http://www.census.gov/population/www/projections/summarytables.html

U.S. Bureau of the Census, Statistical Abstract of the United States. (2011). *Civilian labor force and participation rate with projections, 1980–2018.* Retrieved February 23, 2011, from http://www.census.gov/compendia/statab/2011/tables/11s0585.pdf

U.S. Department of Health and Human Services. (2009). *Healthy People 2010 public meetings.* Atlanta: Author. Retrieved February 23, 2011, from http://www.healthypeople.gov/hp2020/

Objectives/View ProposedObjectives.aspx?
id=37&TopicArea=Older+Adults

U.S. Department of Health and Human Services. (2010). *Healthy People 2020*. Retrieved February 23, 2011, from http://www.healthypeople.gov/2020/default.aspx

Unger, J. B., Johnson, A., & Marks, G. (1997). Functional decline in the elderly: Evidence for direct and stress-buffering protective effects of social interactions and physical activity. *Annals of Behavioral Medicine, 19*, 152–160.

Unger, J. B., McAvay, G., Bruce, M. L., Berkman, L., & Seeman, T. (1999). Variation in the impact of social network characteristics on physical functioning in elderly persons: MacArthur Studies of Successful Aging. *Journal of Gerontology: Social Sciences, 54B*, S245–S251.

Van Willigen, M. (2000). Differential benefits of volunteering across the life course. *Journal of Gerontology: Social Sciences, 55B*, S308–S318.

Verbrugge, L. M. 1991. Risk factors for disability among U.S. adults with arthritis. *Journal of Clinical Epidemiology, 44*(2), 167–182.

Verghese, J., Lipton, R. B., Katz, M. J., Hall, C. B., Derby, C. A., Kuslansky, G., & Buschke, H. (2003). Leisure activities and the risk of dementia in the elderly. *New England Journal of Medicine, 348*, 2508–2516.

Voukelatos, A., Cumming, R. G., Lord, S. R., & Rissel, C. (2007). A randomized, controlled trial of tai chi for the prevention of falls: The Central Sydney Tai Chi Trial. *Journal of the American Geriatric Society, 55*, 1185–1191.

Waldron, D., & Layton, N. (2008). Hard and soft assistive technologies: Defining roles for clinicians. *Australian Occupational Therapy Journal, 55*, 61–64.

Wallace, M. (2008). *Essentials of gerontological nursing*. New York: Springer.

Walter-Ginzburg, A., Blumstein, T., Chetrit, A., & Modan, B. (2002). Social factors and mortality in the old-old in Israel: The CALAS study. *Journals of Gerontology: Psychological Sciences and Social Sciences, 57*, S308–S318.

Wang, H., Karp, A., Winblad, B., & Fratiglioni, L. (2002). Late-life engagement in social and leisure activities is associated with a decreased risk of dementia: A longitudinal study from the Kungsholmen Project. *American Journal of Epidemiology, 155*, 1081–1087.

Wang, L., van Belle, G., Kukull, W. B., & Larson, E. B. (2002). Predictors of functional change: A longitudinal study of nondemented people aged 65 and older. *Journal of the American Geriatrics Society, 50*, 1525–1534.

Wang, C. C., Kosinksi, C. J., Schartzberg, J. G., & Shanklin, A. V. (2003). *Physician's guide to accessing and counseling older drivers*. Washington, DC: National Highway Traffic Safety Administration.

Warsi, B., Wang, P. S., LaValley, M. P., Avorn, J., & Solomon, D. H. (2004). Self-management education programs in chronic disease: A systematic review and methodological critique of the literature. *Archives of Internal Medicine, 164*, 1641–1649.

Welin, L., Larsson, B., Svärdsudd, K., Tibblin, B., & Tibblin, G. (1992). Social network and activities in relation to mortality from cardiovascular diseases, cancer and other causes: A 12-year follow up of the study of men born in 1913 and 1923. *Journal of Epidemiology and Community Health, 46*, 127–132.

Wellman, N. S., Kamp, B., Kirk-Sanchez, N. J., & Johnson, P. M. (2007). Eat better and move more: A community-based program designed to improve diets and increase physical activity among older Americans. *American Journal of Public Health, 97*, 710–717.

Williams, J. H., Drinka, T. J. K., Greenberg, J. R., Farrell-Holtan, J., Euhardy, R., & Schram, M. (1991).

Development and testing of the Assessment of Living Skills and Resources (ALSAR) in community-dwelling veterans. *The Gerontologist, 31,* 84–91.

Willis, S. L., Tennestedt, S. L., Mariske, M., Ball, K., Elias, J., Koepke, K. M., . . .Wright, E. (2006). Long-term effects of cognitive training on everyday functional outcomes in older adults. *JAMA, 296,* 2805–2814.

Wilson, J. (2000). Volunteering. *Annual Review of Sociology, 26,* 215–240.

Wilson, J., & Musick, M. A. (1997). Who cares? Toward an integrated theory of volunteer work. *American Sociological Review, 62,* 694–713.

Wilson, R. S., Mendes de Leon, C. F., Barnes, L. L., Schneider, J. A., Bienias, J. L., Evans, D. A., & Bennett, D. (2002). Participation in cognitively stimulating activities and risk of incident Alzheimer Disease. *JAMA, 287,* 742–748.

Wolf, S. L., Barnhart, H. X., Kutner, N. G., McNeely, E., Coogler, C., & Xu, T. (2003). Selected as the best paper in the 1990s: Reducing frailty and falls in older persons: An investigation of tai chi and computerized balance training. *Journal of the American Geriatrics Society, 51,* 1794–1803.

World Health Organization. (2001). *International classification of functioning, disability and health.* Geneva: Author.

World Health Organization. (2010). *Integrating prevention into health care* (World Health Organization Fact Sheet 172). Retrieved February 27, 2011, from http://www.who.int/mediacentre/factsheets/fs172/en/index.html

Wright, J. (2006). Coaching for workplace success-crisis and opportunity: Coaching older workers in the workplace. *Work, 26*(1), 93–96.

Wu, Y., McCrone, S. H., & Lai, H. J. (2008). Health behaviors and transitions of physical disability among community-dwelling older adults. *Research on Aging, 30,* 572–591.

Xue, Q., Fried, L. P., Glass, T. A., Laffan, A., & Chaves, P. H. M. (2008). Life-space constriction, development of frailty, and the competing risk of mortality. The Women's Health and Aging Study I. *American Journal of Epidemiology, 167,* 240–248.

Yaffe, K., Barnes, D., Nevitt, M., Lui, L-Y., & Covinsky, K. (2001). A prospective study of physical activity and cognitive decline in elderly women: Women who walk. *Archives of Internal Medicine, 161,* 1703–1708.

Yeh, S-C. J., & Lo, S. K. (2004). Living alone, social support, and feeling lonely among the elderly. *Social Behavior and Personality, 32,* 1129–1138.

Yelin, E., Murphy, L., Cisternas, M. G., Foreman, A. J., Pasta, D. J., & Helmick, C. G. (2007). Medical care expenditures and earnings losses among persons with arthritis and other rheumatic conditions in 2003, and comparisons with 1997. *Arthritis and Rheumatism, 56*(5), 1397–1407.

Yen, I. H., Michael, Y. L., & Perdue, L. (2010). Neighborhood environment in studies of health of older adults. *American Journal of Preventative Medicine, 37*(5), 455-463.

Yerxa, E. (1998). Health and the human spirit for occupation. *American Journal of Occupational Therapy, 52,* 412–418.

Yerxa, E. J., Burnett-Beaulieu, S., Stockin, S., & Azen, S. P. (1988). Development of the Satisfaction with Performance scaled questionnaire. *American Journal of Occupational Therapy, 42,* 215–221.

You, K. S., & Lee, H. (2006). The physical, mental, and emotional health of older people who are living alone or with relatives. *Archives of Psychiatric Nursing, 20,* 193–201.

You, K., Lee, H., Fitzpatrick, J., Kim, S., Marui, E., Lee, J., & Cook, P. (2009). Spirituality, depression, living alone, and perceived health among Korean older adults in the community. *Archives of Psychiatric Nursing, 23,* 309–322.

Zhang, W. (2008). Religious participation and mortality risk among the oldest old in China. *Journal of Gerontology: Social Sciences, 63B,* S293–S297.

Ziden, L., Frandin, K., & Kreuter, M. (2008). Home rehabilitation after hip fracture. A randomized controlled study on balance confidence, physical function and everyday activities. *Clinical Rehabilitation, 22,* 1019–1033.

Zijlstra, G. A. R., van Haastregt, J. C. M., Ambergen, T., van Rossum, E., van Eijk, J. Th. M., Tennstedt, S. L., & Kempen, G. I. J. M. (2009). Effects of a multi-component cognitive–behavioral group intervention on fear of falling and activity avoidance in community-dwelling older adults: Results of a randomized controlled trial. *Journal of the American Geriatrics Society, 57,* 2010–2028.

Zijlstra, G. A., van Haagstregt, J. C. M., van Rossum, E., van Eijk, J. T. M., Yardley, L., & Kempen, G. I. J. M. (2007). Interventions to reduce fear of falling in community-living older people: A systematic review. *Journal of the American Geriatric Society, 55*(4), 603–615.